After the War on Crime

After the War on Crime

Race, Democracy, and a New Reconstruction

EDITED BY

*Mary Louise Frampton,
Ian Haney López, and
Jonathan Simon*

New York University Press

NEW YORK AND LONDON

NEW YORK UNIVERSITY PRESS
New York and London
www.nyupress.org

© 2008 by New York University

Library of Congress Cataloging-in-Publication Data
After the war on crime : race, democracy, and a new reconstruction /
edited by Mary Louise Frampton, Ian Haney López, and Jonathan Simon.
p.   cm.
Includes bibliographical references and index.
ISBN-13: 978-0-8147-2760-7 (cl : alk. paper)
ISBN-10: 0-8147-2760-3 (cl : alk. paper)
ISBN-13: 978-0-8147-2761-4 (pb : alk. paper)
ISBN-10: 0-8147-2761-1 (pb : alk. paper)
1. Crime—Government policy—United States. 2. Crime—Political
aspects—United States. 3. Criminal justice, Administration of—
United States. 4. Discrimination in criminal justice administration—
United States.   I. Frampton, Mary Louise. II. Haney-López, Ian.
III. Simon, Jonathan.
HV6789.A3443 2008
364.973—dc22   2007049404

New York University Press books are printed on acid-free paper,
and their binding materials are chosen for strength and durability.

Manufactured in the United States of America

c 10 9 8 7 6 5 4 3 2 1
p 10 9 8 7 6 5 4 3 2 1

Contents

Introduction   1

PART I   Crime, War, and Governance

1   The Place of the Prison in the New Government
    of Poverty   23
    Loïc Wacquant

2   America Doesn't Stop at the Rio Grande: Democracy
    and the War on Crime   37
    Angelina Snodgrass Godoy

3   From the New Deal to the Crime Deal   48
    Jonathan Simon

4   The Great Penal Experiment: Lessons for Social Justice   61
    Todd R. Clear

PART II   A War-Torn Country: Race, Community,
           and Politics

5   The Code of the Streets   73
    Elijah Anderson

6   The Contemporary Penal Subject(s)   89
    Mona Lynch

7   The Punitive City Revisited: The Transformation of
    Urban Social Control   106
    Katherine Beckett and Steve Herbert

8   Frightening Citizens and a Pedagogy of Violence   123
    William Lyons

PART III   A New Reconstruction

9   Smart on Crime   145
     Kamala D. Harris

10   Rebelling against the War on Low-Income, of Color,
     and Immigrant Communities   151
     Gerald P. López

11   Of Taints and Time: The Racial Origins and Effects of
     Florida's Felony Disenfranchisement Law   166
     Jessie Allen

12   The Politics of the War against the Young   187
     Barry Krisberg

13   Transformative Justice and the Dismantling of Slavery's
     Legacy in Post-Modern America   207
     Mary Louise Frampton

     Afterword: Strategies of Resistance   223
     Van Jones

     Contributors   229
     Index   231

Introduction

Jonathan Simon, Ian Haney López, and Mary Louise Frampton

The last three decades have witnessed a Pyrrhic war on crime, with sobering numbers at once chilling and cautionary. Since the 1970s, our imprisoned population has increased five-fold, with a commensurate spike in fiscal costs that many now see as unsupportable into the future. As American society confronts a multitude of new challenges ranging from terrorism to the disappearance of middle-class jobs to global warming, the war on crime may be up for reconsideration for the first time in a generation or more. It is not that the public is no longer concerned about crime; as we shall see, crime remains central to how we have learned to think and act collectively. But, as relatively low crime rates confront scary problems from other sides of the social experience, the mood may be swinging toward declaring victory and moving on.

However, the society-altering impact of this war reaches far beyond the flat numbers; simply moving on is impossible. Over the last thirty-plus years, the government response to social disorder encompassed under the rubric of the war on crime has fundamentally transformed us. The war's impact has been most devastating on those individuals swept up by increased rates and longer terms of incarceration, their families, and the communities bound by strained ties to these prisoners—but it is not confined to them. This impact has instead extended to how society views governance, reshaping not only a wide range of social institutions but also the way we conceive of ourselves. The very concept of policing has changed, as has the place of crime in electoral politics; increasingly, too, schooling, public health, and social welfare overlap with the criminal justice system. Meanwhile, how we view our most basic tasks as individuals—how to raise children, where to live, how to be a good parent, employee, and citizen—also now reflect the spreading logic of crime control. Increasingly, so do our very conceptions of community and even race.

As the war on crime perhaps draws toward a possible diminution in its influence on American democracy and society, it is time to consider the tasks reconstruction must tackle. To do so requires first a critical assessment of how this war has remade our society and then creative thinking about how government, foundations, communities, and activists should respond. This anthology, *After the War on Crime: Race, Democracy, and a New Reconstruction*, aims to accelerate this reassessment by pulling together original essays by a disparate, interdisciplinary group of scholars as well as policy professionals and community activists, many with years of experience working on these issues and some new to the problem. The essayists take a holistic approach, focusing not on the specifics of particular doctrines or studies but on the overarching social consequences of the war on crime and on potential strategies for reconstruction. The volume's immediate goal is to spark a fresh conversation about the war on crime and its consequences; its long-term aspiration is to develop a clear understanding of how we got here and of where we should go.

The War Is Over

It emerged as a slogan more than thirty-five years ago, but, from the first, the "war on crime" was much more than rhetoric. As in the case of the "cold war" and, more recently, the "war on terror," the war on crime produced significant and enduring effects on the entire American population in social, political, economic, constitutional, and, far from least, racial terms. The war on crime targeted hundreds of thousands of persons (mostly young and minority, once mostly boys and men but now including many girls and women), placing them in jails and prisons for extraordinary periods and under ever-more punitive conditions, in turn releasing them to the close scrutiny of supervisory regimes geared toward returning persons to prison rather than promoting reintegration. This campaign mobilized tens of thousands in law enforcement agencies and prison systems and tens of thousands more in the related war industries stimulated by our society's commitment of billions of dollars to this effort. In a nod toward total war, every member of the population has contributed, through federal and state taxes, general revenues, and bond issues, to the most rapid, most thoroughgoing, most extensive buildup in the carceral and police systems this country has ever undertaken. More than merely paying taxes to support the war, though, millions of Americans have adopted war thinking in how they perceive and respond to crime risk as citizens, parents, and economic actors. The war on crime remade our society: it reshaped our cities; transformed our social imagination about the nature of ourselves, our neighbors, and strangers; shifted the distribution of population between urban and rural areas; and ultimately changed the way motor vehicles, housing developments, shopping and office complexes look and operate. Perhaps most important, the war on crime transformed the social meaning of race in ways that make it more difficult than ever to resolve America's constitutive flaw, its legacy of slavery and racial domination and the structural deformation of democracy that these legacies produced.

This war—although currently at or near its peak in terms of imprisonment rates and law enforcement power—is in some important sense over. It is over because while we may continue to fight it, we no longer fight about whether to embark on it. The question of whether it is a good idea to attack America's social problems with a war on crime is in many respects simply behind us. We did that. And now the issues that increasingly come to the fore are those emerging from the consequences of the war on crime itself; its effects are suddenly visible across almost every institution of importance to civic life, including family, schools, the labor market, the political field, and race relations.

The familiar debates of the war-on-crime era—the expanding uses of the death penalty, mandatory prison sentences, absurdly high rates of incarceration, ballooning costs—continue to bedevil our highest courts as well as public debates. But they are now joined by questions that arise primarily from the existence of the war on crime and the strategies of mass incarceration that have been used to fight it. What is happening to the communities in the grip of aggressive policing and from which so many young persons have been extracted? How can we reintegrate into society the more than 600,000 persons a year expected to complete sentences in American prisons under current conditions, many of them after years of being warehoused in violent and racially divided institutions? When will we call a halt to the toll on democracy wreaked by felon disenfranchisement laws that disproportionately diminish the voting strength of identifiable communities such as African Americans, long the traditional victims of state policies aimed at disenfranchisement?

Criminologists in the late 1990s began to focus on a number of issues that have helped to alter the terms of the crime debate. One of the most important is the idea of "mass imprisonment" (Garland 2001). There has long been intense debate about the effects of imprisonment on individuals (see Kruttschnitt and Gartner 2005 for a recent summary). Does prison rehabilitate or does it further embed tendencies toward deviance and antisocial behavior? What became clearer in the 1990s was that the size of the incarcerated population in the United States had reached an unprecedented level and that the scale of this population was itself potentially having effects on American society that went beyond the impact on imprisoned individuals (Zimring and Hawkins 1991; Simon 1993; Clear and Rose 1999).

With close to 3 percent of the adult resident population in correctional custody (prison and jail plus parole and probation) by the mid-1990s, the war on crime had begun to transform the relationship of whole communities to government and to erode the capacity of those communities to sustain economic activity, social reproduction, and informal social control. In the short term, mass imprisonment actually may have boosted the American economy, at least on paper, by reducing the number of unemployed and thus creating the illusion that the United States was outperforming its rivals in Europe and Asia (Western and Beckett 1999). In the long term, however, the collateral consequence of incarceration for future employment opportunity was laying the foundation for an intractable unemployment problem of persons quite literally barred from employment by formal laws and informal economic norms combined with easier access to the criminal record of employment candidates (Pager 2003).

These economic effects are heavily concentrated in inner-city areas already hard pressed to attract employers and sustain middle-class, taxpaying residential communities. The same concentration effects were also undermining forms of social reproduction in these communities. For example, marriage, rates of which plummeted for African Americans in the 1980s and 1990s, was clearly undermined by the removal of large portions of the young adult male population. Worse yet, these economic and social losses did not simply counterbalance gains in security and protection from crime that would presumably redound to the very communities hurt by the concentration effects of incarceration. Instead, criminologists began to document that as young adult males were removed from communities, the capacity of those communities to sustain informal social control over the remaining adolescents further declined, pointing to a downward spiral of insecurity (Clear and Rose 1999).

In the most recent period, the feedback effect of large populations of American prisoners timing out on their substantial prison sentences and returning to American jurisdictions with little effort having been made at rehabilitation or at planning for their reintegration into society has itself become a major source of crime and of further growth in incarceration (Travis, Solomon, and Wahl 2001; Petersilia 2003). This "reentry problem" offers a fundamental reframing of the debate about crime in America. For decades the issue was whether harsher prison sentences could protect Americans from the violent crimes they most fear. Little attention was paid to what happened to the people consigned to years of incarceration. With reentry, the debate has changed to how prisons create crime risks for Americans and what can be done in and after prison to diminish that risk.

With surprising speed, this new discourse has begun to alter the field of political ideas. In his 2004 State of the Union address, President Bush addressed the large numbers of prisoners released and pledged federal money for renewed efforts to give prisoners a real second chance after prison. California Governor Arnold Schwarzenegger, after flexing his crime warrior muscles in beating back a once-popular ballot initiative to amend the state's harsh three-strikes law in the 2004 election, launched a major new effort to reinvent a culture of rehabilitation in California prisons and youth authority facilities, including entering settlements in major lawsuits against the state's prisons and juvenile facilities and commissioning the largest wave of research on corrections the state has seen in thirty years.

After three decades and more, the national mood may be swinging against the war on crime. For the first time in a generation, the consequences of this war, rather than its justifications, are open for public debate. It is time to take up in earnest how America can demobilize and move forward from a costly war that has raged longer than Vietnam, with perhaps greater consequences for American society and institutions.

War Without End

Yet there is no clear sense of where to go from here, or even a clear understanding of where "here" is exactly—the war on crime, after all, not only remade the criminal justice system but also remade much more, altering basic elements of social relations. While there is great opportunity in the reentry and disenfranchisement debates as well as other suggestions that the war on crime has run its course as a political imperative, we cannot move forward without taking stock of what the war has wrought. Perhaps most worrisome is the chance that, far from being over, the war has become perpetual. The material interests of whole economic sectors now depend on a continued expansion of mass policing and incarceration, even as a social zeitgeist of fear and insecurity demand ever-more extreme measures in pursuit of the zephyr of safety. It is crime control as the new face of racial subordination, though, that most threatens to render the war on crime a war without a foreseeable end.

The war on crime began in earnest amid a great national cresting of the legal struggle over civil rights with the adoption of the Civil Rights Act of 1964 and the Voting Rights Act of 1965. These legislative victories culminated more than half a century of efforts by African Americans and their allies on the left of American politics to revive the promise of racial justice made in the Thirteenth, Fourteenth, and Fifteenth amendments of the U.S. Constitution. Yet, rather than representing a resting point, these legislative civil rights victories were mostly opportunities to push forward substantively on the goal of erasing the effects of slavery and its successor regimes of racial domination. Real progress toward that goal would require taking full advantage of new opportunities in a number of directions including moving excluded minorities into parts of the labor market that had been crucial to making white working-class citizens more middle class in their security (like unionized factory jobs and the building trades); forging effective political coalitions (like those among African Americans, Jews, and liberal Catholics that brought pro–civil rights mayors to office in Detroit and Los Angeles); and breaking the hold of the de facto residential segregation that had taken firm hold in the East, in the Midwest, and on the West Coast. It was a moment of great risk as well. Lyndon Johnson's own gamble to give up solid support for the national Democratic Party from conservative white Southerners in exchange for a new majority coalition of African Americans, other minorities, and liberal white Northerners, placed the political machinery that had produced the legislative victories of 1964 and 1965 directly in jeopardy. Within a few short years, advisors to Republican presidential hopeful Richard Nixon would be formulating a "Southern Strategy" based on making those same conservative white Southerners a new base for the Republican Party (Beckett 1997).

The Southern Strategy boiled down to the crafting of a new way to mobilize whites around race, one that could pander to status insecurity and fear without seeming to contradict the newly emergent national consensus that racism was morally wrong. More than outrage against "forced busing" and "reverse discrimination," "crime" became the central discursive cry that whipped whites into a political realignment of historic proportions. Exploited by Nixon but perfected by Ronald Reagan and George H. W. Bush, reference to recidivist violent criminals such as Willie Horton became the most potent weapon in the campaign arsenal of American politicians. The war on crime—with its constituent imagery that melded the burning cities of the 1960s urban riots with the face of Horton as (every) black man, murderer, and rapist of a white woman—remade party affiliations and then remade the parties themselves, as the war came to be embraced and stridently promoted by Republicans and Democrats alike. If only it had remained mere rhetoric. Instead, the war on crime transmogrified from campaign tactic to one of the most far-reaching social experiments in this country. Politicians of both parties tripped over each other in the effort to be the most aggressive in "fighting crime," leading pell-mell to the tectonic shift in policing and incarceration that now distorts American society.

The entry of crime into political discourse and the "war on crime" that was eventually proclaimed by both political parties at precisely the height of the civil rights movement profoundly altered the process of recasting race relations. The language of crime opened an important line of retreat for political defenders of segregation and states' rights. This discursive sanctuary saved the careers of innumerable politicians who were never forced to renounce disgraced political values but could instead restate them as responses to crime. The war on crime allowed the nation to again turn hostile to racial minorities without having to explicitly break support for civil rights.

Meanwhile, the focus on crime led to dramatic increases in levels of reported violence in this period and in turn generated a heightened inter-subjective culture of fear about crime that would have profound consequences for all sides of the political realignment. This may have been particularly devastating for social groups that had been politically key to producing the ideological coherence and support for the liberal pro–civil rights coalition of the 1960s. Urban professional elites were more liberal than their working-class and small business counterparts and had disproportionate influence on government and social welfare institutions in particular (including criminal justice) during the 1960s and 1970s. They proved, however, even more prone to fear of crime (and its consequences for property values and schools), with many retreating toward more segregated suburbs, abandoning their social reform values, and embracing a culture of control that is at best hostile to progress on racial justice.[1]

Today, huge economic and social interests are now tied up with the massive punishment sector, exerting their own gravitational pull on the political process. With nearly two million mostly able-bodied Americans confined to locked penal institutions by the late 1990s, the American economy generates a powerful set of industries and public employees with a financial stake in the expansion of the penal sector. The idea that we now confront a "prison industrial complex," comparable to President Eisenhower's "military-industrial complex," has moved from an idea of the radical left (Parenti 1998) to a widely accepted truth of mass imprisonment. Prison guards form the most powerful union and lobbying organization in California; the prison-building industry generates billions of dollars a year, as does the increasingly privatized dystopia of prison management; rural areas gain political representation, state and federal resources, and high-paying jobs with the location of prisons in their midst and the census allocation of prisoners to their local population numbers. None of these interests care much about improving social welfare through criminal and other policies; they care fervently, though, about perpetuating mass incarceration.

But perhaps the most consequential effect of all has been how the war on crime has directly reconstituted race in the United States. It is not just that the war on crime has its roots in racial politics, fostering a political alignment among many whites predicated on the continued marginalization and subordination of racial minorities. Nor is it simply the tremendously destructive impact this war has had on minorities, especially African Americans. With nearly 10 percent of African American men in prison or jail on any given day, and more than half of them bound to experience a period of incarceration during their lives, the criminal justice system has become a dominant governmental influence on inner-city communities. Rather, it is that the criminal justice system is now integral to keeping ideas of race alive. The war on crime makes race real in America.

Race is not real, of course, or at least not in any biological sense. Race is instead a set of ideas and social practices built lightly on the edifice of physical differences but rooted ultimately in relations of domination and exploitation among socially defined groups. The inertia of past practices is important to the perpetuation of race but not alone sufficient (Fields

1990). For race to continue into the present as a meaningful category of difference, social practices must work to give race continued vitality. The war on crime is one of today's most powerful race-making social institutions.

The war on crime reconstitutes race on both material and symbolic levels. On the material level, the intensive policing of minorities forms part of a new dynamic of social, economic, and political disenfranchisement. Subject to the omnipresent power of the police and prison, many minorities, especially the young, find their lives punctuated and ultimately truncated by legalized violence. A web of neglect has been woven around minority communities, entrapping them amid poor schools, failing infrastructure, deteriorating housing, and the hulking shells of employers long gone. Ensuring that none but the most fortunate can transcend this intense concentration of despair, the war on crime has funded crime control as the preeminent solution to the social ills blighting minority communities. Especially with its commitment to punishment rather than rehabilitation, the war on crime only deepens the misery. Every aspect of the war on crime—the stop and frisk, the arrests, the criminalization of public health issues such as drug use and drunkenness, the violence engendered by overcrowded prisons with no real rehabilitative capacity—combines to virtually guarantee that the marginalization of minority communities will only deepen. In real respects, the war on crime has reversed the gains of the civil rights era and created a new form of racialized domination more intractable in many ways than the mid-twentieth-century versions of Northern ghettos and Southern Jim Crow (Wacquant 2000).

The desperate world of deeply impoverished minorities under the thumb of the law is not, however, something with which the rest of us are completely unfamiliar. Instead, we have images of that world constantly thrust on us by the media, whether as "news" or "entertainment." The mug shots in the morning paper or on the evening local news, as well as every cop show out there, from the fantasy land of *C.S.I.: Crime Scene Investigators* to the verisimilitude of *The Wire*, tell us over and over again about the undeniable concreteness of African American criminality. Most Americans *know* that is what they (African Americans) are really like—know it on some deep level we try to deny in our conscious desire to reject stereotypes if we are racially liberal or otherwise just know as a fact of life. It is in this way that the war on crime constructs race symbolically. The war's wreckage serves as evidence not of misguided social policies but of the fundamentally different nature of "them," the arrested, the incarcerated, the felons, the criminals. Just as the immiseration of minorities has always proved not their long subordination but their inferior natures, so now the disproportionate presence of minorities in the maw of the criminal justice system proves that blacks (and, increasingly, browns and reds) really are different from whites. In this respect, the war on crime not only constructs minorities but also whites. To be white, after all, is to expect and receive courteous treatment from the police, to be innocent until proven guilty, to benefit from the discretion of prosecutors, judges, and juries—and vice versa.

There is no "race" out there, except in our social practices. And among our society's disparate ways of fomenting racial ideas, the war on crime predominates. Its origins and ongoing attraction lie in mobilizing white fears, it perpetuates the material degradation central to racial hierarchy, and it proves at an ideological level the inferiority of blacks and the concomitant superiority of whites. So, it is not just that there are powerful economic interests supporting the war on crime or that a subjective fear of crime now pervades our society. Much more fundamental, the war on crime arose and continues because it is deeply rooted in American racial politics. The war on crime reflects our country's longstanding embrace of racism—but it also perpetuates it, extending racial hierarchy into the future and making it that much harder to ameliorate. Can we end the war on crime without a new racial justice movement?

Imagining a Post–War on Crime America

Despite such pessimism, there are clear signs the war on crime is being reconsidered. The spiraling costs of the war are increasingly being rejected as prohibitive, rehabilitation is back on the table, reentry and felony disenfranchisement are emerging as important debates. These elements alone may not herald the end of the war; indeed, they may do no more than curtail some of its excesses without changing its fundamental direction. Yet, it is also the case that there is some rhetorical value in simply declaring the war over. Maybe saying so will not, by itself, make it so. But saying so, loudly and often and in the context of an extended conversation regarding where we should go from here, can only help.

This book aims to help focus attention on the abundant signs that the political confluence of crime, urban restructuring, and political realignment that produced the war on crime has in important ways run its course. The resultant vast changes in American society and governmental institutions (including criminal justice) will not go away by themselves any time soon without a national conversation about how to redress some of the deformations they have created. Something like that is beginning in a narrower way with the issues of the disenfranchisement and reentry of felons, but the conversation has to be expanded to include the many ways that social ills are reinforced through the war on crime and how relatively privileged populations are poorly served by their own over-valuation of crime security.

Since the 1970s, academics, policy wonks, and political activists have engaged in (often) heated battles over whether harsh prison sentences were the right way to take on America's urban problems. If, after the war on crime, we are to engage in a new conversation about the consequences of the war, we need both to relax the hold of these long-entrenched positions and appreciate how much they misshaped the landscape of our policy imagination. The new discourse should take advantage of the present opportunities in some specific ways.

First, the new discourse should address the ways that the fear of crime and the politics this fear created take shape at the local level of actual cities and neighborhoods. The war on crime represented a nationalizing project that promoted a highly artificial image of a crime problem that was more or less the same everywhere. Not only was this image highly misleading about the actual incidence and prevalence of different kinds of crime problems in different communities, but also it almost certainly created more fear and more readiness to respond harshly (see generally Scheingold 1991).

There is evidence of an emerging shift to the local effects of crime facilitated by new criminological scholarship (e.g., see Western 2007; Clear 2007) and motivated by the rise of new public problems like the reentry of prisoners back into communities from warehouselike prisons that provide little incentive or help to reintegrate, the broad but highly variable "crime decline" of the 1990s (Zimring 2006), and the emergence of terrorism as a prime concern (Tonry 2004). Many of the essays in this volume offer an analysis of the current conjuncture that is grounded in local experiences, often at the city or even neighborhood level.

Second, this new discourse should recognize the emergence of new racialized political identities in America, including Latinos and Asians, that were less central to the early debates on the war on crime but whose political subjectivities have been shaped by it (Haney López 2003). The war on crime simultaneously made race less visible as a set of public problems while having an enormous impact on the construction of race in the United States. Many of the essays in this volume bring race as a constructed and contested dimension back to the center of the debate and seek to imagine racial justice as a central axis to reimagining criminal justice.

Third, this new discourse should reconsider the central goals of a criminal justice system from a perspective that looks beyond criminal justice to broader questions of governance and democracy, both in the United States and in societies confronting criminal justice problems as part of a transition from dictatorship to democracy (Godoy 2003). Many of the essays in this volume focus on specific institutions (from schools and churches to police departments and prosecutors' offices) that govern and that must operate democratically if a society is to be a democracy.

This volume's immediate goal is to spark a fresh conversation about the war on crime and its consequences; the long-term aspiration is to develop a clear understanding of how we got here and of where we should go.

Part I: Crime, War, and Governance

In the years since September 11, 2001, the problems of how governance changes during war and how war differs from the pursuit of criminal justice against lawbreakers often have been on the minds of lawyers, political theorists, and ordinary citizens. These authors have little to say to clarify those conundrums. Instead, they remind us that these problems are rooted in the decades before that terrible day, decades during which Americans were busily reconstructing the meaning of race, the order of communities, democracy, and the institutional practices and mentalities of government around the problems of crime. If we are now haunted by the sense of violence hidden among us and by a sense that the limits of executive power have become alarmingly vague when faced with such violence, this was not the product of terrorism, but it does now shape our response to it.

In Chapter 1, "The Place of the Prison in the New Government of Poverty," Loïc Wacquant outlines a theory of hyper-imprisonment as the latest configuration of the long project of governing race domination. Wacquant argues that the war on crime amounts to a fourth moment in the racial construction and subordination of African Americans: it is the next incarnation of slavery, Jim Crow, and the ghetto as a race-making institution. Wacquant suggests that this analysis identifies accounts for the major appeal of contemporary mass imprisonment, i.e., its promise to physically segregate a population. Furthermore, according to Wacquant, students of contemporary penality who emphasize "mass imprisonment" miss the distinctive concentration of incarceration on African Americans and other non-white minorities seen as similar. Wacquant's account compels us to consider the race effects of criminal justice not as collateral damage but as the core social purposes (and perhaps motivations) of crime policy. The road to racial justice now leads through a direct confrontation with the agencies and operations of the war on crime.

In Chapter 2, "America Doesn't Stop at the Rio Grande: Democracy and the War on Crime," Angelina Snodgrass Godoy locates American punitiveness in a global shift toward expressing conflicts over democracy through the mechanism and metaphors of crime control. Latin American societies share with the wealthier United States a tendency to articulate the new insecurities of the global economy and growing frustrations with democracy in terms of crime insecurity and demands for harsh penal measures. Godoy argues that, while reckoning with the damage that wars on crime have done to democracy both in the United States and Latin America, we must not treat crime as exogenous to the strategies of neo-liberal democracy. Moving alarmed publics in both places away from punitive solutions will take real democratic renewal, not just elite condemnation of punitive policies in terms of human rights.

The centrality of crime to contemporary governance is situated in American history by Chapter 3, "From the New Deal to the Crime Deal." Here Jonathan Simon argues that crime now anchors a whole way of imagining government's role in addressing the needs of post-industrial populations. In the American context, it is the successor to the New Deal, which reshaped American institutions around the promise of large economic structures to distribute risk and promoted a version of freedom tied to participation in just such large structures (unions, partially cartelized industries, etc.). Even if the war on crime is over, the "crime deal" is likely to distort our imagination of how to solve large social problems until we can replace it with a new way of imagining government.

While security has been the main justification for the war on crime, emerging evidence suggests that it has left many communities less capable of producing security. In Chapter 4, "The Great Penal Experiment: Lessons for Social Justice," Todd R. Clear points to four important consequences of "the great penal experiment." They are: (1) prison growth has had only a limited relationship to the amount of crime; (2) prison growth has been the product of intentional penal policy, not natural forces; (3) prison growth has decreased social justice; and (4) prison growth has damaged the well being of poor communities. Today we have a prison population that has outgrown its role in preventing crime and become instead an aggravating factor interfering with social justice and community safety. How can we accept that the very tools of justice might be the wedge that exacerbates injustice?

Part II: A War-Torn Country: Race, Community, and Politics

We are used to thinking of the 1950s and 1960s as decades of both social change and conflict, with vigorous social movements seeking change in courts and in Congress and violent responses of resistance and frustration, including murders, deadly riots, and police use of deadly force. But once the war on crime is taken into account, it is clear that while the decades since the 1970s have been ones of retrenchment in major institutions and diminished social movements, they have also been ones of intense conflict. The high murder rate of the 1960s continued (at least until the steep declines of the 1990s) and violent repression in the form of imprisonment, capital punishment, and police use of deadly force has increased to unprecedented levels.

Like the more optimistic social conflict of the 1950s and 1960s, the conduct of the war on crime has left profound "wounds" in the psyches and social networks of Americans. Nowhere is this more apparent than in race and its formations both in terms of communities and politics. The authors in this section document and deliberate on the ways in which the war on crime has defined racial meanings both in and out of the prison. Their nuanced portraits suggest that the war on crime did not so much reverse the gains of the civil rights movement as it did burden the exercise of the new liberties and subjectivities created by that successful struggle and undermine the capacity of institutions to undertake the hard work of desegregating American communities.

In Chapter 5, "The Code of the Streets," ethnographer Elijah Anderson demonstrates the necessity of breaking the vicious cycle of violence that has formed in our poorest and most disadvantaged communities. Endemic joblessness and persistent racism have alienated young African

American males from the mainstream and encouraged them to develop a "code of the streets," a set of informal rules governing interpersonal behavior that includes violence. A cultural adaptation to a profound lack of faith in the police and the judicial system, this code emphasizes taking care of oneself. Deprived of any other means of obtaining respect, young African American men use this code to assert control and dominance. Although the vast majority of families living in such neighborhoods rejects this code and are decent and law-abiding citizens, the minority dominates the public spaces because of their violent behavior and the ready availability of guns and drugs.

In Chapter 6, "The Contemporary Penal Subject(s)," Mona Lynch reviews the recent history of the prisoner as a subject of state power. A generation ago, prison officials and staff were encouraged to think of themselves as a helping profession engaged in the transformation of deviant subjects, suffering from psychological weaknesses and social disadvantages that could be addressed through prison therapies and parole supervision. Today, the penal subject has been recast as a motivated, rationally acting predator with few restraints on self-fulfillment other than those that can be imposed by coercion. It is this kind of penal subject that has promoted the most dangerous kind of racialization.

In Chapter 7, "The Punitive City Revisited: The Transformation of Urban Social Control," Katherine Beckett and Steve Herbert trace the racializing effects of urban policing strategies during the war on crime through a close look at evolving community police strategies in Seattle, Washington. Over the past two decades, urban governments across the United States have adopted and implemented a range of novel social control techniques. These techniques rely on and reproduce expanded definitions of crime and deviance; have led to a dramatic expansion of the state social control net; and penetrate into the fabric of the urban landscape, blurring the boundaries between guilty and innocent, private and public, inside and out. These new tools are justified in terms of (and are essential to the implementation of) "broken windows policing," an increasingly popular approach to policing that promises to improve community well being and enhance urban residents' "quality of life." This chapter describes these techniques and considers their consequences for democracy and for the governance of urban public spaces in Seattle.

But the disempowering aspects of the war on crime have not only concentrated on communities defined by the negative side of racialized fear and exclusion. In Chapter 8, "Frightening Citizens and a Pedagogy of Violence," William Lyons explores how both urban, minority-majority schools and suburban, white-majority schools have been deformed by the emergence of a zero-tolerance culture that advocates a fear-based approach to any conflict or difference and favors punishment as the primary tool for teachers and administrators. Lyons examines how this culture of fear and control governs schools in both inner-city neighborhoods and wealthy suburban enclaves and describes how 9/11 and right-wing political messaging have exacerbated the problem. By framing school conflicts as just another battleground in the war on crime, the war on drugs, or the war on terror, society is encouraged to view public school children as either uncontrollable or unsuccessfully controlled. This in turn encourages the public to support the steady reduction of investment in public education while spending increasing percentages of taxpayer dollars for prisons.

Part III: A New Reconstruction

A convergence of a number of events at the beginning of this decade, including a dramatic decline in crime throughout most of the 1990s, the emergence of new threats to national security (ranging from terrorism to climate change), and the aging of the baby-boom generation away from crime-prone youth and high-anxiety parenting years, have opened possibilities for renewal and redirection. Nothing is guaranteed. If the essays in part 3 document anything, it is that the war on crime has left enduring structures in the way Americans think about, contest, and act on the conduct of conduct. In this final section, a group of authors, many of them actively engaged in social justice work, reflect on opportunities and risks of the present moment.

In Chapter 9, "Smart on Crime," Kamala D. Harris looks for change in what many would consider the central vortex of the war on crime, i.e., the power of prosecutors to exercise their discretion. Encouraging prosecutors to look beyond the shortest-term strategies of imprisoning the actively destructive, Harris, district attorney of San Francisco, calls for strategies that reach beyond criminal law alone to consider public health and environmental justice as key aspects of community security. Discussing specific tactics that she has embraced as top prosecutor for the County of San Francisco, Harris documents how local prosecutors can regain control of the crime issue from national politicians and policy entrepreneurs.

In Chapter 10, "Rebelling Against the War on Low-Income, of Color, and Immigrant Communities," Gerald P. López advocates for a "rebellious" approach to repairing the harm caused by the war on crime. As founder and director of the Center for Community Problem Solving at New York University Law School, López teams up with low-income, of color, and immigrant communities in New York to improve society's capacity to solve problems on a whole range of issues. This partnership has started a Re-Entry Project, a Re-Entry Orientation Program, the Keeping Our Kids Out of the Criminal Justice System Campaign, and the Campaign to Hire People with Criminal Records. These programs have been instituted in response to the needs identified by those communities themselves rather than by traditional criminal justice experts.

In Chapter 11, "Of Taints and Time: The Racial Origins and Effects of Florida's Felony Disenfranchisement Law," Jessie Allen, a national leader in litigation and legislative efforts to challenge felon disenfranchisement laws, analyzes the racially discriminatory effect of Florida's law and discusses the litigation that sought to dismantle that statutory scheme as unconstitutional. Although most states bar prisoners from voting, Florida was, until 2007, one of only five states that disenfranchise everyone convicted of a felony for a lifetime. Sixteen percent of voting-age African Americans and one in four black males are disenfranchised by this law. Communities with large African American populations have thus witnessed the decline of democracy in their neighborhoods. Despite close historical links between felony disenfranchisement in Florida and efforts after Reconstruction to reduce black suffrage, the litigation challenging the law was ultimately rejected by the federal courts. Despite this, but perhaps facilitated by the attention that the litigation helped draw to this issue, Florida's political branches ultimately acted to redress many of the law's most destructive features.

In Chapter 12, "The Politics of the War Against the Young," Barry Krisberg reviews the specific ways in which the war on crime adversely impacted young people. It considers the forces that make youth especially vulnerable to irresponsible politicians and misguided crime policies. In addition to the sociological analysis of the "war against the young," the chapter describes three case studies in California in which ambitious and cynical politicians used public fear about young people to advance their personal agendas. Last, it reviews recent developments in which community and youth activists have won significant victories on behalf of young people and the lessons learned from these campaigns.

In Chapter 13, "Transformative Justice and the Dismantling of Slavery's Legacy in Post-Modern America," Mary Louise Frampton discusses the philosophy of restorative justice and the new paradigm that this values-driven model offers for our criminal justice system. By focusing on a healing and restoration approach that includes offender accountability and atonement, victim participation, and restitution as well as community involvement and responsibility, this model presents a new lens through which to view criminal justice. It points to the hundreds of local restorative-justice programs around the country that already have been successful in reducing criminal activity as well as the need for incarceration and enhancing victim satisfaction. In doing so, it also discusses a unique experiment that has evolved from the "After the War on Crime" symposium. A criminal justice working group, composed of law professors, social scientists, lawyers, policymakers, community organizations, journalists, and advocates for those most directly affected by the war on crime has been convened by the Boalt Hall Center for Social Justice to research and develop innovative strategies for repairing the harm caused by that war. This chapter discusses the formation and agenda of the group, locating this as one aspect of the emerging movement for restorative justice.

Afterword

If the war on crime has produced its own powerful alliances of interests, change will also require imagining new linkages between groups and interests now separated by that war. In a sharp and provocative afterword, community organizer and racial justice advocate Van Jones proposes a vibrant new resistance to the "shotgun wedding" of the prison-industrial complex and the military-industrial complex that has created a seamless web of repression from West Oakland to Baghdad. In the musical chairs of racial policing, the war on drugs and blacks of the 1990s has become the war on terror, Arabs, and Muslims after 9/11. In response to this unified front, Jones calls on progressives to move beyond the welfare-state approaches that have outlived their usefulness. Instead, he argues, progressives must become the custodians of a community-safety strategy that does not hesitate to expose the incarcerators as profiteers of a bloated monopoly rather than protectors of public safety.

Readers should not expect to find here a seamless or fully worked out vision of a way beyond the war on crime. We offer instead a set of highly original perspectives on the present that share a common desire to get to a better future. They are sharp and at times contending visions that come from highly specific contexts, both in and outside of criminal justice. This is in itself a refusal of the homogenizing and reductionist narratives of crime that have been produced by the war on crime itself (and at times in response to it). They will yield, if we are successful, not simply citations but a broader conversation on how to reinvigorate American cities and democracy.

NOTES

1. David Garland suggests that the demoralization of just this kind of the urban professional elite helps explain the rapid collapse of support for rehabilitation in penal policy during this same time (Garland 2001).

REFERENCES

Beckett, Katherine. 1997. *Making Crime Pay: Law and Order in Contemporary American Politics*. New York: Oxford University Press.

Clear, Todd R., and Dina R. Rose. 1999. "When Neighbors Go to Jail: Impact on Attitudes about Formal and Informal Social Control." National Institute of Justice: Research Preview. Washington, D.C.: National Institute of Justice.

Clear, Todd R. 2007. *Imprisoning Communities: How Mass Incarceration Makes Disadvantaged Neighborhoods Worse*. New York: Oxford University Press.

Fields, Barbara Jeanne. 1990. "Slavery, Race and Ideology in the United States of America." *New Left Review* 181: 95–118.

Garland, David. 2001. *The Culture of Control: Crime and Social Order in a Contemporary Society*. Chicago: University of Chicago Press.

Garland, David, ed. 2001. *Mass Imprisonment: Social Causes and Consequences*. New York: Sage.

Godoy, Angelina. 2003. "When 'Justice' Is Criminal: Crime, Communities, and Lynchings in Contemporary Latin America." Paper prepared for delivery at the 2003 meeting of the Latin American Studies Association, Dallas, Texas, March. 27–29.

Haney López, Ian. 2003. *Racism on Trial: The Chicano Fight for Justice*. Cambridge, Mass.: Harvard University Press.

Kruttschnitt, Candace, and Rosemary Gartner. 2005. *Marking Time in the Golden State: Women's Imprisonment in California*. Cambridge, U.K.: Cambridge University Press.

Pager, Devah. 2003. "The Mark of a Criminal Record." *American Journal of Sociology* 108(5): 937–75.

Parenti, Christian. 1998. *Lockdown America: Police and Prisons in the Age of Crisis.* New York: Henry Holt.

Petersilia, Joan. 2003. *When Prisoners Come Home.* New York: Oxford University Press.

Scheingold, Stuart. 1991. *The Politics of Street Crime.* Philadelphia: Temple University Press.

Simon, Jonathan. 1993. *Poor Discipline: Parole and the Social Control of the Underclass, 1890–1990.* Chicago: University of Chicago Press.

———. 2007. *Governing through Crime: The War on Crime and the Transformation of America.* New York: Oxford University Press.

Tonry, Michael. 2004. *Thinking about Crime: Sense and Sensibility in American Penal Culture.* New York: Oxford University Press.

Travis, Jeremy, Amy L. Solomon, and Michelle Wahl. 2001. *From Prison to Home: The Dimensions and Consequences of Prisoner Reentry.* Washington, D.C.: Urban Institute.

Wacquant, Loïc. 2000. "The New 'Peculiar Institution': On the Prison as Surrogate Ghetto." *Theoretical Criminology* 4(3): 377–89.

Western, Bruce. 2006. *Punishment and Inequality in America.* New York: Russell Sage Foundation.

Western, Bruce, and Katherine Beckett. 1999. "How Unregulated Is the U.S. Labor Market? The Penal System as a Labor Market Institution." *American Journal of Sociology* 104(4): 1030–1062.

Zimring, Franklin E. 2006. *The Great American Crime Decline.* New York: Oxford University Press.

Zimring, Franklin, and Gordon Hawkins. 1991. *The Scale of Imprisonment.* Chicago: University of Chicago Press.

Part I

Crime, War, and Governance

[*Chapter 1*]

The Place of the Prison in the New Government of Poverty[1]

Loïc Wacquant

Grasping the changing roles of the penal state in the post-Fordist and post-Keynesian age requires a double rupture. One must first break out of the dominant paradigm of "crime and punishment," incarnated by criminology and criminal law, which keeps us confined within a narrow law-enforcement perspective that cannot account for the rising punitiveness of the authorities inasmuch as it steadfastly ignores the extra-penological missions of the prison. A simple statistic suffices here to spotlight the glaring and growing disconnect between crime and incarceration in the United States: in 1975 the country locked up twenty-one inmates for every 1,000 serious crimes (homicide, rape, assault, robbery, theft, and car theft counted together); by 1999 this ratio had reached 106 (Bureau of Justice Statistics 2001, 528). Holding crime constant reveals that American society is *five times more punitive now* than it was a quarter of a century ago. But one must similarly sweep aside the oppositional tale of the "prison-industrial complex" elaborated by activists, journalists, and scholars mobilized against penal escalation, who variously misattribute America's carceral boom to the global restructuring of capitalism, intensifying racism, and the frantic search for profit via prison building and the superexploitation of convict labor.

When we stop to think about it, we also realize that the label "War on Crime" is a misnomer on three grounds, rhetorical as well as substantive. First, wars are waged by the military against foreign enemies of the nation whereas confronting lawbreaking, however harshly, involves civilian agencies handling citizens and denizens who are protected by an array of rights and who, instead of being exiled or annihilated on capture, mingle back into society after their stint in penal custody. Second, the so-called war proclaimed by federal and local authorities was never waged on "crime" in general. It was targeted on certain categories of illegalities perpetrated in a definite sector of physical and social space: essentially street crime committed in the segregated lower-class districts of the American metropolis. Third, and most important, activating the fight against crime has been but the *pretext and springboard for a broader remaking of the perimeter and functions of the state*, which has entailed the concurrent and convergent "downsizing" of its welfare component and "upsizing" of its police, courts, and correctional wings.

The Triadic Institutional Nexus of the Prison

Between 1975 and 2000, the carceral stock of the United States exploded from 380,000 to 2 million while the welfare rolls plummeted from 11 million to fewer than 5 million. To quadruple its inmate count between 1980 and 2000 and place some 6.5 million under criminal justice supervision (including parolees and probationers), the United States increased the combined budgets of federal, state, and local correctional administrations by 50 billion dollars and added half-a-million staff, making jails and prisons the country's third largest employer in 1998, behind only Manpower Incorporated and Wal-Mart. Every year since 1985, the nation's custodial expenditures have exceeded the monies allotted to both Food Stamps and Aid to Families with Dependent Children (AFDC): in 1995, on the eve of "welfare reform," the United States spent $46 billion to operate its houses of detention against less than $20 billion for AFDC (Gifford 2002, 8; Committee on Ways and Means 1997, 921). Yet, because public administrations could not expand fast enough to contain the ever-rising tide of convicts, the carceral boom led to the renaissance of private incarceration. In just a decade, for-profit operators captured 7 percent of the "market," offering 120,000 extra beds in 1998, equal to the carceral populations of France, Italy, and Spain combined.

More than the specifics of statistical figures and trends, however, it is this deep-seated logic of this swing from the social to the penal that one must grasp here. Far from contradicting the neoliberal project of deregulation and decay of the public sector, the irresistible rise of the penal state in the United States constitutes, as it were, its negative—in the sense of obverse but also of revelator—since it manifests the implementation of a policy of the *criminalization of poverty that is the indispensable complement to the imposition of precarious and underpaid wage labor* as civic obligation for those trapped at the bottom of the class and caste structure, as well as the redeployment of social-welfare programs in a restrictive and punitive sense that is concomitant with it. At the time of its institutionalization in the United States during the mid-nineteenth century, "imprisonment was above all a method aiming at the control of deviant and dependent populations," and inmates were mainly poor people and European immigrants recently arrived in the New World (Rothman 1971, 254–55). Nowadays, the carceral apparatus of the United States fills an analogous role with respect to those groups rendered superfluous or incongruous by the twofold restructuring of the wage labor relation and state charity: the declining fractions of the working class and poor blacks snared in the dilapidated core of formerly industrial cities. In so doing, the prison has regained a central place in the panoply of instruments for the government of poverty, at the crossroads of the deskilled labor market, the collapsing urban ghetto, and social-welfare services "reformed" with a view to buttressing the discipline of desocialized wage work.

1. Prison and the Deskilled Labor Market

In the first place, the penal system contributes directly to *regulating the lower segments of the labor market*—and it does so in a manner more coercive and consequential than labor legislation, social insurance schemes, and other administrative rules, many of which do not cover insecure work anyway. Its effect on this front is threefold. First, the stupendous prevalence and escalation of penal sanctions helps to discipline the reticent fractions of the working class by raising the cost of strategies of resistance to desocialized wage labor via "exit" into the informal economy. Faced with aggressive policing, severe courts, and the likelihood of brutally long prison sentences for drug offenses and recidivism, many shrink from getting or staying involved in the illegal commerce of the street and submit instead to the dictate of insecure employment. For some of those coming out of "the pen," the tight mesh of post-correctional supervision increases pressure to opt for the "straight" life anchored in work, when it is available (Nelson, Dees, and Allen 1999). On both counts, the criminal justice system acts in concordance with workfare to push its clientele onto the peripheral segments of the deskilled job market.

Second, the carceral apparatus helps to "fluidify" the low-wage sector

and artificially depresses the unemployment rate by forcibly subtract-
ing millions of unskilled men from the labor force. It is estimated that
penal confinement shaved two full percentage points off the U.S. jobless
rate during the 1990s. Indeed, according to Bruce Western and Katherine
Beckett, when the differential between the incarceration level of the two
zones is taken into account, the United States posted an unemployment
rate higher than the average for the European Union during eighteen of
the twenty years between 1974 and 1994, contrary to the view propagated
by the adulators of neoliberalism and critics of "Eurosclerosis" (Western
and Beckett 1999). While it is true that not all inmates would be in the
labor force if free, that gap of 2 percent does not include the Keynesian
stimulus provided by booming public expenditures and employment in
corrections: the number of jail and prison jobs at the local, state, and federal level more than doubled over the past two decades, jumping from
under 300,000 in 1982 to over 716,000 in 1999, when monthly payroll
exceeded $2.1 billion (Gifford 2002, 7).[2] Penal growth has also boosted
employment in the private sector of carceral goods and services, a sector
with a high rate of precarious jobs and turnover and that is rising along
with the privatization of punishment (since the source of the "competitiveness" of correctional firms is the exceedingly low wages and meager
benefits they give their staff).

Western and Beckett argue that carceral hypertrophy is a two-pronged,
delayed mechanism with contradictory effects: while it embellishes the
employment picture in the short run by amputating labor supply at the
bottom of the occupational ladder, in the longer term it can only aggra-
vate it by making millions more or less unemployable. In their view, "incarceration has lowered the U.S. unemployment rate, but . . . sustained
low unemployment in the future will depend on continuing expansion of
the penal system" (Western and Beckett 1999, 1031). But this overlooks a
third impact of hyperincarceration on the labor market, which is to facilitate the development of sub-poverty jobs and the informal economy by
continually (re)generating a large volume of marginal laborers who can
be superexploited at will. Former inmates can hardly lay claim to better
than degraded and degrading work because of their interrupted trajectories, distended social ties, ignominious judicial status, and the manifold
legal restrictions and civil liabilities it carries. The half-million convicts
streaming out of American prisons every year provide the vulnerable
labor power suited to fuel the temporary employment sector, the fast-
est growing segment of the U.S. labor market over the past two decades

(it accounts for one-fifth of all new jobs created since 1984) (Peck and Theodore 1998; Barker and Kristensen 1998). Extreme imprisonment thus feeds contingent employment, which is the spearhead for the flexibilization of wage labor in the lower tier of the jobs distribution. In addition, the proliferation of detention facilities across the country—their number has tripled in thirty years to surpass 4,800—contributes directly to the national growth and diffusion of illicit trafficking (of drugs, prostitution, stolen goods) that are the driving engine of the booty capitalism of the street. Countless small towns in rural areas have lobbied hard to build prisons or bring in inmates from overcrowded urban jails in the hope of stemming economic decline. But, along with convicts, they have unwittingly imported the cultural and economic influences of their visitors and associates, including gangs and the gamut of illegal activities they routinely engage in, for which the carceral population provides a stable consumer base.[3]

2. Prison and the Imploding Ghetto

The massive and growing overrepresentation of lower-class African Americans at every level of the penal apparatus shines a harsh light on the second function assumed by the carceral system in the new government of poverty in America: *to complement and compensate for the collapsing ghetto as device for the confinement* of a population considered deviant, devious, and dangerous as well as superfluous, on an economic plane—Mexican and Asian immigrants make more docile laborers (Waldinger and Lichter 2003)—as well as on a political plane—poor African Americans hardly vote and, in any case, the country's center of electoral gravity has shifted away from declining central cities to well-off white suburbs.[4]

From this angle, incarceration is only the paroxystic manifestation of the logic of ethnoracial exclusion of which the ghetto has been the instrument and product since its historical inception. During the half century (1915–1965) dominated by the Fordist industrial economy to which African Americans contributed an indispensable pool of unskilled labor, i.e., from World War I, which triggered the "Great Migration" from the segregationist states of the South to the worker metropolises of the North, to the civil rights revolution, which finally gave African Americans access to the ballot box a hundred years after the abolition of slavery, the ghetto served as a "social prison" in that it ensured the systematic social ostracization of African Americans while enabling the exploitation of their labor power in the city. Since the debilitating crisis of the ghetto, symbolized by the great wave of urban revolts that swept the country during the mid-1960s, it is the prison that is in turn serving as surrogate "ghetto" by warehousing the fractions of the African American (sub)proletariat that have been marginalized by the transition to the dual-service economy and by state policies of welfare retrenchment and urban withdrawal (Kerner Commission 1969/1989; Harris and Curtis 1998; Wacquant 2007).

The two institutions of ghetto and prison have thus become coupled and they complement each other in that each operates in its own manner to enforce the setting apart (the etymological meaning of *segregare*) of an undesirable category perceived as threatening the metropolis with a twofold menace, inseparably physical and moral. And this structural and functional symbiosis between ghetto and prison finds a striking cultural expression in the lyrics and the lifestyle flouted by "gangsta rap" musicians, as attested by the tragic destiny of the singer-composer Tupac Shakur. Born in prison from an absentee father (his mother, Afeni Shakur, was a member of the Black Panthers), the apostle of "thug life," hero to a multitude of ghetto youths (and hordes of white suburban teens), died in 1996 in Las Vegas, riddled with bullets in a car ambush set up by members of a rival gang, after having himself been accused of shooting at police officers and serving eight months for sexual assault (White 1997/2002).

3. Prison and Welfare-Turned-Workfare

As it was at its birth, the carceral institution is now directly connected to the gamut of organizations and programs entrusted with "assisting" dispossessed populations, in step with the increasing organizational and ideological interpenetration between the social and penal sectors of the post-Keynesian state. On the one side, the panoptic and punitive logic proper to the penal field tends to contaminate and then redefine the objectives and mechanisms of delivery of public aid (Katz 1996, 300–34; Handler and Hasenfeld 1997). Thus, in addition to replacing the right of indigent children to state assistance with the obligation for their parents to work after two years, the "welfare reform" endorsed by President Clinton in 1996 subjects public aid recipients to intrusive practices of lifelong record-keeping and close supervision, and it establishes a strict monitoring of their behaviors—in matters of education, employment, drug consumption, and sexuality—liable to trigger sanctions both administrative and criminal. For example, since October 1998, in central Michigan welfare recipients must submit to periodic drug testing, as do convicts on probation or parole, and their testing is carried out by the state's department of corrections in offices where they mingle with parolees. On the other side, correctional facilities must *nolens volens* face up, under conditions of permanent penury and emergency, to the social and medical hardship that their "clientele" did not manage to resolve on the outside: in the country's major cities, the biggest homeless shelter and the largest mental health facility readily accessible to subproletarians is the county jail (Fuller 1995). And the same population cycles through from one pole of this institutional continuum to the other in a near-closed orbit that entrenches their socioeconomic marginality and intensifies their sense of indignity.

Finally, budgetary constraints and the political fashion for "less government" have converged to push toward the commodification of welfare no less than that of incarceration. Several jurisdictions, such as Texas and Tennessee, already consign a sizable portion of their convicts to private establishments *and* subcontract the administrative handling of public aid recipients to specialized firms because the state does not possess the administrative capacity to implement its new poverty policy. This is a way of making poor people and prisoners (the vast majority of whom were poor on the outside and will be poor again when they get out) "profitable," on the ideological if not on the economic level. What we are witnessing here is the genesis, not of a "prison-industrial complex," as suggested by some criminologists following after journalists and justice activists mobilized against the growth of the penal state (Lilly and Knepper 1993; Schlosser 1998; Goldberg and Evans 1998),[5] but of a truly novel organizational figure, a partially *commercialized, carceral-assistential continuum* that is the spearhead of the nascent liberal-paternalist state. Its mission is to surveil and subjugate, and, if need be, chastise and neutralize, the populations refractory to the new economic order according to a gendered division of labor, with its carceral component handling mainly the men while its assistential component exercises its tutelage over (their) women and children. In keeping with the American political tradition established during the colonial era, this composite institutional ensemble *in statu nascendi* is characterized, on the one hand, by the deep interpenetration of the public and private sectors and, on the other, by the fusion of the functions of branding, moral redress, and repression of the state.

The Demonic Myth of the "Prison-Industrial Complex"

Scholars, activists and ordinary citizens concerned with, or dismayed by, the runaway growth of America's penal system have failed to detect this new triadic institutional nexus of the prison because they have been obsessed by the apparent linkage between incarceration and profit. For the past decade, the refrain of the rise of a "prison-industrial complex" that would have succeeded (or supplemented) the "military-industrial complex" of the cold war era with defense industry giants retooling from supplying arms to the Pentagon to providing surveillance and punishment for the poor, the fear of the "red enemy" of the exterior being replaced by dread for the "black enemy" of the interior, and private operators acting in cahoots with corrections officials and politicians to constitute a shadowy "subgovernment" pushing for limitless carceral expansion aimed at exploiting the booming captive workforce, has been a leitmotiv of the oppositional discourse on prison in the United States (e.g., Donziger 1996; Rosenblatt 1996; Davis and Gordon 1999; Braz et al., 2000). Anchored in a conspiratorial vision of history, this thesis suffers from four major lacunae that undercut its analytical import and ruin its practical pertinence.

First, it reduces the *twofold, conjoint and interactive, transformation of the social and penal components* of the bureaucratic field to the sole "industrialization" of incarceration. But the changing scale of confinement in America is only one element of a broader redefinition of the perimeter and modalities of state action with regard to the "problem populations" residing in the nether regions of social and urban space. It is tightly connected to, and cannot be explained in isolation from, the epochal transition from "welfare" to "workfare" (Wacquant 1996). By contrast, it is very dubious whether it can be tied to the "globalization" of the overly large and vague "-isms" of capitalism and racism—the two favorite culprits in this activist tale of government evil—neither of which provide the necessary and sufficient conditions for America's unprecedented and unrivaled carceral experiment. To start with, carceral inflation in the United States set off well before the acceleration of capital mobility across borders, and other advanced countries that have experienced a similar internationalization of their economy have sported only modest growth in their prison populations fed by the lengthening of sentences and not increased admissions.[6] Next, while the operation of the justice system is stamped by ethnoracial bias, it is hard to see how discrimination could have *intensified* since the 1970s, given the increased stress on due process and legal safeguards instituted in the wake of the civil rights revolution, not to mention the growing presence of black police, judges, guards, wardens, and parole officers at all levels of the penal apparatus.

Second, the imagery of the "prison-industrial complex" accords the role of driving force to the pecuniary interest of firms selling correctional services and wares or allegedly tapping the vast reserves of labor held under lock (Dyer 2000). It maintains that the profit motive is crucial to the onset of mass incarceration when, in reality, the latter pertains first and foremost to a *political logic and project*, namely, the construction of a post-Keynesian, "liberal-paternalistic" state suited to institute desocialized wage labor and propagate the renewed ethic of work and "individual responsibility" that buttress it. Profiteering from corrections is not a primary cause but an incidental and *secondary consequence* of the gargantuan development of the penal apparatus. Indeed, the fact that private concerns are reaping benefits from the expansion of a government function is neither new nor specific to imprisonment: the delivery of every major public good in the United States, from education and housing to safety and health care, grants a vast role to commercial or third-sector parties—relative to medical provision for instance, punishment remains distinctively public (Hacker 2002). Nor is privatization necessary to carceral growth: banning imprisonment for profit did not prevent California from joining the frenzied rush to confine. Between 1980 and 2000, the Golden State saw its convict population skyrocket from 27,000 to 160,000; its correctional budget balloon from $400 million to $4.2 billion; and its correctional staff swell from 8,400 to 48,000, all without opening a single private adult facility. In point of fact, if commercial operators were made to vanish overnight, states and counties would face operational disruptions, increased overcrowding, and short-term obstacles to growth, but the overall prevalence and social physiognomy of incarceration would remain untouched.

Similarly, the ritual denunciation of the superexploitation of inmates under conditions evocative of penal slavery cannot hide the fact that only a minuscule and stagnant fraction of the U.S. carceral population works for outside firms (well under 1 percent by the most generous counts) and that no economic sector relies even marginally on convict laborers. As for the prisoners toiling for state or federal industries behind bars (about 8 percent by the largest estimates), their output is negligible and they are "employed" at a net loss to the government, even though their activity is massively subsidized and heavily protected.[7] Its spectacular growth notwithstanding, it is hard to square the claim made by Goldberg and Evans (1998, 5) that "the prison industrial complex is becoming increasingly central to the growth of the U.S. economy" with the raw statistics of national accounting: the $57 billion that the United States spent on corrections at the local, state, and federal level in 2001 amounted to barely *one-half of 1 percent of the Gross Domestic Product* of $10,128 billion that year. Far from being "an essential component of the U.S. economy," corrections remains insignificant on the production side and acts not as an overall stimulus to corporate profits but a gross drain on the public coffers and a meaningless diversion to financial capital.

Third, this activist vision is premised on a flawed parallelism between the state functions of national defense and penal administration, which overlooks this crucial difference: military policy is highly centralized and coordinated at the federal level, whereas crime control is widely decentralized and dispersed among federal authorities, one hundred state departments of justice and corrections, and thousands of county and city administrations in charge of the police, courts, and jails. The phrase "criminal justice system" hides a loosely coupled web of bureaucratic agencies endowed with wide discretion and devoid of an overarching penal philosophy or policy. Even if some far-sighted ruling group had somehow concocted a nightmarish plan designed to turn the carceral system into a lucrative industry using the bodies of the dark-skinned poor as "raw materials," there is no single lever that it could have seized and used to ensure their delivery. The simplistic thesis that capitalist lucre drives carceral growth leaves unexplained the specific mechanisms that have produced the remarkable convergence of correctional trends across the different jurisdictions of the United States and only adds to the "compound mystery" of nationwide hyperincarceration in the absence of "a distinctive policy precursor" (Zimring and Hawkins 1991, 173).

Finally, constricted by its prosecutorial approach, the woolly notion of "prison-industrial complex" overlooks the wide-ranging effects of the introduction, albeit in a limited and perverted form, of the *welfarist logic within the carceral universe itself.* Correctional institutions have been profoundly transformed over the past three decades, not only by changes in the scale and composition of their clientele, but also by the prisoners' rights movement, the rationalization and professionalization of confinement, and the increasing oversight of the courts (Feeley and Rubin 1998). Thus, judges have demanded of jail and prison authorities that they meet a battery of minimal norms in matters of individual rights and institutional services, entailing for example the provision of education to under-age inmates and psychiatric services on a mass scale. However deficient it remains, correctional health care has improved substantially to the point where it is typically superior to the meager medical services accessible to the poorest convicts on the outside, and it reaches millions yearly—so much so that public health scholars and officials have come to view the carceral system as a crucial point of intervention for detecting and treating a range of infectious diseases common among low-income urban populations (Glaser and Greifinger 1993).

Coda

Breaking out of the angelic law-enforcement paradigm and exorcizing the demonic myth of the "prison-industrial complex" are two necessary and complementary steps required to properly locate the novel functions that the prison shoulders in the reconfigured system of instruments for managing deregulated labor, ethnoracial hierarchy, and urban marginality in the contemporary United States. Taking these two steps reveals that the unleashing of a hypertrophic and hyperactive penal apparatus after the mid-1970s is neither the blunt weapon of a "war on crime" nor the spawn of a devilish collusion between public officials and private corporations intending to profiteer from incarceration. It partakes, rather, of the building of a revamped state suited to imposing the astringent economic and moral requirements of neoliberalism after the discarding of the Fordist-Keynesian social compact and the implosion of the black ghetto. The onset of this new government of poverty mating restrictive workfare and expansive punishment demands that we bring the prison out of the technical domains of criminology and crime policy and place it squarely at the center of political sociology and civic action.

NOTES

1. For all the talk of "lock 'em up and throw away the key," upwards of 95 percent of all convicts entering state and federal prisons eventually come out. "Lifers" and inmates sentenced to death contribute only approximate 5,700 bodies to the country's convict population each year (Bureau of Justice Statistics 1995, 2).

2. This gives the United States 24 correctional employees per 10,000 residents

in full-time equivalents, compared to 4 per 10,000 for France (24,220 staff), 5 for Spain (22,035), and 8 for England and Wales (41,065) (according to data from Tournier 2001, 47).

3. In addition, rural counties have seen their justice system swamped with cases of felonies committed *behind bars*, amounting to one-quarter or one-third of their caseload, which they do not have the resources to handle. As a result, local prosecutors often overlook prison crime committed in their district (Weisheit et al. 1995).

4. For a compressed historical and conceptual elaboration on the coupling of (hyper)ghetto and prison after the ebbing of the civil rights movement, see Wacquant 2000.

5. A trove of activist writings, calls, and information on the topic is on the site www.prisonsucks.com run by the Prison Policy Initiative (based in Northampton, Massachusetts).

6. The international variant of the tale of the "prison-industrial complex" said to ensnare "women of color, immigrants, and indigenous women" all over the globe due to the collusion between states and private prison corporations (Sudbury 2005) is even more implausible than its masculine domestic version.

7. In fiscal 2001, UNICOR, the Federal Prison Industries program, employed 22,600 inmates to produce a variety of goods (law-enforcement uniforms and Kevlar helmets, bedding and draperies, office furniture, laundry services, bindery, vehicular repair, electronics recycling, etc.) sold to the government for a turnover of $583 million. Despite financial subsidies, a captive market (two-thirds of sales are to the Defense Department), and inmate wages averaging a paltry 23 cents to $1.15 an hour, the program turned up a negative cash flow of $5 million dollars (Federal Bureau of Prisons 2001).

REFERENCES

Barker, Kathleen, and Kathleen Kristensen, eds. 1998. *Contingent Work: American Employment Relations in Transition*. Ithaca, N.Y.: Cornell University Press.

Bureau of Justice Statistics. 2001. *Sourcebook of Criminal Justice Statistics 2000*. Washington, D.C.: Government Printing Office.

Bureau of Justice Statistics. 1995. "State Inmates, 1992–1994: Violent Offenders in State Prison: Sentences and Time Served." Washington, D.C.: Government Printing Office. NCJ-154632. http://www.ojp.usdoj.gov/bjs/pub/pdf/vospats.pdf.

Braz, Rose, et al. 2000. "Overview: Critical Resistance to the Prison-Industrial Complex" (introduction to a symposium on "The Prison-Industrial Complex"). *Social Justice* 27(3): 1–5.

Committee on Ways and Means. 1997. *1996 Green Book*. Washington, D.C.: Government Printing Office.

Davis, Angela, and A. F. Gordon. 1999. "Globalism and the Prison-Industrial Complex: An Interview with Angela Davis." *Race and Class* 40(2/3): 145–57.

Donziger, Marc R. 1996. *The Real War on Crime.* New York: Harper Perennial.

Dyer, Joel. 2000. *The Perpetual Prisoner Machine: How America Profits from Crime.* Boulder, Colo.: Westview.

Edsall, Thomas Byrne, and Mary D. Edsall. 1999. *Chain Reaction: The Impact of Race, Rights, and Taxes on American Politics.* New York: W. W. Norton.

Federal Bureau of Prisons. 2001. *UNICOR 2001 Annual Report.* http://www.unicor .gov/information/publications/pdfs/corporate/CATAR2001.pdf.

Feeley, Malcolm, and Edward L. Rubin. 1998. *Judicial Policy Making and the Modern State: How the Courts Reformed America's Prisons.* New York: Oxford University Press.

Fuller, Torrey E. 1995. "Jails and Prisons: America's New Mental Hospitals." *American Journal of Public Health* 85(12): 1611–13.

Gifford, Sidra Lea. 2002. *Justice Expenditures and Employment in the United States, 1999.* Washington, D.C.: Bureau of Justice Statistics, U.S. Department of Justice.

Glaser, Jordan B., and Robert B. Greifinger. 1993. "Correctional Health Care: A Public Health Opportunity." *Annals of Internal Medicine* 118(2): 139–45.

Goldberg, Eve, and Linda Evans. 1998. *The Prison Industrial Complex and the Global Economy.* Boston: Kersplebedeb.

Hacker, Jacob S. 2002. *The Divided Welfare State: The Battle over Public and Private Social Benefits in the United States.* New York: Cambridge University Press.

Handler, Joel, and Yeheskel Hasenfeld. 1997. *We the Poor People: Work, Poverty, and Welfare.* New Haven, Conn.: Yale University Press.

Harris, Fred R., and Lynn Curtis, eds. 1998. *Locked in the Poorhouse: Cities, Race, and Poverty in the United States.* Lanham, Md.: Rowman & Littlefield.

Katz, Michael B. 1996. *In the Shadow of the Poorhouse: A Social History of Welfare in America.* Exp. ed. New York: Basic Books.

Kerner Commission. 1969/1989. The Kerner Report: The 1968 Report of the National Advisory Commission on Civil Disorders. New York: Pantheon.

Lilly, J. Robert, and Paul Knepper. 1993. "The Corrections-Commercial Complex." *Crime and Delinquency* 39(2): 150–66.

Nelson, Marta, Perry Dees, and Charlotte Allen. 1999. *The First Month Out: Post-Incarceration Experiences in New York City.* New York: Vera Institute.

Peck, Jamie, and Nikolas Theodore. 1998. "The Business of Contingent Work: Growth and Restructuring in Chicago's Temporary Employment Industry." *Work, Employment & Society* 12(4): 655–74.

Rosenblatt, Elihu, ed. 1996. *Criminal Injustice: Confronting the Prison Crisis.* Boston: South End Press.

Rothman, David. 1971. *The Discovery of the Asylum: Social Order and Disorder in the New Republic.* Boston: Little, Brown.

Schlosser, Eric. 1998. "The Prison-Industrial Complex." *Atlantic Monthly* 282 (December): 51–77.

Sudbury, Julia. 2005. *Global Lockdown: Race, Gender, and the Prison-Industrial Complex.* New York: Routledge.

Tournier, Pierre V. 2001. *SPACE I (Statistique Pénale Annuelle du Conseil de l'Europe): Enquête 2000 Sur les Populations Pénitentiaires, Version Définitive.* Strasbourg: Conseil de Coopération Pénologique, PC–CP.

Wacquant, Loïc. 1996. "De l'Etat charitable à l'Etat pénal: notes sur le traitement politique de la misère en Amérique." *Regards Sociologiques* 11: 30–38.

———. 2000. "The New 'Peculiar Institution': On the Prison as Surrogate Ghetto," *Theoretical Criminology* 4(3): 377–89.

———. 2007. *Urban Outcasts: A Comparative Sociology of Advanced Marginality.* Cambridge, U.K.: Polity.

Waldinger, Roger, and Michael Lichter. 2003. *How the Other Half Works: Immigration and the Social Organization of Labor.* Berkeley: University of California Press.

Weisheit, Ralph A., L. Edward Wells, and David N. Falcone. 1995. *Crime and Policing in Rural and Small-Town America: An Overview of the Issues.* Washington, D.C.: Bureau of Justice Statistics.

Western, Bruce, and Katherine Beckett. 1999. "How Unregulated Is the U.S. Labor Market? The Penal System as a Labor Market Institution." *American Journal of Sociology* 104(4): 1030–60.

White, Armond. 1997/2002. *Rebel for the Hell of It: Life of Tupac Shakur.* 2nd ed. London: Quartet Books.

Zimring, Franklin E., and Gordon J. Hawkins. 1991. *The Scale of Imprisonment.* Chicago: University of Chicago Press.

Chapter 2

America Doesn't Stop at the Rio Grande
Democracy and the War on Crime

Angelina Snodgrass Godoy

As numerous scholars have shown, the war on crime was launched at a time of decreasing crime rates; its rhetoric reflected specific anxieties about race, class, and the shifting balance of power in contemporary society; and its policies have served as a primary mechanism by which structures of exclusion have been reinforced in recent decades. Although it may be true that some of the rhetorical zeal and political force behind this war appear to have been expended, it also appears that new fronts have opened in the years since its inception. To come to grips with some of these transformations, it may be helpful to place American developments in a broader, global context.

As a sociologist who studies Latin America, I believe there are both empirical and theoretical reasons to undertake such an endeavor. First, America does not stop at the Rio Grande. And I do not mean this only as a reminder that "America" is a pair of continents rather than a single nation—that residents of Buenos Aires or Banff also lay legitimate claim to the title of being American—but, more important, as an attempt to recenter the debate, at least for a moment, in recognition of the transnational dynamics of crime and punishment today. Second, acknowledging the broadening of the war on crime's battlefields invites comparative analysis of the tensions that have given rise to developments in many nations similar to those experienced in America as a result. Not only are globalizing forces arguably exerting a stronger pull today than when the war on crime was launched, but also political conditions within many countries have converged, in some ways, on a common model that pairs the political institutions of democracy with entrenched social exclusion. In today's neoliberal democracies, the criminal justice regime serves to shore up the status quo despite the recent extension of citizenship rights to many previously excluded sectors of the population. I argue here that the war on crime must be understood as a reaction to precisely these developments in contemporary democracies.

Globalized Wars on Crime, Drugs, and Terror

Today, other nations are inescapably enmeshed in the United States' penal order; to talk about crime or punishment without acknowledging the transnational reality of both would be to miss important elements of the contemporary penal regime. This is abundantly clear in Latin America, a region to which the United States has effectively exported criminals by the thousands since the early 1990s. Their activities have contributed to skyrocketing rates of violence in countries such as El Salvador and Guatemala—where young men, many of them schooled in gang culture on the streets of Los Angeles or other U.S. cities, have been returned to their countries of origin despite having spent (in some cases) their entire productive lives in the United States. Not surprising, many have continued their gang activity, knitting together transnational networks involved in drug trafficking, auto theft, and trafficking in persons across the region, with tentacles stretching into the United States. These are the so-called "mega-gangs," the notorious Mara Salvatrucha and M-18 (both of which the F.B.I. convened a task force to combat in early 2005, arresting hundreds of alleged members in cities across the United States).

In response to gang violence and other crime in the region, the United States also exports penal knowledge and technology, as Loïc Wacquant and other scholars have shown. Yet this export is not limited to training or assistance but also includes the dictating of criminal justice policy itself. The paradigmatic example is the war on drugs with its attendant certification process whereby countries' compliance with U.S. expectations for counternarcotics enforcement is assessed, and those failing to "cooperate" in the war on drugs risk exclusion from trade and aid. To avoid such sanctions, countries such as Bolivia have penalized coca production over the objections of their population, effectively surrendering juridical sovereignty in exchange for aid and investment.

And, for that matter, the wars on crime and drugs have begun to blur with the war on terror, too. Speculation has already, in fact, linked al-Qaeda with the Mara Salvatrucha (Arana 2005). In March 2005, U.S. Representative Dan Burton, Chair of the Congressional Subcommittee on the Western Hemisphere, called a congressional hearing on the Central American gang problem, warning, "These gangs represent the very real threat of homegrown terror. [Their] nefarious activities are severely undermining the support for democratic institutions and reforms that we have worked so hard to develop" (U.S. Congressional Committee on International Relations 2005). As fears of crime mingle with concerns about drugs and terrorism, the distinction between external wars fought by armies and internal policing efforts is extraordinarily blurred—if, indeed, it can still be said to exist at all. Given the permeability of these borders, it is difficult to discern whether the war on crime has really ended or perhaps only shifted to new tactics and fronts.

Examining the Latin American experiences of crime and punishment forces us to move beyond assumptions of "American" exceptionalism and reckon with the fact that U.S. trends in punishment may be part of a broader political and economic restructuring. I return to this argument below, after first providing a brief overview of recent trends in Latin America for readers who may be unfamiliar with this context.

Realities of Latin America Today

Transitions from authoritarianism and semiauthoritarian government— the so-called "third wave"—have taken places in many countries of the "developing" world in recent decades; in a good many (perhaps even a majority) of them, these transitions have been accompanied by spikes in crime rates. In some countries, such as the ones I know best in Central America, the word "spike" does not quite do justice to what in fact has been a prolonged, powerful, and very serious crime wave with homicides soaring over 100 per 100,000 in some countries by some estimates. While there exists considerable variation among countries in the region, average homicide rates are higher in Latin America than in any other region of the world, and they continue to climb (Ayres 1998). Some estimates place Latin America's homicide rate at twice the world average (Buvinic, et al. 1999, 2), others as high as five times the world average (Fay 2005, 8). And some individual countries, such as Guatemala and El Salvador, have homicide rates that are on orders of magnitude higher than the regional average.

Alarming as these numbers may be, perhaps we should not be surprised. For while Latin America is not the world's poorest region, it "is the most unequal region in the world" (Jones 2004, 48). Even World Bank researchers have concluded that "countries with more unequal distributions of income tend to have higher crime rates than those with more egalitarian patterns of income distribution," and that "changes in income distribution, not changes in absolute levels of poverty, are associated with changes in violent crime rates" (Lederman and Loayza 1999, 8). The implications of this for Latin America are obvious; clearly, the trend toward income polarization in recent decades has only exacerbated the problem.

Aside from these macroeconomic trends, other explanations abound. In the wake of the widespread and often indiscriminate use of violence by states and guerrilla armies alike, some argue that local populations have become desensitized to violence; this "trivialization of horror" (Torres-Rivas 1999) has effects that far outlast the wars that spawned it. In Central America, for example, the ranks of the unemployed swell with demobilized combatants and former paramilitaries well versed in the use of weapons and skilled in the mounting of clandestine operations. Improved communications and legacies of corruption have facilitated the growth of transnational crime syndicates trafficking in drugs, migrants, stolen property, and small arms. Decades of economic modernization, rural warfare, and deepening agrarian crises have provoked mass migration to metropolitan areas without sufficient social services to absorb, educate, and train recent arrivals for productive employment, making shantytowns fertile breeding ground for criminal activity. State justice systems are woefully overburdened, in part by structures of entrenched impunity erected during the authoritarian period to protect those involved in rights abuses; these patterns continue to stymie prosecution for political and nonpolitical crimes today. While any one of this litany of factors, in isolation, might legitimately be interpreted as fuelling criminal violence, the confluence of so many has converted some countries in the region into cauldrons of criminal activity. These are the unwelcome dividends of democratization.

Perhaps unsurprising then, in reaction to a profound sense of citizen insecurity, many Latin Americans have begun to question the value of democracy itself. A 2004 study by the U.N. Development Programme revealed that Latin American democracies are suffering from a deep crisis in citizen confidence. In response to rampant insecurity, many have willingly acceded to, even clamored for, partial rollbacks in some of the key civil liberties that their countrymen and women struggled and even sacrificed their lives to achieve not so many years before under dictatorships. Today, crime regularly tops lists of citizens' concerns, and the tactics, language, and institutions involved in its combat are all strikingly similar to the period of military rule—indeed, the armies of Central America whose bloated budgets have long exceeded justification (at least in terms of the likelihood of external military threat) are all too happy to have a new mission to carry out to justify their existence; today they hunt so-called "delincuentes" instead of communists, but the similarities are striking, overt, and in many ways intentional. Indeed, one term used to describe a "tough on crime" stance in Latin America—*mano dura*—has its roots in dictatorships' avowed intolerance of dissent and disorder in all its forms. Much of today's "crime talk" reveals a certain nostalgia for authoritarianism, and concern about crime has led to attempts to restart the political careers of some former military leaders famed for their severity.

Guatemala and El Salvador provide apt examples of these dynamics at work. Following bloody civil wars in both countries, hopes of democratic reconstruction dimmed in the face of massive crime waves, fuelled by widening inequality. In both countries, conservative politicians have emerged in recent years with "answers" to crime that sound familiar. In Guatemala, former dictator General Efraín Ríos Montt ran for president in 2003 on a platform emphasizing security and harkening back to the bad old days of the genocide that occurred on his watch by promising *mano dura* against crime; political scientist Dinorah Azpuru has found significant correlations between support for General Montt and fear of crime. In 2007, younger General Otto Pérez Molina designed his entire presidential campaign around the slogan "Urge Mano Dura [*Mano Dura* Urgently Needed]"; even the party's symbol is a raised fist. Crime talk abounds. Today's joint military-police patrols operate in open violation of the peace accords; escalating gang violence has prompted the construction of two maximum security prisons to house growing numbers of inmates held under strict antigang laws; and a majority of the population favors capital punishment.

In neighboring El Salvador, in August 2004 President Antonio Saca of the ARENA party (a party founded by Roberto D'Aubisson, known as the father of the death squads) introduced an antigang initiative known as "Super *Mano Dura*." This controversial program, much of which was eventually struck down as unconstitutional, involved joint military-police sweeps through poor urban slums and the broadening of powers to arrest and detain suspects; wearing a tattoo was grounds for detention on suspicion of "illicit association." The sweeps led to massive overcrowding in the country's jails, yet few prosecutions: of the 4000 detained in the sweeps in the program's first six months, the authorities reported that less than forty had been prosecuted (Harman 2005). Despite objections that such sweeps violate human rights, they have proved very popular among a violence-weary public. To bolster law enforcement efforts in the region, the United States opened a Federal Law Enforcement Training Center in San Salvador in 2005.

Human Rights

When I first started doing research on this topic, the Central American setting seemed very different indeed from the North American one about which many scholars whose work I admired (some of them contributors to this volume) were writing. First of all, Central America faced a serious contemporary crime wave, whereas fear of crime in the United States rose at a time when real crime rates were actually falling. And second, in Central America the recent history of state violence, including state-sponsored genocide, cast a very long shadow; clearly, these legacies must affect how we understand contemporary criminality and the state's responses to it in ways that simply were not true of the United States.

Indeed, because of that recent history of state-sponsored violence and because of Latin America's place in global hierarchies of power, the dominant trope for understanding contemporary violence in postwar Central America was then and continues to be "human rights." For many, late-twentieth-century Latin America conjures up images of steel-jawed generals ruling nations with an iron fist, in which vulnerable citizens were powerless and victimized; from there, many imagine that democracy could remain poorly institutionalized in the region today.

Yet this caricature matched reality better a generation ago. Today, the overwhelming majority of victims of violence are victimized at the hands of private criminal cartels, drug and human smuggling networks, shadowy mafia enterprises with links, via corruption, to various national states but that do the bidding of no single general or military institution. As Dirk Kruijt and Kees Koonings observe, violence in Latin America has "ceased to be the resource of only the traditionally powerful or of the grim uniformed guardians of the nation. [It] increasingly appears as an option for a multitude of actors in pursuit of all kind of goals" (1999, 11).

In this context, the human rights discourse is today struggling to retain relevance in Latin America. Because human rights are framed through liberal theory, which privileges nation states and the individual's negative rights against human rights, "common" crime often falls through the cracks. While human rights organizations and perspectives have long claimed to speak for, or in solidarity with, the everyday people who found themselves victims of grave injustices, historically they have privileged certain types of violence (state violence) and certain types of victims (those targeted for "political" reasons); today, only a small minority of cases meet such criteria.

There are striking points of convergence between the way crime is discussed and understood across the Americas. When I was doing my ethnographic research in Central America, I heard many articulate a sentiment that could be summed up as, "Sure, I think justice and human rights are important. But I'm scared. I'm willing for my government to use force (even lethal force) against criminals if that's what it takes to make me safe." Ultimately, this is the same logic articulated by many in the United States in response to abuses committed by this country in the context of the war on terrorism. It is laced with the same two presumptions: first, this notion of "us vs. them," where "we" and "they" are fundamentally different and one can reliably distinguish between the two; and second, the idea that "we" can then buy our security at the price of "their" liberty or justice, that "we" can deprive "them" of certain rights without affecting the enjoyment of our own rights. I think both of these premises are false, and they need to be contested by a human rights movement that understands fear and insecurity as real concerns and seeks to address them by calling for a new security based on justice as the only truly sustainable model. While human rights organizations have long served as watchdogs that barked at state misdeeds, their challenge today is to engage a broader and more positive debate about justice, security, and democracy, and the role of legal rights in upholding such ideals.

These comments may seem slightly out of place in a volume about the politics of crime and punishment with a primary focus on common, not political, crimes. Yet I think the focus on the United States allows one to maintain an artificial sense of separation between these conceptual categories. When we look at postgenocidal Guatemala, we expect to see politically motivated violence in which the state is a central actor. This is less and less the case, and we mistake that for "progress" even though Guatemala is no less violent. When we look at the United States, we expect to see common crime, problems in our neglected inner cities, in which the state may occasionally rough up a suspect or two, but is not defining violence for political reasons. Yet I think crackdowns in U.S. inner-city communities for "quality of life" crimes, roundups of residents of Middle Eastern descent in the wake of 9/11, or raids on tattooed youth in San Salvador are all mechanisms of neoliberal states governing through crime —crime both "common" and "political" (Simon 2007). In some essential ways these are the same. It is not a coincidence that former Attorney General Alberto Gonzales is noted both for his dismissal of prohibitions on the torture of terrorism suspects and his willful disregard of due process rights for death row inmates in Texas. Nor is it a coincidence that the Antiterrorism and Effective Death Penalty Act of 1996, passed in the wake of the Oklahoma City bombing as an attempt to curb foreign terrorists, mandates deportation of even legal U.S. residents for "aggravated felonies" and eliminates certain appeals for death row inmates. Wars on crime and terrorism have never been separate in Latin America; if we imagine them to be distinct here, we do so at our peril.

Democracy

In a related set of assumptions, because of some Latin American countries' recent experience of political turmoil, many observers tend to imagine that challenges such as crime are related to an incomplete process of "democratization"—there, but somehow not here. Indeed, I believe they are in both places, if we understand democratization as an ongoing process whereby members of a polity, referencing their formal rights under law and their government's stated obligation to uphold those rights, seek to make the commitments to equality, liberty, and justice enshrined in so many constitutions real in lived experience.

At least in theory, democracy provides a mechanism whereby historically disempowered groups, through participation in government, can bring about social policies aimed at leveling the playing field. Yet it seems in practice that concerns about crime often arise precisely at the time when previously excluded groups are granted greater citizenship rights. In Central America, crime emerged as a concern precisely at the time when newly minted constitutions were making rights available to large swaths of the population that had been effectively excluded from citizenship under previous regimes; the need for urgent attention to crime has effectively derailed support for needed socioeconomic reforms. Although concerns about crime were undoubtedly also fueled by real crime rates, conservative actors deftly framed worries about insecurity as qualms that human rights may have "gone too far" in condemning state violence. In this way, fear of crime became one way elites undercut the democratizing potential of formal (legal) structures granting equal rights, and thereby truncating democratic "openings" at their most formal stage.

The United States is not an exception in this regard: here, too, conservative politicians concerned about the transformations wrought by civil rights capitalized on concern about crime. It was these actors, Katherine Beckett (1997) argues, who offered a deeply racialized discourse about crime, often in the same breath as they denounced protest movements, feminism, and other social justice efforts as evidence of a pervasive disorder and creeping cultural permissiveness that required a clampdown. Decades later, the war on crime has stymied minority communities' ability to claim the very rights granted them under existing law, not by contesting inclusion on its merits, but by radically transforming communities through their inscription into an ever more aggressive criminal justice regime.

In this sense, wars on crime do not only have consequences for democracy, they also are driven by it—by its tensions, its struggles, the political tussles it enables through its concession of formal equal rights on substantively unequal population groups. In other words, the attention to or preoccupation with crime is not only something that acts on a democracy in the sense that we often imagine it to, where we note concerns when felony disenfranchisement limits participation of certain groups at the ballot box or three-strikes laws lock up ever greater percentages of nonwhite youth. In assuming that democracy existed and is undermined by the war on crime, we may unwittingly frame crime as exogenous to politics, when in reality the social construction of crime is part and parcel of the social control tactics that enable the side-by-side existence of glittering constitutions studded with lofty promises and a world punctuated by sharper inequality after the "third wave" than before it. In this sense, I suggest the war on crime is constitutive of neoliberal democracy—not a force that threatens it, but the very foil without which it could not function.

If America does not stop at the Rio Grande, it is also because these developments beyond our borders are in very real ways a result of U.S. influence. The model of democracy that appears to be the norm in much (though not all) of Latin America today is also in many ways a U.S. export.

As William Robinson has shown, the United States' "democracy promotion" programs have actually achieved something distinctly undemocratic (at least by the definition of democracy I offer above) in all the countries in which they have been implemented. The polities that such policies have helped shape are characterized by free elections in which elites with ties to transnational corporate power vie for office in ways that not only do not promote, but also actually prevent the formulation of social policies aimed at redistributing resources to remedy the growing inequalities of which criminal violence is a particularly painful indicator. In this context, popular fears about crime serve as the perfect vehicle for delegitimizing political movements of the poor. If the United States has created, in some ways, a penal empire in the Americas, it is not only through the export of ideas about social control itself, but also through the promotion of ostensibly democratic societies patterned on similar notions of curtailed state responsibility for social rights, streamlined economic efficiency, and quiescent publics (Kurtz 2004).

Conclusion

Where does this leave us, then? If wars on crime have emerged in many contexts as an effective means of forestalling social change despite the emergence of important legal precedents—new constitutions, landmark court cases—how can such movements be contested? Recent ballot initiatives decriminalizing some drug offenses may point to chinks in the punitive armor of the neoliberal state. But at the same time, the politics of fear may no longer center on the same imagined enemies; today, the "sum of all fears" may be a gang member with access to a dirty bomb, and the tactics deployed against such real or perceived threats may include military as well as civilian institutions and transnational as well as national and local efforts.

REFERENCES

Arana, Ana. 2005. "How the Street Gangs Took Central America." *Foreign Affairs* 84 (May/June): 98–110.
Ayres, Robert L. 1998. *Crime and Violence as Development Issues in Latin America and the Caribbean*. Washington, D.C.: World Bank.

Beckett, Katherine. 1997. *Making Crime Pay: Law and Order in Contemporary American Politics.* New York: Oxford University Press.

Buvinic, Mayra, Andrew Morrison, and Michael Shifter. 1999. "Violence in Latin America and the Caribbean: A Framework for Action." Inter-American Development Bank. http://www.iadb.org/sds/doc/1073eng.pdf.

Fay, Marianne, ed. 2005. "The Urban Poor in Latin America." The World Bank (Washington, D.C.). http://siteresources.worldbank.org/INTLACREGTOPURBDEV/Home/20843636/UrbanPoorinLA.pdf.

"Gangs and Crime in Latin America." Press release. U.S. Congressional Committee on International Relations. March 16, 2005. http://wwwc.house.gov/international_relations/109/news041905a.htm.

Harman, Danna. 2005. "For Salvadoran Gangs, Jail Is a Revolving Door." *Christian Science Monitor* (March 1). http://www.csmonitor.com/2005/0301/p06s02-woam.html.

Jones, Richard, ed. 2004. "Ideas and Contributions: Democracy in America: Towards a Citizens' Democracy." United Nations Development Programme. http://democracyreport.undp.org/Downloads/Ideas_and_Contributions.pdf.

Kruijt, Dirk, and Kees Koonings. 1999. "Introduction: Violence and Fear in Latin America." In *Societies of Fear: The Legacy of Civil War, Violence and Terror in Latin America*, ed. Kees Koonings and Dirk Kruijt, 1–30. London: Zed Books.

Kurtz, Marcus J. 2004. "The Dilemmas of Democracy in the Open Economy: Lessons from Latin America." *World Politics* 56 (January): 262–302.

Lederman, Daniel, and Norman Loayza. 1999. "What Causes Crime and Violence?" *Violence and Social Capital: Proceedings of the LCSES Seminar Series, 1997–98* (The World Bank LCR Sustainable Development Working Paper No. 5, Urban Peace Program Series), ed. Caroline Moser and Sarah Lister, 7–11. Washington, D.C. http://wbln0018.worldbank.org/LAC/LACInfoClient.nsf/5aaa39a87ab8daf985256cc6006f355b/a7048012ba10182c852567ed0061a1fe/$FILE/Paper-5.doc.

Simon, Jonathan. 2007. *Governing through Crime: How the War on Crime Transformed American Democracy and Created a Culture of Fear.* New York: Oxford University Press.

Torres-Rivas, E. 1999. "Epilogue: Notes on Terror, Fear and Democracy." In *Societies of Fear: The Legacy of Civil War, Violence and Terror in Latin America*, ed. Kees Koonings and Dirk Druijt, 285–300. London: Zed Books.

[*Chapter 3*]

From the New Deal to the
Crime Deal

Jonathan Simon

Introduction: Community, Security, and Liberty

The post-9/11 terrorism policy debate in the United States sometimes sounds as if governance is largely a function of liberty and security. This two-way model is appealing, in part because of its optimism (security can be obtained if only we sacrifice enough liberty), and in part because it fits our dominant convention of addressing policy issues as a matter of purchasing some good at the cost of another (the hamburgers and colas that my micro-economics professor invoked as the commodities in the simplest models of market-clearing transactions). In this essay I want to trouble this model by insisting on the insertion of a third term, community, and then to consider how America's quarter-century obsession with crime, now compounded by fear of terrorism, has altered the nature of our democracy in a way that belongs to the constitutive if not the constitutional.

Since at least the nineteenth century, liberal societies have experienced liberty, security, and community as integrally related to each other in both enabling and destructive ways. Indeed, the problem of governing liberal societies has been increasingly focused on managing the relations among the objectives of liberty, security, and community. Let us just remind ourselves of how many and contradictory these relations are.

Liberty can enable the formation of community. For example, the First Amendment's promise of religious freedom seems to have encouraged the formation of powerful sectarian religious communities throughout American history. Liberty can also create security. During a recent visit to New Haven after an absence of some years, I was struck to find a flourishing youth-oriented club scene along a downtown street. The clubs themselves were of little appeal to this middle-aged visitor, but the liberty-exercising youth made a large swath of surrounding neighborhood feel far safer than it had before. But while liberty can create security, it can also endanger it. The ability to go any place in public, while behaving in conformity with the law's requirements and being free of having to provide an account of oneself makes it harder for law enforcement to prevent some crimes. Liberty also endangers community. The erosion of ethnic and racial segregation in American cities since the 1960s has undermined some of the bonds of solidarity, especially within minority communities that once held bonds across class divides, and where marrying outside of one's religious faith was seen as a threat to minority religions.

Security also provides an essential condition of liberty. Those who fear crime in a neighborhood are less likely to enjoy the liberty of its streets or bring their patronage to local merchants exercising their commercial liberty. But security can also destroy community. The pursuit of defensible space in contemporary residential and commercial developments has made it more difficult for people to experience casual interaction with neighbors and local merchants.

Community can provide security but endanger liberty, as when homogenous religious and ethnic neighborhoods reduce the likelihood of crime in such neighborhoods but also limit the expression of any dissenting ideas through the prospect of near-total surveillance over the public behavior of each other. Community also can provide essential conditions for liberty. Liberty is empty without substantive values that a subject can express or pursue through the exercise of that liberty, and these values almost always come from some community in which the subject has rooted him or herself.

Obviously this sketch cannot do justice to the complexities of any of the concepts of liberty, security, or community. The point is rather to notice that all of these permutations belong to a problem that plays out across our history and which has left its mark over fields such as public health, urban planning, immigration and employment regulation, welfare, and social work; in foreign wars aimed at living space, markets, and national defense; in disciplines such as sociology, criminology, social work, and education; and naturally in constitutional law broadly construed.

It is against this background of relations between liberty, security, and community, and of overlapping institutions and knowledge that we can appreciate the most serious implications of the "war on crime." I contend that the four-decade "war on crime" has radically and perhaps enduringly transformed the relationship of each of these elements and, in the end, how Americans are governed and how they govern themselves (Simon 2007). Crime has always been an important context for the problem of liberty, security, and community, but since the late 1960s it has enjoyed a privileged status that has profoundly altered the ways liberty, security, and community are thought about and acted upon.

The war on crime has also disabled a different way of imagining the relationship between community, security, and liberty, one that crystallized into an effective platform for governing during and as a result of the political changes associated with the New Deal. By eroding confidence in the New Deal's version of the liberty-security-community paradigm and producing a host of dynamic practices, mentalities, and relationships among subjects, what we might call the "Crime Deal" has situated American law and policymaking in a different paradigm, one that I find far less desirable. I will not try to defend those normative intuitions in depth, but I will instead outline these two paradigms briefly and suggest why the Crime Deal is now beginning to create profound problems of governance at all levels. While the New Deal's version of liberty, security, and community may not be recoverable in full, much of its constitutional legacy must be defended if an alternative to the Crime Deal is to be achieved.

Crime and Governance in America

Few developments have had as large an effect on the legal status of Americans over the last quarter century than the emergence of crime as the dominant domestic policy imperative and the punitive policies that have placed more than 3 percent of adult residents of the United States under the jurisdiction of the criminal justice system, including more than two million in confinement. These Americans, in varying degree, have lost their rights to privacy, suffrage, and equal access to markets for housing, jobs, and education.

When we look at the populations most effected by this revolution, especially African Americans, the consequences are shocking (even if well known). With nearly 10 percent of African-American men in prison or jail on any given day and more than half of them bound to experience a period of incarceration during their lives, the criminal justice system has become a dominant governmental institution in inner-city African American communities (Western 2006). The result, according to some criminologists, is a growing crisis of informal social control as the adult elements necessary to form viable economic and child-rearing solidarities within the community are transported to prison (Clear 2007). In real respects this quest for security through crime control has reversed the gains of the civil rights era and created a new form of racialized domination less attractive in many respects than the mid-twentieth century versions of northern ghettos and southern Jim Crow (Wacquant 2000).

This was not the result of a decisive constitutional event such as the Dred Scott decision or the Fourteenth Amendment. In many ways, the constitutional problem of crime has altered in only modest ways since the late 1960s. The efforts of the Burger and Rehnquist courts to weaken the Warren Court's restrictions on law enforcement may have contributed marginally, but most analyses suggest that arrest rates have changed only modestly. Recent efforts to confront penal severity with the proportionality principle of the Eighth Amendment have failed, but even the dissenters of cases in which the later courts removed limitations on police power would never have applied that principle to the sentences under which all but a tiny portion of the two million incarcerated Americans have been confined. The Warren Court itself backed off quickly from any real attempt to limit the criminalizing or punishing capacity of state governments. (It remains unclear how committed Chief Justice Warren, former district attorney of Alameda County, former attorney general of California, and son of a murder victim, was to making significant limitations on crime control).

With rare exceptions, state constitutions also have been silent witnesses to these developments and have often been amended (especially where ballot initiatives make populist fears readily translatable into constitutions' text) to voice punitive demands (such as California's three-strikes law). In short, America is governed through crime by way of powers readily available under almost any conventional interpretation of the Constitution.

But whatever role constitutional developments may have played in raising the salience of crime, its emergence as a master problem of governance has altered America in constitutive ways, particularly in the way we relate liberty, security, and community. That becomes clear once we acknowledge that, in sum, these changes have produced a real threat to the operation of democratic self-governance or the republican form of government that the Constitution promises. We should also be clear that this was not determined by one political party or one segment of the political spectrum. The politicians who have been identified with the war on crime include Republicans like Barry Goldwater, Democrats like Lyndon B. Johnson, conservatives like Ronald Reagan, and liberals like Bobby Kennedy. The religious right has embraced crime as an essential test for government, but so has the feminist left. Some individuals, parties, and ideologies have been more or less adept at playing the rise of crime, but all have participated in it.

Elsewhere I have tried to specify this genealogy in some detail. Here I want to turn to the consequences for American democracy and our constitutional structure and consider briefly the features of the Constitution today and in the future that we might aspire to or worry about. September 11, 2001, and other recent events have opened a potential window of opportunity to confront the disabling aspects of the crime war. After reviewing some of the damage, I want to turn to some adjudicative, legislative, and cultural paths that may help move America away from the Crime Deal.

The New Deal

As befits its continuing importance to our political culture, the New Deal has accumulated many meanings. Here I mean to invoke the broadest sense of the New Deal as a way of imagining American society as a governable problem. Others have persuasively argued that the New Deal as such lacked a coherent political or economic theory (a case that I am ill equipped to challenge and that sounds more or less right), but that does not mean it lacked an effective way of imagining liberty, security, and community, and their relationships to each other. As historian Jennifer Klein has noted, the New Deal "did not simply create a welfare state; it launched a new economy of welfare in which the ideology of security proved a powerful construct" (Klein 2003, 4).[1] This is the essence of Roosevelt's most famous effort to articulate his overall model of liberty, security, and community, that is, his "four freedoms," that was embedded in the United Nation's Universal Declaration of Human Rights.[2]

That politics of security can only be sketched here by its central features. (Klein's book provides a revealing and detailed portrait of this economy of welfare as it played out in the context of health insurance). The main features of the politics of security are

- *Risk spreading* across broad social and economic groups through mechanisms such as worker compensation, social security, and employment-based health, disability, and pension benefits: Spreading risk through large, stable public or private capital funds allowed an enormous expansion of liberty as individuals were freed from one set of communities (a set largely bounded by the bonds of family, ethnicity, and religion) to create all kinds of new communities, both those of the economic marketplace and of the host of lifestyle pursuits (from tango dancing to Evangelical Christianity).
- *Risk prevention* through governmental controls, such as the regulation of banks and employers, focused on large organizations: Regulations were aimed at establishing security through accountability from the top down by putting pressure on corporations and, through the corporate organizational form, on the behavior of front-line supervisors and workers.
- *Risk solidarity* or consciousness through quasi-corporatist forms of community beyond traditional boundaries of language, religion, and ethnicity, including labor unions, business associations, and consumer groups: These forms of community generated a species of civil politics as interest-group competition that sustained a prolonged period of relative civil peace and prosperity, although it was shadowed by nightmares of riots, crimes, and nuclear exchanges.
- *Risk-management strategies* guided by empiricism, pragmatism, and legal realism as dominant forms of political knowledge and expertise relevant to courts, Congress, and administrative agencies: These forms of knowledge promised to allow transparency and continuous adjustment in these relations.

Of course, all of these elements had precedents in earlier periods, but the New Deal brought them into a national programmatic alignment that forced a constitutional moment, forged a transferable model of governance that could be implemented at the state and local level and in private industry, and gave rise to more robust forms of liberty, security, and community than any previous model of liberal governance.

The portrait I have drawn is far too abstract and general to do anything but serve as a contrast to our present moment. But at the same time, I want to acknowledge that the New Deal, as a historical occurrence, left deep and perhaps fatal flaws in its strategy for relating liberty, security, and community. The greatest, most constitutive flaw of all was race and the exclusion by omission and commission of vast portions of the African-American and Latino populations then in the United States.

The Crime Deal

The Crime Deal, if we may for the moment assume that it is as powerful and enduring as the New Deal, has deeply undermined this model of governing the relationship among liberty, security, and community. If the experience of mass economic insecurity associated with the Great Depression formed a major impetus for the New Deal model, it must be agreed that the experience (whether real or imagined, on television or embodied, well-founded or specious) of mass insecurity about violent crime[3] since the late 1960s has provided the impetus for the Crime Deal. Liberty, security, and community have been renegotiated by governing actors and agents of all kinds on the basis of this crime priority.

In place of spreading risk across broad social and economic groups, the Crime Deal has promoted disaggregation of risk that reaches its most potent form in the assignment of a historically unprecedented portion of our population to incarceration,[4] as well as in patterns of consumption, such as the ubiquity of the gated community form of residential subdivision, the high security office park form of business development, and the militarized SUVs with names like Expedition, Armada, and Suburban, which advertise their militant commitment to security and liberty without community.

These new forms of security promise to free the individual from reliance on collective risk-spreading (assuming the taxes are high enough to pay correctional officers) and thus enforce new ways of valorizing liberty, security, and community. At the same time, the relentless focus on crime risk has led many Americans to view the New Deal model of social insurance as invitations to corruption and to view public services from transportation to schools as particularly vulnerable to crime, thus encouraging further disinvestment in its model of liberty, security, and community.

In place of the regulation of large organizations, the Crime Deal has brought the relentless pursuit of security through the sanctioning of individual deviance and misconduct. This has found its perfect expression in the widely copied "broken windows" approach of sanctioning even the most minor violations in order to discourage the appearance of more serious breaches of law and social order. This "zero tolerance" ideal is a bottom approach to social regulation that places the burdens of discipline on individuals and families.

In place of community based on broad economic groupings, the Crime Deal has promoted a model of community anchored in the narrow promise of security through the mass incarceration of whole segments of the population marked as dangerous by their age, gender, race, and social class. The new solidarity means incarceration pursued against whole social groups in institutions that recognize no form of individuality and that aim to affect crime rates by demographically containing whole portions of society, and a kind of neo-Durkheimian pursuit of solidarity through the experience of victimization, violence, and vengeance.

In place of the ideology of empiricism, pragmatism, and legal realism, the Crime Deal has promoted the return of moralism and the postmodern formalism exemplified by the Supreme Court's *habeas* jurisprudence and the repugnant (especially after 9/11) Anti-Terrorism and Effective Death Penalty Act. In both respects, the promise of transparency and accountability has been replaced by a promise of identification with victims and symbolic acts of security.

Worst of all, the Crime Deal has actually built on and expanded the fatal flaw of the New Deal by remaking race into a demoralized construct of risk management, demobilizing the moral advantages of the civil rights movement, and koshering a form of hypersegregation that makes the formation of counter solidarities unlikely.[5] Very few people in America identify with racial purity in schools, but almost everyone can embrace parents doing anything necessary to remove any exposure to crime risk in schools, even if those choices result in the same pattern of racial segregation.

Society Must Be Defended[6]

In the mid-1960s, after Lyndon B. Johnson won an F.D.R.-like landslide re-election and launched a major expansion of social insurance, civil rights, and antipoverty programs, it may have seemed as if the New Deal would last forever—a permanent framework for governing with a range of tactics across which politicians and political parties could compete. By the end of the decade, however, the New Deal and its progeny seemed re-markably vulnerable to catastrophic fractioning of its key constituencies, institutional bases, and forms of political knowledge.

Perhaps from some near future we shall look back on the mid-2000s and see the Crime Deal at just such a moment. Few administrations have more perfectly embodied the key themes of the Crime Deal than the reigning Bush administration, and the war on terror would seem to have handed the administration a perfect way to continue the war on crime beyond the traditional legal restraints of criminal justice and national sov-ereignty. But that same war demands that Americans reconsider the rela-tions of liberty, security, and community, relations that have been carved into quite narrow channels through the Crime Deal. Does the present configuration of mass incarceration for the poor and fortress suburbs for the middle and upper classes make it easier or harder for contemporary families to maintain physical and mental health in the demands of par-enting and working, let alone deal with the threat of mass terrorist attacks like 9/11?

There are signs of popular questioning of the strategy of mass incar-ceration. Even politicians who have strongly supported the war on crime as a legitimate response to the apparent social disintegration of the 1960s through the 1980s now concede that at least some of the consequences of incarceration, such as the effects of voter disenfranchisement and eco-nomic exclusion, must be addressed (e.g., President Bush's call for invest-ment in rehabilitating prisoners in his 2004 State of the Union Address and Senator Clinton's support for a voting rights statute that would bar permanent felon exclusion in federal elections).

The reentry problem "uncovered" by criminologists in the late 1990s has shown a spotlight for the first time on the criminogenic consequences of mass incarceration. The NGO community has "discovered" American prisoners as the newest frontier in the global war for human rights. When considered in total, the net of collateral consequences drawn across some of our most hapless and low-risk prisoners on their release is downright un-American. Who supports denying such people the opportunity to work for a living and support their families? High fuel costs and some at-tention to the health consequences for children of fortress suburbs (obe-sity and automobile accidents) seem good openings to question all the elements of the Crime Deal.

Unfortunately, the Constitution, as read by the courts, does little to dis-able mass incarceration directly. The Thirteenth Amendment itself gives us the explicit assurance that slavery can be reborn so long as it is practiced solely on felons (something the South did almost immediately with the Convict-Lease System). The Eighth Amendment offers little solace either. As long as capital punishment remains constitutional, long prison sentences for crimes such as being a former felon in possession of a firearm are not going to be perceived as "cruel" and they are hardly "unusual."

But while global attacks on the Crime Deal and its equality-eroding and democracy-eroding features are unlikely to find judicial recognition as constitutional principles today, opportunities abound for constitutional struggles over the penal turn in American democracy. One notable example is California's decision to abandon racial classification in its prison reception centers following the Supreme Court's recent remand in *Johnson v. California* (2005). Unfortunately, settlement may have prevented a public discussion of whether it is a good idea for the state to help reproduce a system of racialized gang violence as a way of governing prisons. While the Court is unlikely to go very far in challenging the power of state legislatures to determine the purpose and scale of punishment (at least punishment by imprisonment), it has continued to rule express consideration of race in managing mass incarceration to be out of bounds without justifications that can survive strict scrutiny.

The *Apprendi v. New Jersey* (2000) line of cases and, more recent, the *U.S. v. Booker* (2005) case (in both of which the Court upended the mass imprisonment–enhancing U.S. sentencing guidelines), indicates a growing unease across a broad ideological swath of the Supreme Court at the consequences of governing through crime and its corrosive effects on American democracy (see also *Blakely v. Washington* (2004)). While it is far from clear where the Supreme Court will go next in articulating the meaning of its rejuvenated Sixth Amendment right, it is clear that some portion of its members is very concerned with structural shifts in the way executive, judicial, and legislative branches share the exercise of the state's power to punish. Justice John Paul Stevens's plurality opinion points to changes in sentencing laws in the 1990s that have decoupled the executive's power to enhance punishment beyond the elements of the crime and have left judges unable to control effectively the broad power tied up in their sentencing fact-finding. Whether requiring more specific jury fact-finding or giving judges broader discretion to determine enhancement of punishment is likely to reverse the kind of dynamics that William Stuntz (2001) has described is unclear and will depend on further elaboration by the Court.

The crisis in prison conditions brought on by mass incarceration and fickle state revenues may yet compel more federal courts to intervene directly in state correctional management. Judge Thelton Henderson of the U.S. District Court for the northern district of California has held the state accountable for a broad crisis of governability in the California Department of Corrections and Rehabilitation at a time when the governor and legislature both refuse to take on the politics of fixing a deeply corrupt and expensive system (see *Plata v. Schwarzenegger* (2007)).

Successful political battles also can be raised against efforts to expand the interpretive reach of crime. The most immediate involves resisting the effort of some in Congress to ramp up the criminal treatment of undocumented aliens. In the 1990s (well before 9/11) Congress imposed mandatory deportation and detention on a wide swath of legal resident aliens convicted of crimes (including drug misdemeanors). Recent proposals would make it a felony to be in the United States without proper documentation. The mass demonstrations of immigrants and their citizen supporters in May 2006 seemed mobilized in large part by refusal of this criminal identity and the modes of governance it reinforces.

Challenges to disenfranchisement are unlikely to prevail in courts for the foreseeable future unless they are linked to specific state law peculiarities. But, in the legislative domain, these rules are and can be attacked. Litigation helps make visible the high costs to society of expanding the category of felon to incorporate broad swaths of black markets that are otherwise allowed to flourish.

If there is a constitutional angle to the fight against mass incarceration it may lie in the survival of key elements of the New Deal now being contested, often in constitutional terms. There is irony aplenty here. New Deal precedents on federal power to regulate social conditions under the commerce power have been relied on to support tough anticrime measures aimed at addressing populist concerns while recent efforts to attack some of the substantive criminal laws that sustain mass incarceration have raised the banner of limited federal power.

Moreover, President Franklin Roosevelt and Attorney General Homer Cummings flirted with a war on crime as a hedge against the failure of economic reform that would allow the administration to vigorously address the sense of social collapse during the early stomach-dropping years of the Depression. In its effort to produce compliance with its many regulatory initiatives, the New Deal pushed the use of strict-liability criminal prosecutions to hold executives accountable for faulty consumer products regardless of whether the defendant had any actual knowledge of the particular circumstances.

But the forms of governance that actually emerged from the New Deal (social insurance, organized labor, and regulatory agencies) provided ways of addressing alarming social problems that did not operate primarily on coercive tactics aimed at criminal behavior. Indeed, in some cases, like that of organized labor, the New Deal framework took conflicts that had been channeled into crime and criminal justice (unions were sometimes considered criminal conspiracies, gangs were employed to attack unions and later to protect them) and moved them into a realm of civil law and justice.

Whether or not the social effect of weakening the risk-spreading functions of New Deal governance produces more crime (a difficult question to answer), it seems to have encouraged government itself to view more risks as crimelike and amenable to criminal solutions. In a vicious cycle, the Crime Deal delegitimizes remaining systems of socializing risk. The "No Child Left Behind" law and the new consumer bankruptcy law are only the most recent moves toward dismantling systems of social risk-spreading in the name of isolating and controlling "abusers."

In short, the best way to stop and reverse the destructive effects on democracy of our four-decade-long war on crime is to shore up and reinvigorate the constitutional framework of New Deal governance. Creating effective forms of governance that address important sectors of risk in people's lives, whether cancer, terrorism, or violence, can compete with the attractions of mass incarceration. Society must be defended, but how?

NOTES

1. While Klein mentions only security in this sentence, the New Deal's discourse of security always addressed the other two as well.

2. "Freedom of Speech; Freedom of Religion; Freedom from Want; and Freedom from Fear."

3. Violent crime extends beyond the most feared exposures, up to and including homicide, to acts that are seen as causally related to violence, such as drug possession. On the importance of this systemic slippage from homicide to possession offenses, see Dubber 2002.

4. For the most recent analysis of the demographic scope of that exclusion, see Western 2006.

5. My father, a Jewish juvenile delinquent in working-class Detroit during the

early 1940s could have ended up, at fifteen, living in a Trotskyist commune in the shadows of the auto factories with African American and Appalachian comrades, a pattern virtually impossible to imagine in Detroit today. For Detroit between then and now, see, generally, Sugrue 1996. For national patterns today, see Western 2006.

6. Foucault 2003.

CASES CITED

Apprendi v. New Jersey, 530 U.S. 466 (2000)
Blakely v. Washington, 542 U.S. 296 (2004)
Johnson v. California, 543 U.S. 499 (2005)
Plata v. Schwarzenegger, No. C01-1351 THE (2007), Order Granting Plaintiff's Motion to Convene Three-Judge Panel.
U.S. v. Booker, 543 U.S. 220 (2005)

REFERENCES

Clear, Todd. 2007. *Imprisoning Communities: How Mass Incarceration Makes Disadvantaged Neighborhoods Worse*. New York: Oxford University Press.
Dubber, Markus D. 2002. *Victims in the War on Crime: The Use and Abuse of Victims' Rights*. New York: NYU Press.
Foucault, Michael. 2003. *Society Must Be Defended: Lectures at the College de France, 1975–76*. Translated by David Macey. New York: Picador.
Klein, Jennifer. 2003. *For All These Rights: Business, Labor, and the Shaping of America's Public-Private Welfare State*. Princeton: Princeton University Press.
Simon, Jonathan. 2007. *Governing through Crime: How the War on Crime Transformed American Democracy and Created a Culture of Fear*. New York: Oxford University Press.
Stuntz, William J. 2001. "The Pathological Politics of Criminal Law." *Michigan Law Review* 100(3): 505–600.
Sugrue, Thomas J. 1996. *The Origins of the Urban Crisis: Race and Inequality in Postwar Detroit*. Princeton: Princeton University Press.
Wacquant, Loïc. 2000. "The New 'Peculiar Institution': On the Prison as Surrogate Ghetto." *Theoretical Criminology* 4(3): 377–89.
Western, Bruce. 2006. *Punishment and Inequality in America*. New York: Russell Sage Foundation.

Chapter 4

The Great Penal Experiment
Lessons for Social Justice

Todd R. Clear

The United States has, for more than a generation, engaged in what might be called "the great penal experiment." In 1972, the prison population was about 200,000 and the total incarcerated population was about 300,000. In every year since 1971, the prison population has grown, typically between 4 and 12 percent per year. Today, those numbers are about 750,000 and 1,500,000, respectively. The total incarceration rate grew from 160 per 100,000 citizens in 1971 to 760 per 100,000 today, an increase of 450 percent. At no time in history, and certainly in no other democratic society, has there ever been such a sustained, unrelenting growth in the use of the prison.

In fact, this generation-long penal experiment has followed a pattern of prison population stability that had lasted almost three-quarters of a century. Between 1900 and 1970, the rate of incarceration in the United States fluctuated between 90 and 120 persons per 100,000, going up during times of economic trouble, going down during wars. The pattern was so striking that in the early 1970s, one of America's most esteemed criminologists, Alfred Blumstein, posited a theory that punishment levels are bound by narrow homoeostatic limits and cannot rise or fall outside them (Blumstein and Cohen 1973). He was wrong, but not uniquely so. Nobody foresaw the generation-long expansion of the prison system that has dominated our penal policy.

This expansion is unprecedented—a social experiment of profound significance. In the case of most social experiments, we might speculate about the "results." What has been the heritage of this historically unprecedented national commitment to a sustained growth in prison populations?

Certainly, there have been many consequences of a social upheaval so fundamental as the United States' generation-long social commitment to incarceration. In this paper, I propose for consideration four important consequences—not, nor even close to, an exhaustive list, but a beginning set of what I think are the most important lessons from "the great penal experiment."

Lesson #1: Prison growth has had only a limited relationship to the amount of crime.

The casual observer might say that the growing population has helped produce the decade-long drop in crime in America. But on closer observation, both at the pattern of crime rates and at the way most crimes occur, it becomes clear that the contribution of prison growth to the reduction in crime has been small at best.

The big numbers have to do with the pattern of crime during the prison expansion. Prison populations have grown without exception every year since 1971. Crime has had no consistent pattern over those same years. For the first decade, the Federal Bureau of Investigation reported consistent growth in crime. But beginning in the 1980s, crime rates reversed and dropped for five consecutive years by a total of 15 percent. This short-lived decline was followed by an abrupt rise in crime that lasted into the early 1990s. We are now enjoying the fourteenth consecutive year of dropping crime rates. Thus, we have increased the prison population for more than a generation, during which time there were two "crime waves" lasting a total of eighteen years and two crime declines lasting a total of fifteen years. So, after thirty years of ever-expanding prison populations and a 450-percent-higher rate of prison usage, the overall crime rate today is about what it was in 1972.

Looking more closely, we can see some of the reasons why. Much of the increase in the prison population is driven by the large numbers of people convicted of drug crimes. One in five prisoners is serving time for a drug-related offense, and more than two-thirds of prison or jail commitments arrive on drug charges. It is hard to prevent crime by locking people up for drugs. Typically, when someone is taken off the streets for a drug crime, there stands in the shadows someone ready to take his place, with the results that not only do the drug crimes continue, but also someone who might not have gotten involved in the drug trade is now able to do so. Unless these replacement turn out to be less criminally active over-all than those whose places they take, crime will not be affected much by incarcerating drug felons (Reiss 1988).

This pattern of crime replacement is certainly true for drugs, but so-cial scientists are beginning to discover that it is also true for many other types of crimes. Three-quarters of felonies are committed by young peo-ple (mostly males) acting in groups for which sporadic criminal activity is stimulated by shifting leadership roles. When one (or even two) members of the group are removed from the streets, the group frequently contin-ues to engage in sporadic crime, frequently (again) recruiting replacement participants (for a discussion, see Felson 2003).

Even when incarceration does prevent crimes through incapacitation, we know that the benefits of prison decline as prison populations grow. Prison populations grow either by adding more prisoners or by keeping the same set for longer terms. To the extent that growth is a function of more prisoners, the marginal group added to the prison population always tends to be an increasingly less criminally active group (mostly because the most active criminals are eventually caught and end up in prison any-way), thus increasingly less crime is prevented by these expanding prison entries. On the other hand, when prison populations grow by increasing the length of sentences, the incapacitation benefits diminish because many people are being locked up long after they have aged out of their criminal propensities (see Spelman 1994).

This is not to say that prison has no impact on crime. There is some relationship—smaller than most people think—between the number of prisoners and the amount of crime. Recent review essays summarizing the evidence of the impact of incarceration growth on declining crime rates agree that the total contribution of the prison population to the drop in crime is remarkably small (Blumstein and Wallman 2003; Lynch and Sabol 2004; Spelman 2003; Western 2006). Thus, the best available evidence affirms that prisons have not been the sole, or even the major, source of today's decreases in crime.

Lesson #2: Prison growth has been the product of intentional penal policy, not natural forces.

Why have prison populations been able to grow in ways largely irrelevant to changes in crime? The answer is at once both simple and nuanced: the prison population is completely determined by the number of people entering the prison and their length of stay. Thus, the steady growth of the prison population over the last several decades, without correlation to crime rates, means that the number of individuals entering prison has been increasing, their length of stay has been growing, or some combination of the two.

Patterns of prison entry and length of stay have varied over the last thirty years. Blumstein and Beck (2003) divide the thirty-year period of prison growth into three policy periods, each lasting roughly a decade. For the first ten years, prisons grew because the number of people entering prison grew, mostly as a result of growing crime rates causing more people to be arrested. In the second decade, crime rates played much less of a role in prison growth patterns. A substantial decrease in the use of probation combined with a moderate increase in length of stay accounted for most prison growth, since crime rates first dropped and then rose during that period. The third decade has coincided with sustained drops in crime, so crime has had nothing to do with prison growth. What happened instead was a continuing reduction in the use of probation but a precipitous increase in length of stay (with a steep increase in the use of life sentences). There has also been an increase in the rate of return to prison for those who have been released.

So while prison population trends have been largely disconnected from crime rates, they have been closely connected to developments in penal policy. By the end of the 1970s, public concern about crime led to a series of penal code reforms that swept the country, collectively and substantially reducing the odds of probation terms while also moderately increasing the duration of the penalty. Today, prisons grow despite dropping prison intake nationwide. This growing prison population is sustained by ever-increasing lengths of stay for those who come in on new felonies and a substantially higher chance of return to prison for those who have been recently released and are under closer surveillance (see Jacobson 2005).

In short, we have growing prison populations because we have adopted polices that are designed to produce them. Sociologist Kathryn Beckett and economist Bruce Western (2001) argue that these policies have produced political capital in two important ways. First, until very recently, electoral politics have been dominated by tough-on-crime proposals, with candidates in heated competition to offer increasingly draconian versions of penal reform. Second, the correctional industrial complex has created economic interests that favor prison expansion, with private prison

providers and rural communities lobbying for prison construction legislation. These political interests have decoupled prison population policy
from public safety and created a synthetic pressure for prison expansion
that is increasingly the reason prisons grow in the United States.

Lesson #3: Prison growth has decreased social justice.

Prison growth has been concentrated in certain segments of society in
ways that raise troubling questions of social justice. Men are twelve times
more likely to be locked up than women. African Americans are locked
up at a rate three times the national average and almost six times that
of whites. Prisons house parent-aged adults—over four-fifths of prisoners are between eighteen and forty-five years old. They are disadvantaged.
Nearly two-thirds have not graduated from high school and one-third
do not even have a GED. Prisoners are, as a collective, poor, young-adult
men who have problematic experiences in the job market and limited
human capital (Western 2006).

For these men, going to prison does not improve their life prospects.
Studies show that going to prison reduces lifetime earnings and decreases
long-term employment prospects (Western, Kling, and Weiman 2001).
State and federal laws impose a wide range of collateral costs on the formerly incarcerated as well by restricting job and housing prospects and
limiting access to education and welfare. Prison punishes during incarceration, but the losses the former prisoner feels continue well after the
person has finished the sentence (see Petersilia 2003). The concentration
of these costs of imprisonment fall most heavily on men of color, and this
has resulted in shocking statistics that must give anyone pause. On any
given day, eight percent of African American males between the ages of
twenty and fifty are locked up. An African American male born today has
a 27.8-percent lifetime likelihood of going to prison at least once (Bonczar
and Beck 1997). Recent studies show that incarceration has become one of
the engines driving the growing inequality between middle-class whites
and impoverished blacks (Western 2006).

But prisoners are not the only ones affected. It is estimated that there
are 1.3 million children with an incarcerated parent (Johnson and Waldfogel 2002). Living with an absent parent is surely a disadvantage, but having had a parent imprisoned predicts all manner of detrimental outcomes,
from poorer school performance to juvenile delinquency and, eventually,

inter-generational patterns of incarceration (see Murray 2005; Harris and Miller 2001). The children who suffer an elevated risk of these detrimental outcomes of their parents' imprisonment have been innocent of the crimes used to justify their parents' incarceration. To those who feel that one of the greatest challenges to our democracy is racial inequality, the existence of a growing prison system that reproduces and reinforces the forces of social inequality is deeply troubling.

Lesson #4: Prison growth has damaged the well-being of poor communities.

The existence of widespread, de facto racial segregation in housing means that people of color are concentrated in poor urban areas. As a result, prison is also concentrated there—in some sections of Brooklyn there is one prison or jail admission annually for every eight males aged twenty to forty-five; in some sections of Cleveland, almost one-fifth of the parent-aged adult male population is locked up on any given day (Clear, Waring, and Scully 2005). Prison is a fact of life for the many men who live in these places, but it is just as much a constant factor in the lives of the families, neighbors, and business owners in those places. One study found that every one of 125 Tallahassee residents living in two small, high-incarceration neighborhoods reported having a close relative in prison recently (Rose, Clear, and Ryder 2001).

Numbers of this magnitude describe a concentration of imprisonment in these poor neighborhoods and communities. Incarceration growth, concentrated in the nation's poorest communities, has created war-level rates of missing men. It is easy to see that imprisonment in such levels of heavy concentration might have many unexpected effects for the people who live in these places. What might some of them be?

Recently, Rose and Clear (1998) summarized a broad spectrum of literature regarding community-level effects of social policy and ventured that incarceration concentrated in poor communities might disrupt social networks and systems of social support and weaken the capacities of those support systems to perform functions of informal social control, thus leading to increased crime. A follow-up study (Clear, Rose, Waring, and Scully 2003) found that Tallahassee neighborhoods with the highest incarceration rates experienced increases in crime that were statistically linked to the high rates of removal and return of residents.

These results have prompted a group of researchers to form an incarceration study group investigating various ways in which high rates of incarceration, concentrated in poor communities, might affect those communities detrimentally. Studies are taking place in Baltimore, Portland, Seattle, Durham, Cleveland, Chicago, New York City, Philadelphia, Columbus, Jacksonville, and Buffalo. Studies completed to date suggest that neighborhood-level incarceration rates are linked to sexually transmitted diseases, distrust of the legitimacy of the state, juvenile delinquency, fear of crime, political alienation, and housing deterioration, in addition to crime (see Clear 2007).

One way of looking at the neighborhood-level effects of concentrated incarceration is the pattern of cycling residents through the prison system. On any given day, a substantial percentage of the population is locked up, but the actual people vary from time to time, and over long stretches, everyone in the community is affected one way or another. The prison system consumes residents of these communities as its sustenance, but it also helps produce dynamics of instability that guarantee a continuing flow of potential prisoners.

The Great Penal Experiment and Social Justice

The U.S. prison system has grown inexorably for over thirty years. It has grown in good times and bad, during recessions and economic booms, during war and during peace. It has grown while crime increased and while it decreased. This pattern of growth has no referent in history. It is a social experiment unique to America, unique to the last quarter of the twentieth century, and is now continuing into the twenty-first century. Seen as a social experiment, this astounding growth is the dominant feature of American jurisprudence for a generation of Americans.

Available evidence suggests that (1) the growth has had little to do with crime, (2) the growth has been a conscious political policy, (3) the growth has exacerbated social inequality for poor people of color, and (4) the growth has sustained powerful destabilizing forces in our poorest neighborhoods that serve to entrench the disadvantages they suffer.

Could there be anything more troubling about our criminal justice system than that it may be visiting generations of hardships on our poorest citizens, many of whom have never been convicted of a crime? Today we have a prison population that has outgrown its role in preventing crime and become an aggravating factor interfering with social justice and community safety. How can we accept that the very tools of justice might be the wedge that exacerbates injustice?

While the overall picture painted by this essay is pessimistic about change, there are glimmers of change on the horizon. There is a growing scholarly consensus that further increases in the size of the prison population will have no appreciable impact on crime (see Liedka, Piehl, and Useem 2006; Western 2006). A broader adoption of viable penal code reforms—policies that are already in use in at least one state or large city—would reduce the prison population by up to half (Austin et al. 2007). Even those who have been strong voices for more imprisonment have concluded that more prison growth is a mistake (see, e.g., DiIulio 1999). It is fair to say that in scholarly circles, informed opinion now holds that the burgeoning prison population is less of a crime control strategy and more of a social problem in need of repair.

In the world of politics, there is also reason for optimism. Crime is waning as an organizing paradigm in political campaigns, being replaced by terrorism and illegal immigration. It is unlikely that the feel of politics will improve with this change, but at least the worst instincts regarding crime policy have less visceral appeal than they once did. For example, in the most recent presidential campaigns, "crime" was a word rarely mentioned, and crime policy proposals had almost no limelight.

But inaction will not work. Absent new penal policy, the prison system will continue to grow for the next decade, even in the face of dropping crime rates (Austin, Naro, and Fabelo 2007). The two most important questions are whether a popular movement to roll back prison populations can catch the public imagination and whether realistic proposals to do so can have sufficiently broad support.

REFERENCES

Austin, James, Troy Duster, Todd Clear, David Greenberg, John Irwin, Candace McCoy, Alan Mobley, Barbara Owen, and Joshua Page. 2007. *Unlocking America: Why and How to Reduce America's Prison Population.* Santa Barbara, CA: J.F.A. Associates.

Austin, James, Wendy Naro, and Tony Fabelo. 2007. "The 2006 National Prison Population Forecast." Report of the J.F.A. Institute. Philadelphia: Pew Charitable Trust.

Beckett, Kathryn, and Bruce Western. 2001. "Governing Social Marginality: Welfare, Incarceration, and the Transformation of State Policy." *Punishment & Society* 3(1): 43–59.

Blumstein, Alfred, and Allen J. Beck. 2005. "Reentry as a Transient State between Liberty and Recommitment." In *Prisoner Reentry and Crime in America*, Jeremy Travis and Christy Visher, eds., 50–79. New York: Cambridge University Press.

Blumstein, Alfred, and Jacqueline Cohen. 1973. "A Theory of the Stability of Punishment." *Journal of Criminal Law & Criminology* 64: 198–207.

Blumstein, Alfred, and Joel Wallman, eds. 2003. *The Crime Drop in America*. New York: Cambridge University Press.

Bonczar, Thomas P., and Allen J. Beck. 1997. "Lifetime Likelihood of Going to State or Federal Prison." Bureau of Justice Statistics, U.S. Department of Justice (March).

Clear, Todd R. 2007. *Imprisoning Communities: How Mass Incarceration Makes Disadvantaged Neighborhoods Worse*. New York: Oxford University Press.

Clear, Todd R., Elin Waring, and Kristen Scully. 2005. "Communities and Reentry: Concentrated Reentry Cycling." In *Prisoner Reentry and Crime in America*, Jeremy Travis and Christy Visher, eds., 179–208. New York: Cambridge University Press.

Clear, Todd R., Dina R. Rose, Elin Waring, and Kristen Scully. 2003. "Coercive Mobility and Crime: A Preliminary Examination of Concentrated Incarceration and Social Disorganization." *Justice Quarterly* 20(1): 33–64.

Clear, Todd R., Dina R. Rose, and Judith A. Ryder. 2001. "Incarceration and Community: The Problem of Removing and Returning Offenders." *Crime and Delinquency* 47(3): 335–51.

DiIulio, John. 1999. "Two Million Prisoners Are Enough." *Wall Street Journal*, March 12: 1.

Felson, Marcus. 2003. "The Process of Co-Offending." In *Theory for Practice in Situational Crime Prevention*, Vol. 16, Martha J. Smith and Derek B. Cornish, eds. Monsey, NY: Criminal Justice Press.

Harris, Othello, and R. Robin Miller. 2001. *Impacts of Incarceration on the African American Family*. New Brunswick, NJ: Transaction.

Jacobson, Michael. 2005. *Downsizing Prisons: How to Reduce Crime and End Mass Incarceration*. New York: NYU Press.

Johnson, Elizabeth Inez, and Jane Waldfogel. 2002. "Children of Incarcerated Parents: Cumulative Risks and Children's Living Arrangements." Unpublished paper, Columbia University.

Liedka, Raymond V., Anne Morrison Piehl, and Bert Useem. 2006. "The Crime Control Effect of Incarceration: Does Scale Matter?" *Criminology & Public Policy* 5(2): 245–76.

Lynch, James, and William Sabol. 2004. "Assessing the Effects of Mass Incarceration on Informal Social Control in Poor Communities." *Criminology & Public Policy* 3(2): 267–94.

Murray, Joseph. 2005. "The Effects of Imprisonment on the Families and Children of Prisoners." In *The Effects of Imprisonment*, Allison Liebling and Shadd Maruna, eds., 442–92. Cullompton, UK: Willan.

Petersilia, Joan. 2003. *When Prisoners Come Home*. New York: Oxford University Press.

Reiss, Albert J. 1988. "Co-Offending and Criminal Careers." In *Crime and Justice: A Review of Research*, Vol. 10, Michael Tonry and Norval Morris, eds., 117–70. Chicago: University of Chicago Press.

Rose, Dina R., and Todd R. Clear. 1998. "Incarceration, Social Capital and Crime: Examining the Unintended Consequences of Incarceration." *Criminology* 36:3 (August): 441–79.

Rose, Dina R., Todd R. Clear, and Judith Ryder. 2001. "Addressing the Unintended Consequences of Incarceration through Community-Oriented Services at the Neighborhood Level. *Corrections Management Quarterly* (5)3: 62–71.

Spelman, William. 2003. "The Limited Importance of Prison Expansion." In *The Crime Drop in America*, Alfred Blumstein and Joel Wallman, eds., 97–129. New York: Cambridge University Press.

———. 1994. *Criminal Incapacitation*. New York: Plenum.

Western, Bruce. 2006. *Punishment and Inequality in America*. New York: Russell Sage Foundation.

Western, Bruce, Jeffery Kling, and David Weiman. 2001. "The Labor Market Consequences of Incarceration." *Crime and Delinquency* 43(3): 410–28.

Part II

A War-Torn Country
Race, Community, and Politics

Chapter 5

The Code of the Streets*

Elijah Anderson

Of all the problems besetting the poor, inner-city, African American community, none is more pressing than that of interpersonal violence and
aggression. It wreaks havoc daily with the lives of community residents
and increasingly spills over into downtown and residential middle-class
areas. Muggings, burglaries, carjackings, and drug-related shootings, all of
which may leave their victims (including innocent bystanders) dead, are
now common enough to concern all urban and many suburban residents.
The inclination to violence springs from the circumstances of life among
the ghetto poor: the lack of jobs that pay a living wage, the stigma of race,
the fallout from rampant drug use and drug trafficking, and the resulting
alienation and lack of hope for the future.

Simply living in such an environment places young people at special
risk of falling victim to aggressive behavior. Although there are often
forces in the community that can counteract the negative influences, by far
the most powerful being a strong, loving, "decent" (as inner-city residents
put it) family committed to middle-class values, the despair is pervasive
enough to have spawned an oppositional culture, that of "the streets," the
norms of which are often consciously opposed to those of mainstream society. These two orientations, decent and street, socially organize the community, and their coexistence has important consequences for residents,
particularly children growing up in the inner city. Above all, this environment means that even youngsters whose home lives reflect mainstream
values (and the majority of homes in the community do) must be able to
handle themselves in a street-oriented environment.

* Adapted from "The Code of the Street," *Atlantic Monthly* (May 1994).

This is because the street culture has evolved what may be called a "code of the streets," which amounts to a set of informal rules governing interpersonal public behavior, including violence. The rules prescribe both a proper comportment and the proper way to respond if challenged. They regulate the use of violence and so supply a rationale that allows those who are inclined to aggression to precipitate violent encounters in an approved way. The rules have been established and are enforced mainly by the street-oriented, but on the streets the distinction between street and decent is often irrelevant; everybody knows that if the rules are violated, there are penalties. Knowledge of the code is thus largely defensive; it is literally necessary for operating in public. Therefore, even though families with an orientation of decency are usually opposed to the values of the code, they often reluctantly encourage their children's familiarity with it to enable them to negotiate the inner-city environment.

At the heart of the code is the issue of respect, loosely defined as being treated "right" or granted the deference one deserves. However, in the troublesome public environment of the inner city, as people increasingly feel buffeted by forces beyond their control, what one deserves in the way of respect becomes more and more problematic and uncertain. This in turn further opens the issue of respect to sometimes intense, interpersonal negotiation. In the street culture, especially among young people, respect is viewed as almost an external entity that is hard-won but easily lost and so must constantly be guarded. The rules of the code in fact provide a framework for negotiating respect. The person whose very appearance, including his clothing, demeanor, and way of moving, deters transgressions, and allows that person to feel that he possesses (and may be considered by others to possess) a measure of respect. With the right appearance, for instance, he can avoid being "bothered" in public. If he is bothered, not only may he be in physical danger but also he has been disgraced or "dissed" (disrespected). Many of the forms dissing can take might seem petty to middle-class people (maintaining eye contact for too long, for example), but to those invested in the street code, these actions become serious indications of the other person's intentions. Consequently, such people become very sensitive to advances and slights, which could well serve as warnings of imminent physical confrontation.

This hard reality can be traced to the profound sense of alienation from mainstream society and its institutions felt by many poor, inner-city, African Americans, particularly the young. The code of the streets is actually a cultural adaptation to a profound lack of faith in the police and the judicial system. The police are most often seen as representing the dominant white society and not interested in protecting inner-city residents. When called, they may not respond, which is one reason many residents feel they must be prepared to take extraordinary measures to defend themselves and their loved ones against those who are inclined to aggression. In fact, lack of police accountability has been incorporated into the status system: the person who is believed capable of "taking care of himself" is accorded a certain deference, which translates into a sense of physical and psychological control. Thus, the street code emerges where the influence of the police ends and personal responsibility for one's safety is felt to begin. Exacerbated by the proliferation of drugs and easy access to guns, this volatile situation results in the ability of the street-oriented minority (or those who effectively "go for bad") to dominate the public spaces.

Decent and Street Families

Although almost everyone in the poor inner-city neighborhood is struggling financially and therefore feels a certain distance from the rest of America, the decent and the street families in a real sense represent two poles of value orientation, two contrasting conceptual categories. The labels "decent" and "street," which the residents themselves use, amount to evaluative judgments that confer status on local residents. The labeling is often the result of a social contest between individuals and families of the neighborhood. Individuals of the two orientations often coexist in the same extended family. Decent residents judge themselves to be so while judging others to be of the street, and street individuals often present themselves as decent, drawing distinctions between themselves and other people. In addition, there is quite a bit of circumstantial behavior; that is, one person may at different times exhibit both decent and street orientations depending on the circumstances. Although these designations result from much social jockeying, there do exist concrete features that define each conceptual category.

Generally, so-called decent families tend to accept mainstream values more fully and attempt to instill them in their children. Whether married couples with children or single-parent (usually female) households, they are generally "working poor" and so tend to be relatively better off financially than their street-oriented neighbors. They value hard work and self-reliance and are willing to sacrifice for their children. Because they have a certain amount of faith in mainstream society, they harbor hopes for a better future for their children, if not for themselves. Many of them go to church and take a strong interest in their children's schooling. Rather than dwell on the real hardships and inequities facing them, many such decent people, particularly the increasing number of grandmothers raising grandchildren, sometimes see their difficult situation as a test from God and derive great support from their faith and from the church community.

Extremely aware of the problematic and often dangerous environment in which they reside, decent parents tend to be strict in their childrearing practices, encouraging children to respect authority and walk a straight moral line. They have an almost obsessive concern with trouble of any kind and remind their children to be on the lookout for people and situations that might lead to it. At the same time, they are themselves polite and considerate of others and teach their children to be the same way. At home, at work, and in church, they work hard to maintain a positive mental attitude and a spirit of cooperation.

So-called street parents, in contrast, often show a lack of consideration for other people and have a rather superficial sense of family and community. Though they may love their children, many of them are unable to cope with the physical and emotional demands of parenthood and find it difficult to reconcile their needs with those of their children. These families, who are more fully invested in the code of the streets than the decent families are, may aggressively socialize their children into it in a normative way. They believe in the code and judge themselves and others according to its values.

In fact, the overwhelming majority of families in the inner-city community try to approximate the decent-family model, but there are many others who clearly represent the worst fears of the decent family. Not only are their financial resources extremely limited, but also what little they have may be easily misused. The lives of the street-oriented individuals and families are often marked by disorganization. In the most desperate circumstances, people often have a limited understanding of priorities and consequences, and so frustrations mount over bills, food, and, at times, drink, cigarettes, and drugs. Some tend toward self-destructive behavior; many street-oriented women are crack-addicted ("on the pipe"), alcoholic, or repeatedly involved in complicated relationships with men who abuse them. In addition, the seeming intractability of their situation, caused in large part by the lack of well-paying jobs and the persistence of racial discrimination, has engendered deep-seated bitterness and anger in many of the most desperate and poorest African Americans, especially young people. The need both to exercise a measure of control and to lash out at somebody is often played out in the adults' relations with their children. At the least, the frustrations of persistent poverty shorten the fuse in such people, thereby contributing to a lack of patience with anyone, child or adult, who irritates them.

In these circumstances, a woman (or a man, although men are less consistently present in children's lives) can be quite aggressive with children, yelling at and striking them for the least little infraction of the rules she has set down. Often little, if any, serious explanation follows the verbal and physical punishment. This response teaches children a particular lesson. They learn that to solve any kind of interpersonal problem one must quickly resort to hitting or other violent behavior. Actual peace and quiet, and also the appearance of calm, respectful children conveyed to her neighbors and friends, are often what the young mother most desires, but at times she can be very aggressive in trying to make them that way. Thus, she may be quick to beat her children, especially if they defy her law, not because she hates them but because this is the way she knows to control them. In fact, many street-oriented women love their children dearly. Many mothers in the community subscribe to the notion that there is a "devil in the boy" that must be beaten out of him or that socially "fast girls need to be whupped." Thus, much of what borders on child abuse in the view of social authorities is acceptable parental punishment in the view of these mothers.

Many street-oriented women are sporadic mothers whose children learn to fend for themselves when necessary, foraging for food and money any way they can get it. The children are sometimes employed by drug dealers or become addicted themselves. These children of the street, growing up with little supervision, are said to "come up hard." They often learn to fight at an early age, sometimes using short-tempered adults around them as role models. The street-oriented home may be fraught with anger, verbal disputes, physical aggression, and even mayhem. The children observe these goings-on, learning the lesson that might makes right. They quickly learn to hit those who cross them, and the dog-eat-dog mentality prevails. In order to survive, to protect oneself, it is necessary to marshal inner resources and be ready to deal with adversity in a hands-on way. In these circumstances, physical prowess takes on great significance.

In some of the most desperate cases, a street-oriented mother may simply leave her young children alone and unattended while she goes out. The most irresponsible women can be found at local bars and crack houses, getting high and socializing with other adults. Sometimes a troubled woman will leave very young children alone for days at a time. Reports of crack addicts abandoning their children have become common in drug-infested inner-city communities. Neighbors or relatives discover the abandoned children, often hungry and distraught over the absence of their mother. After repeated absences, a friend and relative, particularly a grandmother, will often step in to care for the young children, sometimes petitioning the authorities to send her, as guardian of the children, the mother's welfare check, if the mother gets one. By this time, however, the children may well have learned the first lesson of the streets: survival itself, let alone respect, cannot be taken for granted; you have to fight for your place in the world.

Campaigning for Respect

These realities of inner-city life are largely absorbed on the streets. At an early age, often even before they start school, children from street-oriented homes gravitate to the streets, where they "hang," or socialize, with their peers. Children from these generally permissive homes have a great deal of latitude and are allowed to "rip and run" up and down the street. They often come home from school, put their books down, and go right back out the door. On school nights, eight- and nine-year-olds remain out until nine or ten o'clock (and teenagers typically come in whenever they want to). On the streets, they play in groups that often become the source of their primary social bonds. Children from decent homes tend to be more carefully supervised and are thus likely to have curfews and to be taught how to stay out of trouble.

When decent and street kids come together, a kind of social shuffle occurs in which a child has the chance to go either way. Tension builds as a child comes to realize that he must choose an orientation. The kind of home he comes from influences but does not determine the way he will ultimately turn out—although it is unlikely that a child from a thoroughly street-oriented family will easily absorb decent values on the streets. Youth who emerge from street-oriented families but develop a decency orientation almost always learn those values in another setting, such as in school, in a youth group, or in church. Often it is the result of their involvement with a caring "old head" (adult role model).

In the street, through their play, children pour their individual life experiences into a common knowledge pool, affirming, confirming, and elaborating on what they have observed in the home and matching their skills against those of others. And they learn to fight. Even small children test one another, pushing and shoving, and are ready to hit other children over circumstances not to their liking. In turn, they are readily hit by other children, and the child who is toughest prevails. Thus, the violent resolution of disputes, the hitting and cursing, gains social reinforcement. In effect, the child is initiated into a system that is really a way of campaigning for respect.

In addition, younger children witness the disputes of older children, which are often resolved through cursing and abusive talk, if not aggression or outright violence. They see that one child succumbs to the greater physical and mental abilities of the other. They are also alert and attentive witnesses to the verbal and physical fights of adults, after which they compare notes and share their own interpretations of the event. In almost every incident, the victor is the person who physically won the altercation, and this person often enjoys the esteem and respect of onlookers. These experiences reinforce the lessons the children have learned at home: might makes right, and toughness is a virtue while humility is not. When it is left virtually unchallenged, this understanding becomes an ever-more important part of the child's working conception of the world. Over time, the code of the streets becomes refined.

Those street-oriented adults with whom children come in contact, including mothers, fathers, brothers, sisters, girlfriends, boyfriends, cousins, neighbors, and friends, help them along in forming this understanding by verbalizing the messages they are getting through experience: "Watch your back." "Protect yourself." "Don't punk out." "If somebody messes with you, you got to pay them back." "If someone disses you, you got to straighten them out." Many parents actually impose sanctions if a child is not sufficiently aggressive. For example, if a child loses a fight and comes home upset, the parent might respond, "Don't you come in here crying that somebody beat you up; you better get back out there and whup his ass. I didn't raise no punks! Get back out there and whup his ass. If you don't whup his ass, I'll whup your ass when you come home." Thus, the child obtains reinforcement for being tough and showing nerve.

While fighting, some children cry as though they are doing something about which they are ambivalent. The fight may be against their wishes, yet they may feel constrained to fight or face the consequences, not just from peers but also from caretakers or parents, who may administer another beating if they back down. Some adults recall receiving such lessons from their own parents and justify repeating them to their children as a way to toughen them up. Looking capable of taking care of oneself as a form of self-defense is a dominant theme among both street-oriented and decent adults who worry about the safety of their children. Thus, at times there is a convergence in their childrearing practices, although the rationales behind them may differ.

Self-Image Based on "Juice"

By the time they are teenagers, most youth have either internalized the code of the streets or at least learned the need to comport themselves in accordance with its rules, which chiefly have to do with interpersonal communication. The code revolves around the presentation of self. Its basic requirement is the display of a certain predisposition to violence. Accordingly, one's bearing must send the unmistakable if sometimes subtle message to "the next person" in public that one is capable of violence and mayhem when the situation requires it and that one can take care of oneself. The nature of this communication is largely determined by the demands of the circumstances but can include facial expressions, gait, and verbal expressions, all of which is geared mainly to deter aggression. Physical appearance, including clothes, jewelry, and grooming, also plays an important part in how a person is viewed; to be respected, it is important to have the right look.

Even so, there are no guarantees against challenges, because there are always people around looking for a fight to increase their share of respect, or "juice," as it is sometimes called on the street. Moreover, if a person is assaulted, it is important, not only in the eyes of his opponent but also in the eyes of his "running buddies," for him to avenge himself. Otherwise he risks being "tried" (challenged) or "moved on" by any number of others. To maintain his honor he must show he is not someone to be "messed with" or "dissed." In general, the person must "keep himself straight" by managing his possession of respect among others; this involves in part his self-image, which is shaped by what he thinks others are thinking of him in relation to his peers.

Objects play an important and complicated role in establishing self-image. Jackets, sneakers, and gold jewelry reflect not just a person's taste, which tends to be tightly regulated among adolescents of all social classes, but also a willingness to possess things that may require defending. A boy wearing a fashionable, expensive jacket, for example, is vulnerable to attack by another who covets the jacket and either cannot afford to buy one or wants the added satisfaction of depriving someone else of his. However, if a boy forgoes the desirable jacket and wears one that isn't "hip," he runs the risk of being teased and possibly even assaulted as an unworthy person. To be allowed to hang with certain prestigious crowds, a boy must wear a different set of expensive clothes, sneakers, and athletic suit every day. Not doing so might make him appear socially deficient. The youth comes to covet such items, especially when he sees easy prey wearing them.

In acquiring valued things, therefore, a person shores up his identity, but since it is an identity based on having something, it is highly precarious. But this very precariousness gives a heightened sense of urgency to staying even with peers, with whom the person is actually competing. Young men and women who are able to command respect through their presentation of self, by allowing their possessions and their body language to speak for them, may not have to campaign for regard but rather may gain it by the force of their manner. Those who are unable to command respect in this way must actively campaign for it and are thus particularly alive to slights.

One way of campaigning for status is by taking the possessions of others. In this context, seemingly ordinary objects can become trophies imbued with symbolic value that far exceeds their monetary worth. Possession of the trophy can symbolize the ability to violate somebody, "to get in his face," to take something of value from him, to "diss" him, and thus to enhance one's own worth by stealing someone else's. The trophy does not have to be something material. It can be another person's sense of honor, snatched away with a derogatory remark. It can be the outcome of a fight. It can be the imposition of a certain standard, such as a girl establishing herself as the most beautiful and being recognized as such. Material things, however, fit easily into the pattern. Things such as sneakers, a pistol, even somebody else's girlfriend, can become a trophy. When a person can take something from another and then flaunt it, he gains a certain regard by being the owner, or the controller, of that thing. But this display of ownership can then provoke other people to challenge him. This game of who controls what is thus constantly being played out on inner-city streets, and the trophy, extrinsic or intrinsic, tangible or intangible, identifies the current winner.

An important aspect of this often violent give-and-take is its zero-sum quality. That is, the extent to which one person can raise himself up depends on how he can put another person down. This underscores the alienation that permeates the inner-city ghetto community. There is a generalized sense that very little respect is to be had, and therefore everyone competes to get what affirmation he can of the little that is available. The resulting craving for respect gives people thin skins. Shows of deference by others can be highly soothing, contributing to a sense of security, comfort, self-confidence, and self-respect. Transgressions by others that go unanswered diminish these feelings and are believed to encourage further transgressions. Hence, one must be ever vigilant against the transgressions of others or even *appearing* as if transgressions will be tolerated. Among young people, whose self-esteem is particularly vulnerable, there is an especially heightened concern with being disrespected. Many inner-city young men in particular crave respect to such a degree that they will risk their lives to gain and maintain it.

The issue of respect is thus closely tied to whether a person has an inclination to be violent, even as a victim. In the wider society, people may not feel required to retaliate physically after an attack, even though they are aware that they have been degraded or taken advantage of. Middle-class people may feel a great need to defend themselves *during* an attack, or to behave in such a way as to deter aggression (middle-class people certainly can and do become victims of street-oriented youths), but they are much more likely than street-oriented people to feel they can walk away from a possible altercation with their self-esteem intact. Some people may even have the strength of character to flee, without any thought that their self-respect or esteem will be diminished.

In impoverished inner-city African American communities, however, particularly among young males and perhaps increasingly among females, such flight would be extremely difficult. To run away would likely leave one's self-esteem in tatters. Hence people often feel constrained not only to stand up and at least attempt to resist during an assault but also to "pay back," to seek revenge, after a successful assault on their person. This may include going to get a weapon or even getting relatives involved. Their very identity and self-respect, their honor, is often intricately tied up with the way they perform on the streets during and after such encounters.

This outlook reveals the circumscribed opportunities of the inner-city poor. Generally people outside the ghetto have other ways of gaining status and regard and do not feel so dependent on such physical displays.

By Trial of Manhood

Among males on the street, concerns about possessions and identity have come to be expressed in the concept of "manhood." Manhood in the inner city means having the prerogatives of men and having everyone—strangers, other men, women—acknowledge an individual male's right to those privileges and distinguish him as a man. It implies physicality and a certain ruthlessness. Regard and respect are associated with this concept in large part because of its practical application: if others have little or no regard for a person's manhood, his very life and that of his loved ones could be in jeopardy. But there is a chicken-and-egg aspect to this situation: one's physical safety is more likely to be jeopardized in public *because* manhood is associated with respect. In other words, an existential link has been created between the idea of manhood and one's self-esteem so that it is hard to say which is primary. For many inner-city youth, manhood and respect are flip sides of the same coin; physical and psychological well-being are inseparable, and both require a sense of control, of being in charge.

The operating assumption is that a man, especially a "real" man, knows what other men know—the code of the streets. And if one is not a real man, one is somehow diminished as a person, and there are certain valued things one simply does not deserve. Thus, there is believed to be a certain justice to the code because it is considered that everyone has the opportunity to know it. Implicit in this is that everyone is held responsible for being familiar with the code. If the victim of a mugging, for example, does not know the code and so responds incorrectly, the perpetrator may feel justified even in killing him and may feel no remorse. He may think, "Too bad, but it's his fault. He should have known better."

So when a person ventures outside, he must adopt the code—a kind of shield, really, to prevent others from "messing" with him. In these circumstances it is easy for people to think they are being tried or tested by others even when this is not the case. When it is sensed that something extremely valuable is at stake in every interaction, people are encouraged to rise to the occasion, particularly with strangers. For people who are unfamiliar with the code (generally people who live outside the inner city), the concern with respect in the most ordinary interactions can be frightening and incomprehensible. But for those who are invested in the code, the clear object of their demeanor is to discourage strangers from even thinking about testing their manhood. And the sense of power that attends the ability to deter others can be alluring even to those who know the code without being heavily invested in it, e.g., the decent inner-city youth. Thus, a boy who has been leading a basically decent life can, in trying circumstances, suddenly resort to deadly force.

Central to the issue of manhood is the widespread belief that one of the most effective ways of gaining respect is to manifest "nerve." Nerve is shown when someone takes a person's possessions (the more valuable, the better), "messes with" someone's woman, throws the first punch, "gets in someone's face," or pulls a trigger. Its proper display helps on the spot to check others who would violate one's person and also helps to build a reputation that works to prevent future challenges. But since such a show of nerve is a forceful expression of disrespect toward the person on the receiving end, the victim may be greatly offended and seek to retaliate with equal if not greater force. A display of nerve, therefore, can easily provoke a life-threatening response, and the background knowledge of that possibility has often been incorporated into the concept of nerve.

True nerve exposes a lack of a real fear of dying. Many feel that it is acceptable to risk dying over the principle of respect. In fact, among the hard-core street-oriented, the clear risk of violent death may be preferable to being "dissed" by another. The youth who have internalized this attitude and convincingly display it in their public bearing are among the most threatening people of all, for it is commonly assumed that they fear no man. As the people of the community say, "They are the baddest dudes on the street." They often lead an existential life that may acquire meaning only when faced with the possibility of imminent death. Not to be afraid to die is, by implication, to have few compunctions about taking someone else's life. Not to be afraid to die is the quid pro quo of being able to take another's life, for the right reasons, if the situation demands it. When others believe this is someone's position, it gives that person a real sense of power on the streets. Such credibility is what many inner-city youths strive to achieve, whether they are decent or street-oriented, both because of its practical defensive value and because of the positive way it makes them feel about themselves. The difference between the decent and the street-oriented youth is that the decent youth makes a conscious decision to appear tough and manly; in another setting, with teachers, for instance, or at his part-time job, the same young man can be polite and deferential. The street-oriented youth, on the other hand, has made the concept of manhood a part of his very identity; he has difficulty manipulating it, and it often controls him.

Girls and Boys

Increasingly, teenage girls are mimicking the males and trying to have their own version of "manhood." Their goal is the same: to get respect, to be recognized as capable of setting or maintaining a certain standard. They try to achieve this end in the ways that have been established by the males, including posturing, abusive language, and the use of violence to resolve disputes, but the issues for the girls are different. Although conflicts over turf and status exist among the girls, the majority of disputes seem rooted in assessments of beauty (which girl in a group is "the cutest"), competition over boyfriends, and the attempts to regulate other people's knowledge of and opinions about a girl's behavior or that of someone close to her, especially her mother.

A major cause of conflicts among girls is "he say, she say." This practice begins in the early school years and continues through high school. It occurs when "people," particularly girls, talk about others, thereby putting their "business in the streets." Usually one girl will say something negative about another in the group, most often behind the person's back. The remarks will then get back to the person talked about. She may retaliate or her friends may feel required to "take up for" her. In essence, this is a form of group gossiping in which individuals are negatively assessed and evaluated. As with much gossip, the things said may or may not be true, but the point is that such imputations can cast aspersions on a person's good name. The accused is required to defend herself against the slander, which can result in arguments and fights, often over little of real substance. Here again is the problem of low self-esteem, which encourages youngsters to be highly sensitive to slights and to be vulnerable to feeling easily "dissed." To avenge the dissing, a fight is usually necessary.

Because boys are believed to control violence, girls tend to defer to them in situations of conflict. Often, if a girl is attacked or feels slighted, she will get a brother, uncle, or cousin to do her fighting for her. Increasingly, however, girls are doing their own fighting and are even asking their male relatives to teach them how to fight. Some girls form groups that attack other girls or take things from them. A hard-core segment of inner-city girls inclined to violence seems to be developing. As one thirteen-year-old girl in a detention center for youth who have committed violent acts told me, "To get people to leave you alone, you gotta fight. Talking don't always get you out of stuff." One major difference between girls and boys: girls rarely use guns. Their fights are therefore not life-or-death struggles. Girls are not often willing to put their lives on the line for "manhood." The ultimate form of respect on the male-dominated inner-city streets is thus reserved for men.

"Going for Bad"

In the most fearsome youth, such a cavalier attitude toward death grows out of a very limited view of life. Many are uncertain about how long they are going to live and believe they could die violently at any time. They accept this fate; they live on the edge. Their manner conveys the message that nothing intimidates them; whatever turn the encounter takes, they maintain their attack, rather like a pit bull, whose spirit many such boys admire. The demonstration of such tenacity "shows heart" and earns their respect.

This fearlessness has implications for law enforcement. Many street-oriented boys are much more concerned about the threat of "justice" at the hands of a peer than at the hands of the police. Moreover, many feel not only that they have little to lose by going to prison but also that they have something to gain. The toughening-up one experiences in prison can actually enhance one's reputation on the streets. Hence the system loses influence over the hard core who are without jobs and with little perceptible stake in the system. If mainstream society has done nothing *for* them, they counter by making sure it can likewise do nothing *to* them.

At the same time, however, a competing view maintains that true nerve consists in backing down, walking away from a fight, and going on with one's business. One fights only in self-defense. This view emerges from the decent philosophy that life is precious, and it is an important part of the socialization process common in decent homes. It discourages violence as the primary means of resolving disputes and encourages youngsters to accept nonviolence and talk as confrontational strategies. But "if the deal goes down," self-defense is greatly encouraged. When there is enough positive support for this orientation, either in the home or among one's peers, then nonviolence has a chance to prevail. But it prevails at the cost of relinquishing a claim to being bad and tough, and therefore sets a young person up as alienated from street-oriented peers and quite possibly a target of derision or even violence.

Although the nonviolent orientation rarely overcomes the impulse to strike back in an encounter, it does introduce a certain confusion and so can prompt a measure of soul-searching or even profound ambivalence. Did the person back down with his respect intact or did he back down only to be judged a "punk," viz., a person lacking manhood? Should he or she have acted? Should he or she have hit the other person in the mouth? These questions beset many young men and women during public confrontations. What is the "right" thing to do? In the quest for honor, respect, and local status, which few young people are uninterested in, common sense most often prevails, which leads many to opt for the tough approach, enacting their own particular versions of the display of nerve. The presentation of oneself as rough and tough is very often quite acceptable until one is tested. And then that presentation may help the person pass the test, because it will cause fewer questions to be asked about what he did and why. It is harder for a person to explain why he lost the fight or why he backed down. Hence, many will strive to appear to "go for bad," while hoping they will never be tested. But when they are tested, the outcome of the situation may be out of their hands, as they become wrapped up in the circumstances of the moment.

An Oppositional Culture

The attitudes of the wider society are deeply implicated in the code of the streets. Most people in inner-city communities are not totally invested in the code, but the significant minority of hard-core street youth who are have to maintain the code in order to establish reputations, because they have, or feel they have, few other ways to assert themselves. For these young people, the standards of the street code are the "only game in town." The extent to which some children, particularly those who through upbringing have become most alienated and those lacking in strong and conventional social support, experience and internalize racist rejection and contempt from mainstream society may strongly encourage them to express contempt for the more conventional society in turn. In dealing with this contempt and rejection, some youngsters will consciously invest themselves and their considerable mental resources in what amounts to an oppositional culture to preserve themselves and their self-respect. Once they do, any respect they might be able to garner in the wider system pales in comparison with the respect available in the local system; thus, they often lose interest in even attempting to negotiate the mainstream system.

At the same time, many less-alienated young African Americans have assumed a street-oriented demeanor as a way of expressing their blackness while really embracing a much more moderate way of life; they, too, want a nonviolent setting in which to live and raise a family. These decent people are trying hard to be part of the mainstream culture, but the racism, real and perceived, that they encounter helps to legitimate the oppositional culture. And so, on occasion, they adopt street behavior. In fact, depending on the demands of the situation, many people in the community slip back and forth between decent and street behavior.

A vicious cycle has been formed. The hopelessness and alienation many young inner-city African American men and women feel, largely as a result of endemic joblessness and persistent racism, fuels the violence they engage in. This violence serves to confirm the negative feelings many whites and some middle-class African Americans harbor toward the ghetto poor, further legitimating the oppositional culture and the code of the streets in the eyes of many poor young African Americans. Unless this cycle is broken, attitudes on both sides will become increasingly entrenched, and the violence, which claims victims black and white, poor and affluent, will only escalate.

[Chapter 6]

The Contemporary Penal Subject(s)

Mona Lynch

Introduction

The well-documented late-twentieth-century war on crime in America and the explosion in the use of highly punitive sanctions that came with it has spawned new conceptualizations of the criminal/penal subject across a number of arenas. These constructions differ in fundamental ways from those of the old penological subject and have had dramatic consequences for penal policy and practices. The ways in which the population that is to be punished is imagined by policy makers, court personnel, penal administrators, and others who are in the business of state punishment necessarily shapes the kinds of investments states have made in their penal machinery. And while this category has always held an amalgam of prototypes, depending on who is doing the conceiving and what kind of offender is being conceived, there has been a marked change over the past four or five decades in the overall composition of the "mixed bag" of penal subject constructions.[1]

Indeed, we have moved from a set of conceptions that prominently featured psychologically complex and innately human characterizations of the punished subject to a set that, for the most part, envisions the penal subject as an almost nonpsychological being who does not deserve the kind of examination and understanding that criminal offenders had previously warranted. Thus, at present, there is a cold-hearted simplicity to how penal policy makers and practitioners tend to construct those to be subjected to penal intervention.

In this essay, I will explore some specific ways that the penal subject, as constructed in several arenas, has been transformed in recent years. To do so, I will examine the relationship between the punitive state and the punished subject. I will begin with a discussion of the "old," pre-1960s penal subject and then move on to describe the transitional stage of penal subjectivity. I will then flesh out several prototypes of the contemporary penal subject, distinguished by type of offender and context of construction. I will conclude by discussing signs of change—openings to a new discourse about punishment and its subjects that may contribute to a productive approach to the post–war on crime reconstruction.

The "Old" Penal Subject

Much has been written about the pre–war on crime penology that dominated twentieth-century American corrections into the 1960s, and what it meant in terms of how the recipients of punishment were viewed. Very simply, underlying the prevailing penal philosophy of that time was a conception of the offender/convict as a reformable being and the state as the appropriate entity to engage in such reform. David Garland refers to the ideology of this period as "penal-welfarism," which he describes as a hybrid intellectual structure that combines philosophies of legal liberalism and proportionality with "a more correctionalist commitment to rehabilitation, welfare, and criminological expertise" (Garland 2001, 27). Thus, penal welfarism represented, at least in its ideal form, an optimistic commitment to improving the lives of those at the lowest rungs of society through the governmental implementation of relatively generous, albeit somewhat paternalistic and intrusive programs that aimed to eradicate various social ills, including unemployment, educational deficiencies, deviance, and criminality.

In a related manner, Feeley and Simon (1992) describe the "old penology" as being concerned with offenders as individuals who need to be known and understood in order to be reformed or even simply to be punished. Such a conception meant that penal interventions were best individualized, often with a concern for remediating the root causes of offending behavior. Underlying many conceptions of the "old" penal subject was the implicit understanding that the offender fell within the larger category of personhood—with all of the psychological and sociological complexity inherent in being human. Thus, the criminal/penal subject merely deviated on one or more scales from an idealized norm, rather than belonging in a qualitatively different category of being. And since the penal subject's offending behavior or deviant acts fell within a continuum of human behavior, this conception of the penal subject held the potential for productive change and was generally viewed as worthy of state efforts to impel that change.

Of course, within the subgroup of criminal deviants, there has long existed the notion that some offenders are beyond hope for redemption, and punishments such as the death penalty were reserved for this small, irredeemable group. Yet, in contrast to the current era, even at that far end of the continuum, individual penal/criminal subjects still could at least inspire debate about the possibility for reform and redemption (see, for example, Theodore Hamm's (2001) discussion of Caryl Chessman). Indicative of this sense of hope was the fact that all those subject to penal law, including the most serious and violent offenders (save for those unusual few who were sentenced and put to death), had the real and probable chance that they would be set free to try to live a law abiding life after incarceration. Thus, a prominent feature of this penology was the view that those subject to penal intervention held, except in rare and extreme cases, the potential to move toward the middle of the scale into the range of normal and law abiding.

Borne from this construction was the notion that the punished subject was, in a sense, psychologically weak or ailing, and in need of expert intervention. This prompted two things. First, it required that the state penal system invest in expertise. Diagnosis of the underlying problems that led the offender to behave in a criminal manner, intervention strategy, and prognosis for rehabilitation all required the reliance on experts in human behavior, employed by the state to aid in the reformative task. Such individualized, expert "treatment" allowed for the emergence over the course of the twentieth century of a variety of new sanctions, designed to meet a range of offenders' needs. The ascension of probation and parole as alternative sanctions, then later, the development of mental health–oriented correctional institutions, residential and community training centers, halfway houses, and so on were all at least in part predicated on the understanding of the offender as a flawed but fixable individual.

The Transitional Penal Subject: Moving from Continua to Discrete Categories

The hegemony of rehabilitation as a means and goal of American punishment began to falter in the late 1960s, spurring the disintegration of the predominant construction of the penal subject. There emerged, during a transition decade or so, a number of new penal subject constructions —the punished person was no longer simply someone who needed state-supplied intervention to set him on a proper life course; he or she also became increasingly identified in political, legal, and institutional realms as a political being, a subversively free-willed actor, a product of structural inequality, and a victim of a negative label, among multiple other new identities. This fragmentation of what was a more holistic understanding of penal subjectivity contributed to the crisis in the state's expressed confidence in its ability to correct offenders.

Contradictory calls for penal reform that dominated this period underscored the competing and disparate new constructions of the punished subject that emerged. Those involved in the prisoners' rights movement, both inside and outside of state institutions, demanded that prisoners be treated as autonomous and able adults by courts and penal administrators and rejected the "prisoner as infirm" model that was asserted by a paternalistic "therapeutic" state (e.g., American Friends Service Committee 1971). Academic criminologists joined the critique of the previously dominant penal paradigm, some suggesting that crime is largely a socially constructed category that works to maintain racial, ethnic, and class divisions; thus "criminal offender" was merely a label used by those with power to denigrate various subcultural and countercultural members (see, e.g., Becker 1963; Quinney 1970; and Cohen 1972 for several different varieties of this theoretical thrust).

On the other side of the spectrum, political figures, especially at the state and national levels, significantly stepped up the use of crime as political fodder. As Beckett (1997) points out, starting in the 1960s, conservative presidential candidates began to use calls for law and order as a powerful heuristic to delegitimate a range of political activism taking place. Those fighting for various civil rights, particularly for racial equality, were often reduced, in this rhetoric, to simple outlaws and criminals, which required a powerful and punitive criminal justice system to contain. This political tactic, then, helped shape a new construction of the penal subject as one who, on the one hand, was autonomous and responsible for his actions, but who, on the other, was a much more significant threat to the nation's well-being than previously conceived. It also played a major role in racializing penal subjectivity in the American imagination.

As Sloop (1996) illustrates in his analysis of popular cultural representations of the prisoner, the convict of this period was still predominantly portrayed as redeemable and human, yet the fragmented subidentities of this constructed prototype opened up the possibility of the coming "new" penal subject. There were several components to this process. First, it is in this period that the penal subject increasingly became identified as a person of color, who, in turn, became identified with the increasing level of violence that was occurring in American prisons. Thus, according to Sloop (1996), in the 1960s, the male prisoner identity became somewhat bifurcated—the weak but redeemable white inmate was joined by a newly constructed image of the more violent (in sympathetic conceptions, as a product of his oppressed status), more irrational, and less redeemable African American convict. By the late 1970s, the African American prisoner prototype spun off a third, new version of the penal subject: a wholly irredeemable "other," primarily identified as African American, who is best incarcerated to protect society.

Previous work of mine that examined correctional industry advertising campaigns over a fifty-year period also illustrates this transformative process. Penal products manufacturers and service industries alike began to reconstruct the image of the prisoner in their advertising to fit with this prototypical new, dangerous convict. A concern with security and containment of inmates within institutions became evident in the advertising campaigns of the 1970s, replacing the previous emphasis in the ads on bridging the institution (and its residents) and the larger community. Visual depictions of the (almost exclusively male) inmate transformed from one who was exclusively white in ethnicity, often smiling, passive in posture, and small in stature relative to the accompanying images of correctional officers, to a bulky, muscled figure with a darker skin tone (without always clearly identifying race or ethnicity), a surly or menacing facial expression, and frequently depicted as trying to escape, incite a riot, or make other serious trouble (Lynch 2002a).

During this period, a more salient cultural construction of the female prisoner also emerges, and she is clearly a product of gendered stereotypes—she is "bad" due to weakness and male influence, underdeveloped morality, and/or her prior status as a victim of abuse—and she is reformable through state-assisted programs (Sloop 1996). Thus, she is essentially an era behind the male prisoner and functions in many ways like the "old" male penological subject. Yet because state punishment was (and continues to be) predominantly aimed at men, the emergence of these transitional male penal subjects had major implications for how punishment would be transformed. As Sloop (1996) has argued, the splintering of the convict's cultural identity in this period ultimately encouraged a "construction of difference" that comes to dominate the conceptualization of penal subjects by the 1980s.

The New Penal Subject(s)

Literally by the start of the 1980s, punishment in the United States had been massively transformed, and there was little competition for the tough-on-crime rhetoric that propelled almost all criminal justice policy in the country. The emerging penal subject, as imagined by most mainstream individuals and groups, reflected the ascension of this new harsh punitiveness. The imagined prototypical offender in popular, political, and even justice policy circles tended to be the scariest (although statistically rarest) type of criminal, who need not be understood or corrected but who must at any cost be contained and disempowered.

The narrative of this late-twentieth-century penal shift—from the explosion in U.S. incarceration rates and the re-emergence of the death penalty as a popular punishment to the bizarre, showy, and demeaning penal innovations like the resurgence of chain gangs, the "invention" of chemical castrations, various shaming punishments, and so on—has been well told by many, so I will not go into detail here. Nonetheless, this phenomenon clearly had major implications for how those to be punished were being conceived and characterized in a number of venues.

David Garland (2001) has suggested a new bifurcated criminal/penal subject emerged in this "late modern" period. In his view, the contemporary criminal falls into one of two polar categories that lead to very different state responses: on one side is the normal, rational, opportunistic actor who tends not to inspire too much public or political furor (i.e., common burglars, low-level thieves, vice offenders, drug dealers, etc.); at the opposite end is the "alien other" (Garland, 2001, 134)—the brutal murderer, the sex offender, and so on—whose construction lurks behind much of the draconian policymaking from the 1980s onward. So, according to Garland, in the first case, deviance tended to be defined downward and sanctions have been lightened over time and, in the second case, punitive response has generally ratcheted upward.[2]

Nonetheless, I would argue, the underlying psychological being in both cases has certain common characteristics that distinguish this construction of the criminal/penal subject from earlier incarnations. Specifically, the new subject is conceived of as relatively simple, rational, and free willed in making his behavioral choices. As such, he has, in many important ways, lost the psychological complexity and imagined vulnerability of the previous prototypes.

Of course, there is a longstanding assumption in modern criminal law that those subject to legal punishment *are* (with a few specified exceptions) rational actors who make choices as a product of their own free will (Connolly 1999). Yet in recent decades, this "rational choice" criminal/penal actor has become a dominant figure across a landscape of criminal justice domains, from academic scholarship to justice policymaking, and the more sociologically and psychologically informed construction of the penal subject nearly vanished in this period. One small but telling indicator of this trend has been the diminishing and even the demise, in many jurisdictions, of social-psychological and mental-health legal justifications/defenses to criminal behavior such as diminished capacity and insanity.[3]

And this simplified contemporary penal subject—stripped of the complex, rich, multi-layered identities and motivations that we continue to recognize and often celebrate in ourselves and our in-group members—has abetted the dramatic spiraling up of punitive sanctions characteristic of state and federal criminal justice policy since the 1980s. If the person to be punished has freely made choices, whether those choices were the product of opportunity, greed, or an evil disposition, punishment, at best, need only function as a deterrent and/or incapacitator to redirect or block the decision to commit crime by offenders (Garland 2001; Lynch 2001).

And because it is inherent in the rational-choice conceptualization that offenders have chosen their fate by exercising their free will in choosing to commit crime, the pains of punishment they must endure in increasingly harsh and austere facilities is a consequence of their own doing. Indeed, as I have illustrated previously, criminal justice personnel and political figures in recent years have increasingly cast the punishment experience itself as a choice made by offenders, rather than something imposed on them (Lynch 2000b; Lynch 2001). Consequently, as the conceptualization of punishment and its subjects changed, state investment in penal machinery shifted away from an emphasis on various forms of individualized programming, expertise, and the development of life-improving opportunities for offenders to an emphasis on cheap but secure housing and various forms of hardware to contain and incapacitate offenders behind fortified walls.

Even the most serious and threatening offenders—those who in the earlier era would be viewed as crippled by all kinds of psychological and sociological impediments—are increasingly characterized as simple yet rational (albeit evil) beings. As I have suggested before (Lynch 2005), borrowing from Garland's conceptualization, this contemporary serious offender/convict prototype might be best characterized as a rational "other." So, in contrast to previous conceptions, where various defects and impediments were seen as the root cause of criminality, the rationality and free will of the contemporary serious criminal is now seen as contributing to his perceived threat and inherent evilness. He chooses to wreak criminal havoc for pleasure, greed, or other selfish and immoral purposes, so he deserves no help or intervention to facilitate law-abiding behavior (Lynch 2005). And indeed, it is generally not worth the state's time, trouble, or resources to even try to understand this being; rather the assumption should simply be made that he chooses to be "evil" and thus must be prevented from making his malevolent choices in the most efficient manner possible (see, e.g., Wilson 1975).

For example, as Craig Haney and I (Lynch and Haney 1998) have found in work that examines how attorneys characterize capital defendants in their closing arguments at trial, prosecutors uniformly construct this hybrid rational "other" criminal subject—a cold, calculating, free-willed actor who chooses evil in killing and harming others—to argue for the most extreme penal response, capital punishment. Simply put, in contemporary prosecutorial rhetoric, since the defendant himself chose to do evil, he chose his own fate. The resulting punishment imperative is that offenders have made the choices that have exposed themselves to penal intervention, and the prudent response is ultimate containment through a sentence of death.

Simon (1998) makes a related argument about the construction of the contemporary sex offender as a subject of state punishment. For Simon, this category of offender reflects the major transformations in the meaning and purpose of punishment that emerged as paradigmatic by the 1980s. Today's sex offender is, at once, a modern-day monster that inspires extreme degrees of populist punitiveness, but, at the same time, is merely one in a "class" of high-risk management problems, inferentially assumed to offend as a matter of his own twisted choice. Thus, the psychiatrically informed individualism that helped define earlier constructions of the sex offender and shaped the kinds of rehabilitative interventions used to help normalize him (Lynch 2000) has given way to an understanding of the sex offender as a simply dangerous, seemingly insatiable actor who must be incapacitated at all costs. His psyche need not be known in order for the state to respond to him; he merely must be identified by the level of risk he poses and be managed by increasingly coercive and constitutionally suspect tools of the state (Simon 1998).

Ultimately, the contemporary adherence to the rational actor/other perspective allows legal and policy decision makers to eschew any complex inquiry into the nature of human behavior; it assumes that behavior is simply a product of individual rational choices "disembodied from all social context" (Cohen 1996, 5). Thus, structural forces, situational and contextual influences, and even individual psychodynamic factors underlying the "crime problem" have little bearing on the assessments that shape official responses to deal with it. As a result, state penal administrators and policymakers have shifted responsibility for dealing with the problem of crime onto those subjected to criminal victimization and those subject to punishment. The job of the state has been reduced to ensuring that identified offenders are contained, incapacitated, monitored, and immobilized by efficient yet punitive means; the job of reducing crime falls on would-be crime victims who are told how to minimize their risks of victimization (Garland 2001), and the offenders are increasingly told to simply "choose" to obey the law (Lynch 2001).

This contemporary construction is now, more than ever, differentially defined by race and class. As Feeley and Simon (1992) have argued, underpinning the nonindividualized new penology is the notion that the growing and intractable underclass population (which disproportionately come into contact with the penal system) can and should merely be managed, not reformed. A number of poorer, darker-skinned subpopulations of criminal "threat" are especially likely to be conceived of as categories of free-willed "bad" actors, drawn in stereotyped and simple terms. For instance, those involved in the illegal drug market are predominantly represented as young men from the ghettos and barrios who choose their illicit trade over honest work out of indolence or avarice, not as a consequence of limited opportunities or longstanding structural barriers.[4] The "gang" problem, which has inspired a slew of extremely punitive policies in the last two decades in jurisdictions across the nation, is similarly conceived of as a problem of bad choices of association made by young men and women of color, disembodied from the structural conditions that clearly underpin gang proliferation. Additionally, especially since the 1980s, undocumented immigrants of color, particularly from south of the

U.S. border, are portrayed as a problem group that must be prevented from choosing to reside in our nation, and have been increasingly subject to new penological-style detention and punitive risk-management techniques (Welch 2002). And, indeed, the most recent "war on terror" is driven by a construction of a very dangerous, threatening, ethnically and religiously different "other" who must not be understood in order to defuse and mitigate the risk posed by him, but must solely be identified and contained through whatever extreme measures it takes.

This is not to say that there does not concurrently exist a rhetoric of the reformable penal subject. This construction is just not at all dominant anymore and, in its current incarnation, is less psychologically and sociologically complex than its predecessor. As Sloop's (1996) analysis indicated, there still exists a version of the reformable offender (albeit more infrequently invoked than in earlier eras), but this portrayal is always of a man or a woman (who is also almost always portrayed as white) who has chosen to avail her/himself of the state's reformative opportunities to be a better person. Thus, behavioral "choice" is now central even to this construction. The contemporary penal subject of color is someone who typically chooses not to reform himself, and simply deserves punishment, not redemption.

From Unique Individuals to Stereotyped Categories: Further Consequences of the New Penal Subject Construction

The predominant rendering of the contemporary penal subject is notable, then, for several distinctive features. First, the individuality formerly ascribed to offenders has nearly vanished. In its place is a broad, near caricaturelike construction of the punished offender that relies on simple, disposition-based understandings of criminality and a variety of racial, cultural, class-based, and gendered stereotypes as its basis. Second, the "offender," and especially the "serious offender," now more than ever falls in a discrete category of being that is rigidly distinguished from the "law abiding"; as several commentators have noted, he is a criminal "other," and severe and incapacitative punishment is necessary to contain and control him. The punished offender is thus distanced from the (ostensibly) noncriminal population in terms of his basic humanity and is broadly understood as not having the same needs, desires, strengths, vulnerabilities, and psychological complexities as the rest of us.

In addition, this construction has contributed in many ways to the rise of a new role that the prototypical penal subject has taken on—that of commodity. I have made the argument before (Lynch 2004) that there is an increasing tendency to view offenders generally and prisoners in particular as a kind of fodder to be (figuratively) consumed by media audiences in a number of ways. Images of and stories about certain offenders and their bad deeds have become as marketable as candid photographs of and gossip about celebrities. One only needs to turn to Nancy Grace on CNN once (and I recommend against any more than that) to illustrate this phenomenon.

The caricatures of criminal offenders as bogeymen blamed for a variety of social ills that predominated news and reality-based mass media in the late 1980s and 1990s drastically impacted penal policy (Anderson 1995), and we are still dealing with the consequences of that rash of faulty policies. With massive transformations in popular mass media that have occurred in more recent years—from the further blurring of the lines between fiction and reality in television programming to the ascension of the Internet as a mode of mass communication—the rendering of the penal subject for mass audiences has had a profound effect on knowledge about and reactions to state punishment policies and its recipients.[5] As I have argued earlier (Lynch 2004), the proliferation of visual forms of electronic mass media has catalyzed the rise of the penal icon, where mass broadcast images have taken on whole sets of meaning beyond the simple image itself (see also Valier 2003). It may take the form of transmitted images of suspect mug shots, used to encapsulate and symbolize the evils of violent crime, particularly in racialized (Anderson 1995) and gendered (Valier 2003) ways; visual representations of penal machinery and other hardware used to reflect our appropriately harsh responses to crime (Lynch 2000b); or streamed video images, such as those sent through the "Jail Cam" used in Arizona and elsewhere, which take on a life of their own in cyberspace (Lynch 2004). These iconic mass-produced penal images feed, shape, reproduce, and reinforce a form of populist culture of punishment and entertainment that in turn feed back into penal policy and practices.

In short, integral to the transformation of punishment and its subjects has been a sustained interactive loop between various forms of the mass media, public action/reaction and the political and policymaking process. In states like California, where citizens directly impact law and policy through the initiative process, the impact of this iterative process is even more apparent. And once the criminal/penal subject has been reduced to imagery and is the source of thrills and entertainment (generally in the form of a horror story "bad guy"), the dehumanization process of the penal subject is nearly total and complete. Thus, in the United States especially, talk of penal subjects—prisoners and condemned convicts particularly—as bearing and deserving of human rights is absolutely foreign.[6]

As I pointed out earlier, this characterization not only justifies the increasingly harsh treatment to which offenders are subjected by our penal system on the basis that offenders choose their penal fate by their malevolent choices in committing crime, but it also contributes to the growing disregard for prisoners—as humans—that has been expressed by legislators, penal administrators, courts, the public, and even mainstream academics in the United States. The predominant discourse around the problems associated with punishment policies and practices will often address such issues as escalating costs, space constraints, staffing problems, efficacy and efficiency in population management, administrative challenges, and so on, but it is rare to find mention within such discourse about the true impact of punishment on its subjects.[7] One generally must turn to critical scholars and activists within the United States, or to sources outside our borders to find any meaningful evaluation of the degrading and damaging aspects of various penal practices or discussions about how to maintain the mental and physical well being, much less the dignity, of those we punish from an ethical or humanistic perspective.[8]

Signs of Change

There are several small signs of change that may indicate some reshaping of the way the punished are being conceived in the early twenty-first century. Two recent examples are illustrative—one emerging from my state, California, and the other from across the world in Iraq.

First, in the fall of 2005, the question of whether Stanley "Tookie" Williams, who had been on death row in California for more than two decades, deserved to be spared from execution was widely debated in distinctly "old" penological terms. As many may be aware, Williams was a founder of the notorious Crips gang in Los Angeles and had a long, violent criminal history when he was convicted of capital murder. He became a leading antigang activist on death row, writing children's books that steered kids away from gangs, and was widely recognized for his positive impact. His appeal for clemency was primarily debated around this fact—should he be allowed to live because he indeed had been reformed and, in the process, had transformed others in meaningful ways. The ideals of rehabilitation and reform and the possibility for redemption were central to discussions about this case occurring on talk radio, on a variety of television news programs, on the Internet, in secondary school and college classrooms, and in various community venues. Ultimately, California's governor rejected clemency and Williams was executed, but the depth and breadth of the discussion about Williams as a human with the potential for positive change was quite reminiscent of an older (and seemingly more thoughtful) era. Indeed, a debate of this intensity over the possibility of redemption in the case of a condemned man has not been seen since Caryl Chessman's execution more than forty years earlier in the same prison (again, see Hamm 2001 on Chessman's case).[9]

The Abu Ghraib prisoner/detainee abuse scandal is, if nothing else, ironic. The digital images of the degrading and tortuous acts imposed on prisoners and detainees in this U.S.-run prison clearly became a form of commodity, as they were transmitted around the world by news media and traveled all around cyberspace to and from any number of audiences. Yet, largely because of their wide and uncontrolled distribution, these penal images sparked intense reaction to and debate about the impact of punishment (albeit excessive, abusive forms of punishment) on its *human* subjects. Despite the official federal response, which first sought to downplay the severity of the acts, then sought to contain the matter by blaming individual, low level, "rogue" prison guards as it became impossible to deny the brutality of what was occurring in Abu Ghraib, a broader dialogue about the effects of punishment emerged. The insights of the 1970s Stanford Prison Experiment were resurrected and discussed on a range of mainstream news programs, and "prisoner abuse," "ethics," and "values" were all raised as concerns within the same sentence by a range of media and political commentators. While these incidents and subsequent outrage on the part of many constituencies did not directly impact domestic, civilian penal practices, they did seem to open up a dialogue about captive prisoners as human subjects of punishment that was much broader and more encompassing than what we have seen and heard in recent years.

The Abu Ghraib incidents catalyzed considerable pressure from American and international groups and organizations on the U.S. government to shut down the facility, ultimately resulting in its closure in 2006. Furthermore, those incidents as well as other disclosures about the use of torture against detainees in our "war on terror" have prompted a number of American legislators and other political figures (as well as individuals and groups) to demand that the administration close the scandal-ridden detention facility at Guantanamo Bay, Cuba, and cease the practice of sending terror detainees to countries that practice torture.[10] This kind of vocal and concerted political pressure would be inconceivable even three years earlier when standing up for basic human rights for detainees, including opposing the use of torture as a tool of the "war on terror," would have been equated with being soft on terrorism.

The final sign of change is in the relative downturn in the volume of "crime hysteria," particularly in the political realm at the state level, that we are beginning to experience. Perhaps only as a consequence of unresolvable budgetary crises, state-level political actors in a number of diverse jurisdictions have cooled on the crime rhetoric in their election campaigns and have even quietly begun to work on reforms that in small ways will turn back from the more punitive (and expensive) policies that were widely enacted in the 1980s and 1990s. "Smart on crime" as a state-level policy slogan is beginning to replace the "tough on crime" slogan that predominated ten years ago (Greene 2003). As crime and punishment begin to diminish as central political issues, the punished subject may well be restored as a more complex, multivaried human subject than the prevailing contemporary prototype.

NOTES

1. Throughout this essay, I will generally use the masculine pronoun when referring to the punished because the predominant conceptualization of criminal offenders/convicts, especially the more serious ones, tends to be male.

2. Although the evidence in the American case does not seem to support this assertion. Sanctions across many of these lower level offenses have on the whole increased rather than decreased since the late 1970s, particularly for drug related offenses at the federal level.

3. Just as it would have been illogical and inconceivable to have life without parole (LWOP) sentences in the previous era, it would also have been inconceivable and absurd to have a "guilty but insane" verdict available to jurors. Both of these contemporary legal inventions seem to be direct products of the current disdain for sociologically and psychologically based understandings of criminality.

4. On this issue, see Moore and Haggerty (2001) who describe the differential understanding and consequent treatment of the youth drug "problem" by race

and class. For upper- and middle-class youth, various forms of drug offending are increasingly handled as private, noncriminal matters: home drug-testing equipment is utilized by families to detect and control use, and insurance eligible "programs" are accessed to treat youthful offenders of means. For the poor, the state has become increasingly punitive, and distinctly nontherapeutic, in dealing with poor, young drug offenders.

5. Few of us who teach about crime and punishment have escaped having college students in our classes cite television shows like "Law and Order" as their authoritative sources of understanding particular aspects of justice. The Internet is fast replacing the more traditional forms of media as a source of knowledge and interactive avenue for visually and textually communicating about crime and punishment. The interactive nature of the World Wide Web allows not only for passive learning but also has become an important mode of mobilizing action on a variety of issues. See Lynch (2002a, 2002b, 2002c, 2004) on this process for those who use the Internet to communicate and provoke activism about crime and punishment issues.

6. "Foreign" is used in several senses of the word—there is widespread interest in our treatment of prisoners and our execution policies from outside our borders, where the issue is explicitly discussed within a human rights framework. Within our borders, though, little or no discussion in such a way occurs in mainstream media or among penal policy-makers and practitioners.

7. To illustrate with just one of many recent examples, in their otherwise thoughtfully written analysis of the "theory and practice of supermax prisons," Mears and Reisig (2006) almost completely ignore the issue of whether the use of the supermax prison, regardless of its contribution to order in correctional systems, might inflict a huge human cost on those prisoners so confined to make it, at the very least, an *unethical* practice as currently implemented, and thus problematic by default. The human cost—the psychological and emotional damage to offenders and their loved ones that is increasingly evident as punishment becomes harsher—is rarely a factor in the cost-benefit equations among academic policy experts who evaluate such the efficacy of such things.

8. These issues may be raised as a matter of concern for instrumental reasons, such as to minimize liability or to comply with a set of rules, standards, or legal mandates that have been imposed on the penal system in question.

9. Arguably, Karla Tucker's execution in Texas inspired a similar level of debate, but this discourse was highly gendered and would not likely have occurred at all if Tucker had been a man (Heberle 1999).

10. Undoubtedly, some but not all of this political will is the product of the major congressional victories by Democrats in November 2006 when that party regained control of both the House and Senate. Voter disenchantment with the war in Iraq is thought to have played a decisive role in the Democrats' election successes.

REFERENCES

American Friends Service Committee. 1971. *Struggle for Justice: A Report on Crime and Punishment*. New York: Hill and Wang.

Anderson, David. 1995. *Crime and the Politics of Hysteria: How the Willie Horton Story Changed American Justice*. New York: Time Books.

Becker, Howard. 1963. *Outsiders: Studies in the Sociology of Deviance*. New York: Free Press.

Beckett, Katherine. 1997. *Making Crime Pay: Law and Order in Contemporary American Politics*. New York: Oxford University Press.

Braman, Donald. 2004. *Doing Time on the Outside: Incarceration and Family Life in Urban America*. Ann Arbor: University of Michigan Press.

Cohen, Stanley. 1972. *Folk Devils and Moral Panic*. London: Paladin.

———. 1996. "Crime and Politics: Spot the Difference." *British Journal of Sociology* 47: 1–21.

Connolly, William. 1999. "The Will, Capital Punishment, and Cultural War." In *The Killing State*, ed. Austin Sarat, 187–205. New York: Oxford University Press.

Feeley, Malcolm, and Jonathan Simon. 1992. "The New Penology: Notes on the Emerging Strategy of Corrections and its Implications." *Criminology* 30(4): 449–74.

Garland, David. 2001. *The Culture of Control: Crime and Social Order in Contemporary Society*. Chicago: University of Chicago Press.

Greene, Judith. 2003. Smart on Crime: Positive Trends in State-Level Sentencing and Corrections Policy. Washington, DC: Families Against Mandatory Minimums.

Hamm, Theodore. 2001. *Rebel and a Cause: Caryl Chessman and the Politics of the Death Penalty in Postwar California, 1948–1974*. Berkeley: University of California Press.

Haney, Craig. 2006. *Reforming Punishment: Psychological Limits to the Pains of Imprisonment*. Washington, DC: American Psychological Association.

Heberle, Renee. 1999. "Disciplining Gender; or, Are Women Getting Away with Murder?" *Signs* 24(4): 1103–12.

Hughes, Timothy, Doris Wilson, and Allen Beck. 2001. *Trends in State Parole, 1990–2000*. Bureau of Justice Statistics Special Report. Washington, DC: U.S. Department of Justice. http://www.ojp.usdoj.gov/bjs/pub/pdf/tsp00.pdf.

Lynch, Mona. 2000a. "Rehabilitation as Rhetoric: The Reformable Individual in Contemporary Parole Discourse and Practices." *Punishment and Society* 2: 41–65.

———. 2000b. "On-Line Executions: The Symbolic Use of the Electric Chair in Cyberspace." *PoLAR: Political and Legal Anthropology Review* 23(2): 1–20.

———. 2001. "From the Punitive City to the Gated Community: Security and

Segregation across the Social and Penal Landscape." *Miami Law Review* 56(1): 601–23.

———. 2002a. "Selling 'Securityware': Transformations in Prison Commodities Advertising, 1949–1999." *Punishment and Society* 4: 305–20.

———. 2002b. "Pedophiles and Cyber-Predators as Contaminating Forces: The Language of Disgust, Pollution, and Boundary Invasions in Federal Debates on Sex Offender Legislation." *Law and Social Inquiry* 27: 529–66.

———. 2002c. "Capital Punishment as Moral Imperative: Pro–Death Penalty Discourse and Activism on the Internet." *Punishment and Society* 4: 213–36.

———. 2004. "Punishing Images: Jail Cam and the Changing Penal Enterprise." *Punishment and Society* 6: 255–70.

———. 2005. "Supermax Meets Death Row: Legal Struggles around the New Punitiveness in the USA." In *The New Punitiveness: Current Trends, Theories, Perspectives*, eds. John Pratt, David Brown, Simon Hallsworth, Mark Brown and Wayne Morrison, 66–84. Devon, UK: Willan.

Lynch, Mona, and Craig Haney. 1998. "Impelling/Impeding the Momentum toward Death: A Contextual Analysis of Attorneys' Final Arguments in California Capital Penalty Phase Trials. Unpublished manuscript.

Mauer, Mark, and Meda Chesney-Lind, eds. 2002. *Invisible Punishment: The Collateral Consequences of Mass Imprisonment*. New York: New Press.

Mears, Daniel, and Michael Reisig. 2006. "The Theory and Practice of Supermax Prisons." *Punishment and Society* 8(1): 33–57.

Mehl, Christopher, and Teresa Miller, eds. 2005. *Civil Penalties, Social Consequences*. New York: Routledge.

Moore, Dawn, and Kevin Haggerty. 2001. "Bring It On Home: Home Drug Testing and the Relocation of the War on Drugs." *Social & Legal Studies* 10(3): 377–95.

Quinney, Richard. 1970. *The Social Reality of Crime*. Boston: Little, Brown.

Simon, Jonathan. 1998. "Managing the Monstrous: Sex Offenders and the New Penology." *Psychology, Public Policy, and Law* 4: 452–67.

Sloop, John. 1996. *The Cultural Prison*. Tuscaloosa: University of Alabama Press.

Tonry, Michael. 1996. *Malign Neglect: Race, Crime, and Punishment in America*. New York: Oxford University Press.

Valier, Claire. 2003. *Crime and Punishment in Contemporary Culture*. London: Routledge.

Welch, Michael. 2002. *Detained: Immigration Laws and the Expanding I.N.S. Jail Complex*. Philadelphia: Temple University Press.

Wilson, James Q. 1975. *Thinking about Crime*. New York: Basic Books.

[*Chapter 7*]

The Punitive City Revisited
The Transformation of Urban Social Control

Katherine Beckett and Steve Herbert

Nearly thirty years ago, in a provocative essay titled, "The Punitive City," Stanley Cohen identified the emergence and characteristics of a new model of "community-based control." This community-based regime, he argued, increasingly supplemented traditional state control institutions yet diverged from them in important ways. Whereas traditional mechanisms such as the prison drew sharp spatial and social distinctions, the new control techniques blurred several important boundaries—between inside and out, guilty and innocent, ordinary deviance and serious crime. This new social control regime, he suggested, was both intrusive and expansive, spreading formal social control mechanisms well beyond prison walls. Although couched in the language of community and motivated by the best of intentions, this new community-based regime created a social-control apparatus that was both broad and deep, extending well past the traditional state apparatus (Cohen 1979; see also Lynch 2001).

As Mona Lynch (2001) points out, Cohen's essay did not anticipate one of the most notable social-control developments of the twentieth and twenty-first centuries: the dramatic expansion of the U.S. criminal justice system. Although the political frenzy around crime has subsided, current U.S. incarceration and community supervision rates are historically unprecedented (Western 2006). The incarceration boom disproportionately affects people of color and has altered the very fabric of social life in many poor communities (Mauer and Chesney-Lind 2003; Patillo, Weiman, and Western 2004; Roberts 2004). Moreover, as Lynch suggests, the expansion of these custodial institutions has been a critical component of a broader cultural trend in which security and segregation are linked. Fences, gates, and walls, she argues, are increasingly pervasive symbols of our security-conscious society.

Lynch's essay provides an important corrective to Cohen's emphases on nonstate institutions and blurred boundaries. As she argues, the state's role in social control remains shockingly robust, and the expansion of U.S. prisons and jails does indeed represent a singularly important development in both practical and symbolic terms. The logic of segregation and exclusion, so vividly exemplified by mass incarceration, appears to be ever more entrenched.

Nonetheless, we argue in this chapter that Cohen's account of the emerging control system was, in many ways, prescient. Over the past two decades, and in the shadow of mass incarceration, local governments across the United States have implemented a range of new social-control techniques that have dispersed the logic and operations of spatial control beyond prison walls. For example, in many cities, people convicted of drug or prostitution-related offenses must, as a condition of a suspended sentence or probation, remain out of large sections of their city of residence. Violations of these "off-limits orders" may lead to reincarceration. Similarly, in Seattle and some other municipalities, authorities are able to "trespass admonish" people from increasingly large areas. No evidence of criminal wrongdoing is required to sustain these exclusions, though violations of these civil exclusion orders are a criminal offense.

These and other similar control innovations build on the "civility" laws that were adopted by many cities in the 1990s. Like the civility laws, they are aimed primarily at excluding those deemed disorderly from particular urban spaces. As was the case with the civility laws, our data suggest it is overwhelmingly people of color, the poor, and the homeless who are ensnared by the new regime (see also Fagan and Davies 2000; Roberts 1999).

Yet the new techniques possess several important and novel characteristics. Each infuses criminal law with civil and administrative legal authority yet expands definitions of crime and deviance. Each imposes spatial restrictions that are dispersed throughout the urban landscape. Each expands the social-control net. And each blurs the boundaries between guilty and innocent, private and public, inside and out, criminal and civil. Contra Cohen, however, these techniques are based in state rather than community institutions. Promoted as an alternative to incarceration, they are attractive to city authorities eager to enhance urban "civility" but constrained by the costs associated with mass incarceration.

We use this chapter to describe and analyze these new urban social-control practices. We draw primarily on research we have conducted in Seattle, as well as secondary sources regarding similar developments elsewhere. The chapter moves through two main sections. In the first, we situate the emergence of the new techniques in their historical context and identify three converging dynamics that help to explain these developments. These include the transformation of the post-industrial urban economy and landscape, the Supreme Court's invalidation of vagrancy-related statutes and the ensuing quest for alternatives to them, and the constraints imposed by mass incarceration. In the second section, we describe a number of the new urban social-control techniques on display in municipalities across the county. In the conclusion, we identify their novel characteristics and suggest that, without resistance, a state-centered version of the dystopian prophesy offered by Cohen may indeed be realized, buttressed by one of the largest incarcerative systems the world has ever known.

The Origins of the New Urban Social-Control Techniques

The new social-control techniques with which we are concerned are sufficiently pervasive to suggest the existence of broad, systemic causes. In what follows, we suggest that the origins of this trend lie in three related developments: the transformation of the urban economy; an invalidation of vagrancy laws and the ensuing quest for alternative disorder-management "tools"; and the constraints imposed by mass incarceration.

The Post-Industrial Urban Economy

As many scholars have noted, the export of much of the U.S. manufacturing industry has significantly impacted urban economies. The increased mobility of industry and finance has led many cities to compete with each other to create the most hospitable environment for corporate investment and headquarters, "luxury-living" facilities, tourism, and retail operations (Gibson 2003; Hackworth 2007; Harvey 2005; Mitchell 2003; Parenti 1999). As a result of these developments, cities increasingly host two distinct post-industrial service economies, one focused on generating and managing information connected to financial flows, the other focused on the retail and tourist sectors. This type of economic development creates an urban landscape of pronounced economic and social differentiation

(Dreier et al. 2001; Goldsmith and Blakely 1992; Wilson 1987). Moreover, as the retail and tourist sectors become more central to the health of urban economies, post-industrial cities increasingly compete to attract potential investors, tourists, and shoppers.

At the same time, federal and local government policies have become increasingly focused on economic growth rather than redistribution (Gibson 2003). U.S. social policy is primarily and increasingly guided by the perceived need to enhance corporate competitiveness, capital accumulation, deregulation, and privatization rather than to reduce inequality and alleviate poverty. These neoliberal social policies, along with the expansion of the penal system, have exacerbated social inequality and rendered life increasingly difficult for the socially and economically marginal (Gowan 2002; Wacquant 2000; Wacquant and Wilson 1989; Western 2006). The inequality and social misery caused by these economic and policy developments fuels participation in the informal economy (Duneier 1999; Gowan 2002; Wacquant 2000). At the same time, cuts in federal housing assistance, wage reductions, and the demolition of low-income housing in the name of urban renewal have deprived a large number of U.S. residents of permanent housing (Feldman 2004; Gibson 2003; Wolch and Dear 1993). Particularly in cities that depend on tourists and suburban shoppers for their economic well-being, the "environment" on commercial streets has become the subject of much official attention.

In this context, city governments often engage in what Timothy Gibson (2003) calls "projects of reassurance": efforts to counter widespread images of cities as sites of decay and danger with sanitized images of urban consumer utopias. The presence of large numbers of homeless people and others involved in the informal economy is highly inconsistent with these images. Since the 1980s, the war on drugs has provided an important means of regulating and controlling these urban spaces. However, as the number of homeless and transient persons has increased, concern over a range of even more minor forms of disorder and the desire for a broader range of legal "tools" to "clean up" particular urban spaces has intensified.

The Politics of Disorder

While efforts to "cleanse" urban areas of "disorder" and vice are a venerable American tradition, both of the socio-economic developments discussed above and recent legal developments have intensified those initiatives and triggered a quest for alternative "tools" by which this might be accomplished. These legal developments are described below.

In the 1960s and 70s, a series of Supreme Court decisions invalidated local ordinances that defined public drunkenness, vagrancy, and loitering as crimes. In these decisions (including *Robinson v. California* (1962) and *Powell v. Texas* (1968)), the Supreme Court ruled that penalizing people for behaviors over which they had no control—that were, in legal terms, based on status—was unconstitutional. Shortly thereafter, many U.S. cities witnessed a dramatic upsurge in homelessness.

In response to these twin developments, urban governments across the United States adopted a range of criminal statutes that, at least in theory, criminalize behavior rather than status. These ordinances include prohibitions against sitting on sidewalks or in bus shelters, sleeping in parks and other public spaces, urinating and drinking in public, and begging. Proponents of these measures call them "civility laws" to promote the idea that their enforcement will restore "civility" to the urban landscape. Regardless of their intent, these laws have the effect of criminalizing noncriminal behaviors—such as drinking, sleeping, and urinating—only when they occur in public spaces, and therefore have a disproportionate impact on the unstably housed (Feldman 2004; Foscarinis 1996; Gowan 2002). In addition, these ordinances provide the police with an important set of tools for general order maintenance (and have been widely used to police not only the homeless, but political protests as well).

The adoption of the civility laws was legitimated by the claims and frames associated with "broken windows policing." Broken windows policing was first articulated by James Q. Wilson in a short *Atlantic Monthly* article in 1982, and has become wildly popular in U.S. urban police departments in the intervening years (Herbert 2001). Broken windows policing calls for a fundamental reorientation of policing, one that offers city governments an even broader and more flexible means of regulating public spaces and removing those deemed "disorderly."

The argument is by now quite familiar: neighborhoods that fail to fix broken windows or address other manifestations of "disorder" display a lack of informal social control and thereby invite the criminally minded into their midst (see also Skogan 1990). Although the theory ostensibly concentrates on the built environment, it also emphasizes unwanted human behavior, particularly that which is engaged in by "disreputable or obstreperous or unpredictable people: panhandlers, drunks, addicts, rowdy teenagers, prostitutes, loiterers, the mentally disturbed" (Wilson and Kelling 1982, 32). It logically follows that strong policing is necessary, and the police are encouraged to consider misdemeanor offenses such as public drunkenness as very serious matters. The appeal of this approach to city and law enforcement officials is clear: broken windows policing promises to enhance the security of urban voters and to facilitate the "revitalization" of urban downtowns.[1] Broken windows policing and related ordinances are analogous, in their effects and goals, to the vagrancy and loitering statutes adopted by southern states in the late nineteenth century (see Bass 2001; Stewart 1998).

Although the civility laws have at least in some cases enabled authorities to push marginal populations away from what David Snow and Michael Mulcahy (2001) call "prime" urban spaces to more peripheral and less visible areas, this effect has been far from complete. In many cities, the civility codes have not led to the successful relocation of the homeless and others who spend time on the streets. Moreover, those arrested under these laws are entitled to legal representation, and many civility laws have been successfully challenged in the courts (Coalition of the Homeless 2006). Despite rendering the lives of many homeless people more precarious, these "failures" have been quite productive (in the Foucauldian sense). In Seattle and elsewhere, the quest for more expansive and invulnerable social-control mechanisms that infuse criminal law with civil and administrative legal authority, thereby reducing the chances that they will be challenged and diminishing the rights-bearing capacity of their targets, has been quite successful.

The New Urban Social-Control Techniques

The post-industrial city is characterized by a complex and often bewildering array of new social-control measures. Below, we describe some of those that seem to be particularly central to the management of urban "disorder." Although there is significant variation in the degree to which these measures are being imposed, and Seattle appears to be something of a leader in this regard, each of the techniques we describe below is employed in numerous localities. Our discussion focuses on three of the most important new control measures—off-limits orders, novel applications of trespass law, and parks exclusion statutes.

Off-Limits Orders

In Seattle and many other cities, judges and/or correctional officers may order people convicted of drug- and prostitution-related offenses to stay out of particular sections of their city of residence (Flanagan 2003; Hill 2005; Sanchez 2001). These administrative tools rest on the combined principles of trespass and zoning law (Flanagan 2003). In some cities, including Portland, Oregon, and Cincinnati, Ohio, these orders were initially authorized by city statute and were imposed by the police at the time of arrest rather than conviction (Sanchez 2001; see also *Johnson v. City of Cincinnati* (6th Cir. 2002)). Challenges to these ordinances were successful. As a result, off-limits orders are now imposed as a condition of a deferred or imposed sentence or of community supervision (Moser 2001; Hill 2005). In Seattle, these orders are called "Stay Out of Drug Area" (SODA) and "Stay Out of Areas of Prostitution" (SOAP) orders.

In some cities, the "high drug" and "high prostitution" areas from which people are banned comprise significant parts of the city and may include the downtown core in which social and legal services are concentrated. According to the most recent data available in Seattle, for example, roughly half of the city's terrain, including all of downtown, is defined as a "high drug area" from which someone might be banned. Those subject to these off-limits orders are generally prohibited from being in the proscribed areas for any reason.[2] Violations may be considered separate crimes worthy of an additional year of jail.

The enforcement of off-limits orders has been enabled, in part, by the transformation of probation. In 1999, the Manhattan Institute released a report titled "Broken Windows Probation: The Next Step in Fighting Crime." Noting that the probation population has grown rapidly—over four million U.S. residents are now on probation (Bureau of Justice Statistics n.d.)—and that many probationers are readmitted to prison or jail, the report advocated a fundamental reorientation of probation. Probation, the report urged, must be primarily seen as a mechanism for achieving public safety rather than rehabilitation (Center for Civic Innovation at the Manhattan Institute 1999, 5). In order to undermine probationers' expectation that they get two or more "free" violations, the report argues that "this permissive practice must be abandoned. All conditions of a probation sentence must be enforced, and all violations must be responded to in a timely fashion" (7). Furthermore, arguing that effective supervision of millions of probationers cannot be achieved from within the probation office during normal business hours, the report urged that the "neighbor-hood should be the place of supervision," and this supervision should take place "around the clock" (6). Toward these ends, different versions of "Broken Windows Probation" have been implemented in cities across the United States (see Parent and Snyder 1999).

A number of Department of Corrections (DOC) officials and analysts have since argued that DOC patrols are the best way to enhance supervi-sion of probationers and, in some cases, parolees. Some advocates, not-ing that "Probation officers have broad authority to stop and question offenders and immediately revoke their probation if they violate its re-quirements," stress the "advantages of combining forces" with the police (Reichert 2002, 2). In Boston, for example, fifty police officers and fifty probation officers have patrolled together seven nights a week for several years (Reichert 2002). In Seattle, a dedicated team of probation officers now patrols the city, and units consisting of one or more probation offi-cers and a police officer often ride together as part of the city's "Neighbor-hoods Corrections Initiative" (NCI) An important part of the NCI teams' function is the enforcement of SODA orders (Murakami 2004). The NCI teams not only enforce off-limits orders but also various new spatial re-strictions associated with novel uses of trespass law.

Innovations in Trespass Law

In Seattle and elsewhere, trespass laws have been implemented in a variety of novel ways. In particular, trespass law is increasingly used to regulate access to both private and publicly owned places normally open to the public, such as public transportation facilities, libraries, public-housing facilities, and commercial establishments (Goldstein 2003; Mitchell 2005). In order to be arrested for trespass in a public space or on private prop-erty that is normally open to the public, a person must be forewarned, either by posted regulations or in the form of a trespass warning or ad-monishment. Over time, these admonishments have evolved to extend the period of time one is excluded and the range of spaces from which one is excluded.

In a growing number of municipalities, for example, nonresidents of public housing facilities, including the parents of resident children, may be trespass-admonished from those facilities and arrested for criminal trespass if they subsequently return (Mitchell 2005). In *Virginia v. Hicks*

(2002), the U.S. Supreme Court affirmed the right of local governments to enforce laws such as trespass-exclusions, arguing that those practices reflect "legitimate state interests in maintaining comprehensive controls over harmful, constitutionally unprotected conduct."[3]

In Taylor, Texas, a resident recently sued the Taylor Housing Authority in the federal courts over its criminal trespass policy. The policy in question did not specify the behaviors that could trigger exclusion, did not provide an opportunity to appeal an exclusion order, and did not place time constraints on any exclusions issued. This lawsuit was eventually settled and the trespass policy modified (Austin Tenants Council 2001). Yet similar polices remain in place in many other jurisdictions. Indeed, many no-trespass policies enacted by public housing authorities ban nearly all nonresidents, not just those who are unwelcome or uninvited by residents (Goldstein 2003). In New York City, the adoption of a trespass program in NYCPH and other apartment complexes appears to have resulted in a jump in trespass arrests (Adame 2004; Parascandola 2007; Tabachnick 2007).

Trespass admonishments are also used to limit access to other kinds of properties that are normally open to the public. In Seattle, for example, people are routinely trespass-admonished from public parks, libraries, recreation centers, the public transportation system, college campuses, hospitals, religious institutions, social service agencies, and commercial establishments. The bans are typically in effect for one year. Because there is little regulation of the circumstances under which these "admonishments" are issued, critics worry that their use and enforcement may be discriminatory. In a recent case in Hawaii, for example, a trespass exclusion program was challenged by a plaintiff who alleged that he was banned from a public library for one year because he viewed gay-themed websites on the library computer. Other plaintiffs alleged that the Hawaiian statute—Act 50—was used to remove homeless people from public beaches and parks (*The Center v. Lingle* (2004)).

In Seattle, several initiatives have significantly expanded the number of trespass admonishments issued, as well as their spatial consequences. The first initiative involves the reallocation from private individuals to the police of the authority to ban persons from specific premises. Under this initiative, business owners are encouraged to authorize the police department to ban people from places normally open to the public even in the absence of evidence of criminal wrongdoing.[4] In recent years, the Seattle Police Department (SPD) has issued thousands of "trespass admonishments" restricting access to a range of places normally open to the public, including shops, apartment and public housing complexes, college campuses, hospitals, libraries, and the public transportation system.

As a result of a second major initiative undertaken by the city of Seattle, the size of the physical spaces from which many people are banned has also increased. Dubbed "Trespass Programs," these initiatives group participating and geographically proximate businesses together as part of particular Trespass Programs. Where these programs exist, anyone banned from any of the participating businesses is banned from all of the participating establishments. Seattle's Aurora Motel Trespass Program is one example. Under this program, someone banned from one of the participating hotels is effectively banned from all of the hotels that have agreed to participate in the program. Similarly, the West Precinct Parking Lot Trespass Program includes 320 downtown parking lots.[5] Anyone excluded from one of the participating parking lots is simultaneously excluded from all of them and is subject to arrest for walking through one of the 320 participating parking lots.

In many cities, including Seattle, police officers and others issuing "civil" trespass admonishments are not required to record the reason for the exclusion. Our four-month sample of trespass admonishments issued by the SPD includes 2,606 admonishment records. No reason for the admonishment was given in 58 percent of the records. Some "reasons" given include noncriminal behavior, such as loitering, panhandling, and "staying in the bathroom too long." The banished person does not have an opportunity to contest his or her exclusion. Violation of these "civil" exclusion orders is a criminal offense, punishable by up to one year in jail.

Parks Exclusion Laws

The adoption (in Seattle; Portland, Oregon; and other municipalities) of "parks exclusion" laws has also been an important social-control development.[6] Parks exclusion laws authorize police and parks officials to ban persons for committing minor infractions (such as being present after hours, having an unleashed pet, camping, urinating, littering, or possessing an open container of alcohol) from one, some, or all public city parks for up to one year (depending on the number and type of violation). Prior to the adoption of these laws, individuals could be removed from public parks only if there was probable cause that they had committed a criminal

offense; more minor rule violations, such as being in the park after closing time, resulted in a citation. Although the exclusion order is defined as
civil rather than criminal in nature, violation of a parks exclusion order is
a misdemeanor criminal offense (in Seattle, Trespass in the Parks).

Two aspects of the debate over Seattle's parks exclusion ordinance are
particularly noteworthy. The first is the question of due process. As many
critics of the law pointed out, the ordinance authorizes the police to exclude an alleged rule-violator without providing any evidence of wrongdoing. As one critic put it, the law authorizes "the police to act as prosecutor, judge and executioner."[7]

Proponents of the law insist that this denial of due process is not inap-
propriate because "under the ordinance individuals are excluded from a
park, not arrested. Thus, due process is—and should be—less than for a
criminal arrest."[8] The law's supporters thus emphasized the fact that the
legal authority to exclude was based on civil (or, in some versions, administrative) law rather than criminal law, as well as the noncriminal nature
of the (initial) sanction imposed on violators, to justify the denial of due
process.

Yet this emphasis on the noncriminal nature of the exclusion order obscures the fact that the ordinance created a new crime. Those who have
been excluded from the parks are subject to arrest for simply being in a
public park during operating hours. Furthermore, the fact that a person
might have been previously excluded means that for some, simply being
in a public park may be sufficient basis for a police stop. The parks exclusion law has thus enhanced police authority to stop and question "un-
desirables," led to the exclusion of many from significant public spaces for
extended periods of time, and, our data suggest, is the basis of a significant number of arrests each year.

Conclusion

The new tools described above possess a number of novel characteristics.
First, by defining mere presence in urban spaces as a potential crime, they
broaden the range of behaviors that can lead to criminal justice intervention. Indeed, we suggest that by making it a crime for a person with a
particular status (banished) to be some place in the city, these broad spatial exclusions essentially (re)criminalize status. Second, by combining
elements of criminal, civil, and administrative law, the new tools provide

minimal or no avenues for contestation. This denial of rights is legitimated through the discursive construction of certain people as embodiments of disorder who must be geographically relocated (and, sometimes, as clients in need of instruction and help). Notably absent from this discourse is the notion that those targeted are citizens with rights. The denial of rights is further legitimated by the construction of the new tools as "civil" mechanisms for enhancing neighborhood security rather than punishing particular behaviors. This construction obscures the ways in which the new tools diminish the rights of many urban residents, broaden definitions of crime, and contribute to the overcrowding of the courts and jails. Last, the new tools are resolutely territorial: they are primarily aimed at removing perceived disorder from particular geographic locations. While the police have long acted as territorial agents, this spatial goal increasingly trumps rehabilitative and even punitive aspirations as a matter of policy.

Like the civility laws that preceded them, the new social-control tools described here are legitimated by the claims and frames associated with broken windows policing. They offer an additional advantage to city authorities concerned about disorder: they promise to "cleanse" urban areas of disorder in a way that is comparatively difficult to challenge and does not rely (solely) on arrest and incarceration. Although the claim that these tools are an alternative to criminal justice intervention is exaggerated, it is true that the new tools disperse formal social-control mechanisms throughout the urban landscape.

Taken together, these and related new social-control techniques represent a dramatic extension of the state's authority and surveillance capacity throughout the urban landscape. This landscape is increasingly characterized by a social-control apparatus that embodies the characteristics outlined by Cohen: blurred spatial boundaries between inside and outside and legal boundaries between guilty and innocent; broadened and increasingly "fuzzy" definitions of crime; an expanded social-control net; and dispersed and penetrating social-control mechanisms that operate beyond prison walls. Although sometimes justified in terms of "community policing" and "community prosecution," the origins and authority for these new social-control mechanisms lie not in the community, but in the state. The punitive city of twenty-first-century America is one in which an increasing number of acts are regulated and criminalized; the state's ability to search, detain, regulate, and monitor is expanded; and a system of invisible yet highly consequential gates and barriers increasingly regulates the movement of some urbanites in public space.

Once in place, the new regime is likely to have long-lasting effects. Expanded definitions of crime, enhanced police authority, and the expansion of spatial regulation mean that misdemeanor arrests and correctional "violations" are likely to skyrocket. Once arrested, defendants are subject to an increasing array of spatial and behavioral regulations (see also Fischer 2003). Any re-arrests that do occur, of course, drive up local arrest rates, a reality that helps to justify the perpetuation of trespass and off-limits zones. Moreover, enforcement of the new tools often displaces the socially marginal into adjacent neighborhoods, which, in turn, advocate for expanded exclusion zones. This is, then, very likely to be an expansionary social-control regime. It works much as Cohen predicted, but unfolds largely at the direction of state institutions. The contemporary city is indeed punitive, but it is the formal social-control apparatus, now erecting a series of invisible but powerful fences and barriers, that is exerting the most significant and pernicious force.

NOTES

1. Indeed, former New York Mayor Rudolph Giuliani indicated that the removal of poor people in areas slated for redevelopment was "not an unspoken part of our strategy. That [was] our strategy" (quoted in Body-Gendrot 2000).

2. In Seattle, exceptions may be granted if people live, work, or have other "legitimate" reasons to be in the proscribed areas. However, judges' willingness to grant such exceptions apparently varies a good deal, and our interviews with both probationers and prosecutors indicate that these exemptions do not show up in the police database.

3. In this case, the defendant was arrested for trespassing when delivering diapers to his daughter; he did not receive formal notification of his banishment until after his second such arrest (see Mitchell 2005).

4. Other authorities, including metro transit police, public housing authorities, and public library staff, also have the right to exclude alleged rule-breakers.

5. See http://www.cityofseattle.net/law/precinct_liaisons/newsletters/Revised linksSpring05.pdf.

6. The formal title of the Seattle ordinance is the "Parks Enhanced Code Enforcement Ordinance" (SMC 18.12.278). For a partial list of other Washington State cities that have similar laws, see http://www.mrsc.org/Subjects/Parks/adminpg. aspx#Enforcehttp://www.mrsc.org/Subjects/Parks/adminpg.aspx#Enforcehttp:// www.mrsc.org/Subjects/Parks/adminpg.aspx#Enforce.

7. Unlike those who are (criminal) trespass admonished, those who are issued a parks exclusion order for more than seven days have the right to appeal the

order. Yet there are several important barriers to appealing: the accused does not have the right to legal representation; the written appeal must be post-marked within one week of the exclusion order; and the telephone number that is provided on the form for those who have questions about submitting an appeal is, at the time of this writing, the telephone number of a community center, the staff of which knows nothing about submitting an appeal. According to Seattle Parks Security, only ten to twelve people have appealed their exclusion in the decade or so since the legislation was adopted; in only two such cases the appeal was successful. Personal communication, Larry Campbell, Seattle Parks Security Officer, June 6, 2007.

8. Letter from Assistant Chief Harv Ferguson to Councilmember Nick Licata re: "Proposed Amendment to Parks Exclusion Ordinance," September 29, 1998.

CASES CITED

Johnson v. City of Cincinnati, 310 F.3d 484, 2002 WL 31119105 (6th Cir. 2002)
Robinson v. California, 370 U.S. 660 (1962)
Papachristou v. Jacksonville, 405 U.S. 156 (1972)
Powell v. Texas, 392 U.S. 514 (1968)
State of Washington vs. Michael Thomas (WA NO. C06975UW)
The Center v. Lingle, No. 04-537 KSC (D. Haw. 2004)
Virginia v. Hicks, U.S. No. 02-371 (2002)

REFERENCES

Adame, Jaime. 2004. "Operation Safe Housing." *Gotham Gazette*, August 17. http://www.gothamgazette.com/article/crime/20040817/4/1087.
The Austin's Tenants' Council. 2001. "Suit Results in Changes to Criminal Trespass Policy." *Housing Rights Advocate* 20 (Fall): 1–2.
Bass, Sandra. 2001. "Policing Space, Policing Race: Social Control Imperatives and Police Discretionary Decisions." *Social Justice* 28(1): 156–76.
Body-Gendrot, Sophie. 2000. *The Social Control of Cities: A Comparative Perspective*. Oxford, UK: Blackwell.
Bureau of Justice Statistics. n.d. "Adult Correctional Population 1980–2004." http://www.ojp.usdoj.gov/bjs/glance/corr2.htm.
Cohen, Stanley. 1979. "The Punitive City: Notes on the Dispersal of Social Control." *Contemporary Crises* 3: 339–63.
Dreier, Peter, John Mollenkopf, and Todd Swanstrom. 2001. *Place Matters*. Lawrence: University Press of Kansas.
Duneier, Mitchell. 1999. *Sidewalk*. New York: Farrar, Straus, and Giroux.

Ellickson, Robert C. 1996. "Controlling Chronic Misconduct in City Spaces: Of Panhandlers, Skid Rows, and Public-Space Zoning." *Yale Law Journal* 105(5): 1165.

Fagan, Jeffrey, and Garth Davies. 2000. "Street Stops and Broken Windows: Terry, Race and Disorder in New York City." *Fordham Urban Law Journal* 28: 457–504.

Feldman, Leonard C. 2004. *Citizens without Shelter: Homelessness, Democracy, and Political Exclusion*. Ithaca, NY: Cornell University Press.

Fischer, Benedikt. 2003. "Doing Good with a Vengeance: A Critical Assessment of the Practices, Effects and Implications of Drug Treatment Courts in North America." *Criminal Justice* 3(3): 227–48.

Flanagan, Peter M. 2003. "Trespass-Zoning: Ensuring Neighborhoods a Safer Future by Excluding Those with a Criminal Past." *Notre Dame L. Rev.* 79: 327–87.

Foscarinis, Maria. 1996. "Downward Spiral: Homelessness and Its Criminalization." *Yale Law & Policy Review.* 14: 1–63.

Gibson, Timothy A. 2003. *Securing the Spectacular City: The Politics of Revitalization and Homelessness in Downtown Seattle*. New York: Rowman & Littlefield.

Goldstein, Elena. 2003. "Kept Out: Responding to Public Housing No-Trespass Policies," *Harvard Civil Rights–Civil Liberties Journal* 38: 215–45.

Gowan, Teresa. 2002. "The Nexus: Homelessness and Incarceration in Two American Cities." *Ethnography* 3(4): 500–34.

Goldsmith, William, and Edward Blakely. 1992. *Separate Societies: Poverty and Inequality in U.S. Cities*. Philadelphia: Temple University Press.

Hackworth, Jason. 2007. *The Neoliberal City: Governance, Ideology and Development in American Urbanism*. Ithaca, NY: Cornell University Press.

Harvey, David. 2005. *A Brief History of Neoliberalism*. Oxford: Oxford University Press.

Herbert, Steve. 2001. "Policing the Contemporary City: Fixing Broken Windows or Shoring Up Neo-Liberalism?" *Theoretical Criminology* 5: 445–66.

Hill, Gordon. 2005. "The Use of Pre-Existing Exclusionary Zones as Probationary Conditions for Prostitution Offenses: A Call for the Sincere Application of Heightened Scrutiny." *Seattle University Law Review* 28(1): 173–209.

Kelling, George L., and Catherine M. Coles. 1996. *Fixing Broken Windows*. New York: Martin Kessler Books.

Lynch, Mona. 2001. "From the Punitive City to the Gated Community: Security and Segregation across the Social and Penal Landscape." *U. Miami Law Review* 56: 89–112.

Manhattan Institute, Center for Civic Innovation. 1999. "Broken Windows Probation: The Next Step in Fighting Crime." Civic Report No. 7.

Mauer, Marc, and Meda Chesney-Lind, eds. 2003. *Invisible Punishment: The Collateral Consequences of Mass Imprisonment*. New York: New Press.

Mitchell, Don. 2003. *The Right to the City: Social Justice and the Fight for Public Space*. New York: Guilford.

———. 2005. "Property Rights, the First Amendment, and Judicial Anti-Urbanism: The Strange Case of *Hicks v. Virginia.*" *Urban Geography* 26(7): 565–86.

Moser, Sandra L. 2001. "Anti-Prostitution Zones: Justifications for Abolition," *Journal of Criminal Law and Criminology* 91: 1101–37.

Murakami, Kery. 2004. "Program Aims to Get Drug Users off Street." *Seattle Post-Intelligencer*, November 9.

Parascandola, Rocco. 2007. "Trespass Arrests Under Attack." *Newsday*, April 13, 2007.

Parent, Dale, and Brad Snyder. 1999. *"Police-Corrections Partnerships."* Issues and Practices in Criminal Justice series, National Institute of Justice.

Parenti, Christian. 1999. *Lockdown America: Police and Prisons in the Age of Crisis*. New York: Verso.

Patillo, Mary, David Weiman, and Bruce Western, eds. 2004. *Imprisoning America: The Social Effects of Mass Incarceration*. New York: Russell Sage Foundation.

Reichert, Kent. 2002. "Police-Probation Partnerships: Boston's Operation Night Light." http://www.sas.upenn.edu/jerrylee/programs/fjc/paper_maro2.pdf.

Roberts, Dorothy E. 1999. "Race, Vagueness, and the Social Meaning of Order-Maintenance Policing." *J. Crim. L. & Criminology* 89: 775–836.

———. 2004. "The Social and Moral Costs of Mass Incarceration in African American Communities." *Stanford Law Review* 56(5): 127–62.

Sanchez, Lisa. 2001. "Enclosure Acts and Exclusionary Practices: Neighborhood Associations, Community Police, and the Expulsion of the Sexual Outlaw." In *Between Law and Culture: Relocating Legal Studies*, David Theo Goldberg, Michael Musheno, and Lisa C. Bower, eds., 122–40. Minneapolis: University of Minnesota Press.

Simon, Harry. 1992. "Towns without Pity: A Constitutional and Historical Analysis of Official Efforts to Drive Homeless Persons from American Cities." *Tulane Law Review* 66(4): 631–76.

Skogan, Wesley G. 1990. *Disorder and Decline: Crime and the Spiral of Decay in American Neighborhoods*. Berkeley: University of California Press.

Snow, David, and Michael Mulcahy. 2001. "Space, Politics, and the Survival Strategies of the Homeless." *American Behavioral Scientist* 45: 149–69.

Stewart, Gary. 1998. "Black Codes and Broken Windows: The Legacy of Racial Hegemony in Anti-Gang Civil Injunctions." *Yale Law Journal* 107: 2249–79.

Tabachnick, Cara. 2007. "Jump in Trespassing Arrests Draws Anger." *Newsday*, April 10.

Wacquant, Loïc. 2000. "The New 'Peculiar Institution': On the Prison as Surrogate Ghetto." *Theoretical Criminology* 4(3): 377–89.

Wacquant, Loïc, and William J. Wilson. 1989. "The Cost of Racial and Class Exclusion in the Inner City." *Annals of the American Academy of Political and Social Science* 501: 825–35.

Western, Bruce. 2006. *Punishment and Inequality in America*. New York: Russell Sage Foundation.

Wilson, William J. 1987. *The Truly Disadvantaged: The Inner City, the Underclass, and Public Policy*. Chicago: University of Chicago Press.

Wilson, James Q., and George E. Kelling. 1982. "Broken Windows: The Police and Neighborhood Safety." *Atlantic Monthly* (March): 29–38.

Wolch, Jennifer, and Michael Dear. 1993. *Malign Neglect: Homelessness in an American City*. San Francisco: Jossey-Bass.

[*Chapter 8*]

Frightening Citizens and a Pedagogy of Violence

William Lyons

Our son, Brian, took mostly honors classes as a high school senior. His observation about the teacher in one of his regular courses, however, illustrates the depth of the problems we face in education today. "This teacher is crazy," he told us. "It is like asking a question is against the rules. I try to participate in the class and I get punished for it. In my other classes asking questions and arguing points is taken as a sign of paying attention and working, but in this class it seems to be seen as being a troublemaker." When asking questions in class becomes a form of deviance, a critical examination of the relationship between our love of punishment and our approach to education is long past due.

Our son's experience is not unique but is one aspect of what a coauthor and I call "punishing schools" (Lyons and Drew 2006). We mean "punishing" in two interrelated senses: first, we are increasingly willing to punish our public schools by impoverishing them, diverting large chunks of their already-limited funding to less innovative, less parent-friendly, and more poorly performing charter schools and at the same time imposing enormous unfunded mandates that redirect our reformist energies from improving education to enforcing pedagogically dubious forms of teacher accountability in ever more draconian fashion. Second, these same schools, public and charter, are increasingly driven to focus their energies on punishing our children, as Anne Ferguson so powerfully documents in her book, *Bad Boys* (2000), and mobilizing fear and violence as pedagogies for controlling rather than educating our young.

A recent *Law & Society* article, for example, documents our now routine framing of schools as social spaces that manifest our failure to control our children, demanding increasingly punitive approaches to education:

> For nearly three decades, stories of youth violence have claimed front-page news. Early accounts depicted urban youths of color as gangsters and violent predators. . . . Recent stories shifted attention to a string of white student shootings in suburban high schools. . . . Taken together, these stories —about gang warfare, school-yard murders, and bullying—yield images of adolescents as either *uncontrollable* or *unsuccessfully controlled* by school, family, religious, and legal institutions (Morrill et al. 2000, 522, italics in original).

Framing school conflicts as just another battleground in a war on crime, a war on drugs, or a war on terror, is part of the reason so many of us now see public school children as uncontrollable or unsuccessfully controlled and one of the ways that schools—urban and suburban—are punished by our steady disinvestment in public education, the criminalization of youth, the mass-mediated amplification of some citizen fears (and the muting of others), and a zero-tolerance approach to difference and conflict that is eroding the conceptual and material distance between the prison and the school.

Our examination of the relationship between education and our national fascination with wars on difference that are policy failures but political achievements focuses on how this relationship is playing out at one urban and one suburban school in adjacent Midwestern school districts, and highlights the emergence of what we call a zero-tolerance political culture. This culture is driven by the kind of cultural politics described so powerfully in Tom Frank's *What's the Matter with Kansas? (How Conservatives Won the Heart of America)*. It is driven by an elite-led electoral coalition constructed to make a particular package of largely cultural conflicts salient as the metaconflicts that dominate public discourse by saturating communication channels with familiar (if often contradictory and sometimes misleading) images. These images are constructed by sound-bite saboteurs to divide the public in ways expected to favor those whose political fortunes are likely to be advanced by expanding the scope of these particular conflicts.

What Edelman (1977) called "words that succeed and policies that fail" divide the public in ways that remake some constituents as virtuous citizens in law-abiding communities targeted for job creation and political patronage. At the same time, policy failures such as our various wars on crime construct other citizens as disruptive subjects appropriately targeted for punishment with foreseeably disparate racial and class impacts (Tonry 1995). This lethal combination of amplifying the fears of some to patronize them as "the community" and mute the fears of others to punish them as the most salient threat to "the community" can constitute a political success irrespective of its policy outcome—when it mobilizes citizens into electoral coalitions. The political, economic, and cultural messages delivered when public and private leaders target metaphorical broken windows for tending and those actually experiencing broken windows for punishment, suggest that what we call punishing schools is an articulation of a zero-tolerance culture grounded in fear as a form of punishment, patronage, and pedagogy that draws our attention to the ways that current approaches to school conflict exclude inner-city communities targeted for punishment and include suburban communities in ways that disempower both.

Fear as Punishment, Patronage, and Pedagogy

In terms of the cases we examine, the fears of affluent, white, suburban parents are amplified—economic anxieties, fears of change and conflict, and virtual fears of the African American, poor, underclass. Other fears —inner-city parents' fears—are muted and marginalized. Suburban parents are constructed as the community patrons at the foundation of a crime-control state governing through fear. Inner-city parents and their kids are cast in the role of lazy troublemakers to be punished. There is political utility in amplifying and ignoring, mobilizing and redirecting citizen fear—fear as a punishment for the marginalized, a form of patronage for middle-class taxpayers, creating via a pedagogy of violence frightened citizens receptive to a zero-tolerance political culture. One central aspect of this pedagogy is the cultivation of citizen identities that are inattentive to power, frightened and frightening citizens who are more vulnerable to elites seeking to determine our fears.[1] As Glassner (1999) demonstrates, Americans often fear lesser harms made salient by elites interested in displacing more serious harms from the public-policy agenda, such as the decline of living-wage jobs, lack of adequate health insurance, environmental degradation, and the three harms briefly noted below.

Distribution of Income and Wealth

The proportion of total U.S. income going to the top 1 percent of our population has steadily increased over the past twenty years. In 1981, it was 9.3 percent. In 1997, it had risen to 15.8 percent, bringing it back up to pre-1929 levels. When we examine family wealth, rather than income, the data is even more telling. The top 1 percent of American families controlled 19.9 percent of total family wealth in 1976, but that has risen steadily since that time to again reach a level not seen since 1929—such that in 1998, the top 1 percent of American families controlled more than 38 percent of total family wealth. The land of equal opportunity now stands, according to World Bank data, as a nation with more extreme economic inequality than that found in any of our closest allies, a gap that has grown through Republican and Democratic presidencies.[2]

Distribution of Tax Burden

When we compare the relative tax burdens that prevailed in the four decades following World War II, we get a more accurate sense of what nostalgia for the fifties ought to really mean. In 1950, corporations paid 26.5 percent of total taxes collected and payroll taxes were only 6.9 percent of the total. In 2000, corporations paid 10.2 percent (*before* the Bush administrations' enormous tax cuts for the wealthiest individuals and corporations) and payroll taxes made up 31.1 percent of total taxes collected (Phillips 2002, 149). In this context, it is not difficult to imagine a political utility in citizen identities distracting our attention from fears that point to the powerful, with fears for our children that target teachers' unions, stranger predators, and political correctness (Glassner 1999).

Distribution of Risk and Harm

Mary Douglas (1992) argues that societies have an infinite number of dangers to select from and points to a selection process that focuses on what enables the criticism of disliked groups. This process allows us to transform our guilt over our own leadership failures into angry attacks on the underclass in ways that intersect with the enormous money making opportunities increasingly available to those patronized by a growing penal-industrial complex. This selection process determines fears that make us inattentive to trends likely to be more harmful to us and our children. For instance, around 65,000 Americans suffer workplace deaths or debilitating injury each year (Herbert and Landrigan 2000, 541), compared to an average of 21,000 homicides per year from 1976 to 2000, but we have no war on the unsafe workplace, war on irresponsible corporate leadership, war on the automobile (43,220 deaths in 2003, according to the National Highway Safety Administration), or even a war on lethal violence as suggested by Zimring and Hawkins (1997).

The mixture of amplified and muted fears bred by a zero-tolerance pedagogy reflects a culture in which leaders encourage us all to cultivate identities inattentive to these harms, indeed inattentive to political conflicts and governance in general, breeding more dependent citizens who demand more aggressive and less accountable forms of state and corporate agency (Taylor 1982; Tocqueville 1956). Affluent inattentiveness to bomb-making in the basements of the Harris and Klebold homes, or in palacelike schools experienced as prisonlike warehouses, was driven, at least in part, by amplified fears of lazy, African American, and criminal students in inner-city schools and paralyzing fears of economic insecurity. Power-poor inattentiveness was similarly driven by economic imperatives: the balancing of three jobs without benefits (or, like in our more affluent communities, family-and-community-destroying addictions of one sort or another) that makes P.T.A. meetings or parent-teacher conferences a mighty challenge.

The steadily eroding New Deal electoral coalition is being replaced with an emerging zero-tolerance coalition that governs through amplifying some fears and patronizing the communities mobilized by these fears and muting other fears to justify punishing the already most victimized communities more likely to articulate these muted fears. This is a political, economic, and cultural strategy for reinforcing a plutocratic vision of governance limited to combinations of patronage and punishment insulated from the need for policy-related and data-driven justification or the critical public scrutiny and informed deliberations that ought to drive democratic decision making and governance. And the zero-tolerance culture that this is enabling is transforming our schools—inner city and suburban—into warehouses more focused on control than education, animated by an anti-intellectual pedagogy that constructs student identities that are inattentive to power, uninterested in understanding the most harmful conflicts characteristic of our everyday lives because they have not learned the intellectual or relational skills needed to manage conflicts as productive democratic citizens, making them afraid of conflict and more dependent on the state.

The emergence of a zero-tolerance culture in our schools is animated by a politically right, utopian, antidemocratic vision of limited government, driven by a cultural (and sometimes electoral) coalition intent on governing through crime and fear.[3] This zero-tolerance coalition seeks to dissipate public energies by focusing citizens on those lesser fears that draw our attentiveness not to power but to blaming—and more intensively punishing—the power-poor. A zero-tolerance culture cultivates citizen identities as inattentive to failed leadership, amplifying fears that divide and paralyze us—insulating us within a passive and dependent articulation of citizen agency as consuming subjects—reinforcing state agency and a vision of limited government limited to punishment.

We argue that what began as a Republican strategy to mobilize a punitive, law and order, electoral coalition has become a political culture as comfortable with Bill Clinton as George Bush. It is built on an elite-led, extralegal, and often violent intolerance for the disorder inherent in active citizen agency and a democratic public sphere, a political culture that punishes the poor for the challenges they face as energetically as it insulates corporate corruption from critical public scrutiny and justifies less accountable but more aggressive forms of state agency as democratic responses to elite-amplified citizen fears. It is a political culture that enables world record income gaps between the rich and poor, even as our economic strength declines more rapidly in response to an overextended military—where a globalized, indiscriminate, and unilateral war on terror reflects a zero-tolerance approach to managing international conflict and a zero-tolerance vision of democratic society: a political culture reflected and reproduced by the kinds of punishing schools observed in both an inner-city and a suburban neighborhood in adjacent Midwestern school districts.[4]

Patronizing Suburban Fears

At our suburban school site ("Suburban High"), the differences we found were less physically visible and more emotionally stark than initially expected. There were almost no black bodies and even the poorest students were from solidly middle-class families. But difference still cast a long shadow over the school in three ways. First, even without black bodies to target, the fear of association with blackness remained present in the stories we heard from Suburban's students, teachers, parents, and administrators. In the absence of black bodies, we read these stories as evidence of the presence at Suburban of mass-mediated images of being black, poor, dangerous, and frighteningly undeserving of anything other than punishment through the criminal justice system and decaying inner-city schools. Second, in the fear-driven war against this absent-yet-present form of difference—where locals constructed identity and agency around amplifying being white, heterosexual, consumers—other fears were constructed as worthy of informal punishment in school hallways. These were the fears of any student groups whose sense of identity challenged white, heterosexual normativity or whose sense of agency was not limited to their purchasing power. The absence of visible differences led to a greater, and more relentless, pursuit of invisible differences, constituting a culture of zero tolerance.

Taken together, these two factors contribute to a third way the construction of invisible differences cast a shadow within Suburban High. In a culture that cultivated inattention to power as the privileged form of citizen identity, power relations were less openly contested, and the possibility of subjecting various forms of unaccountable power to critical public scrutiny was structurally and behaviorally constrained by fears of invisible, mass-mediated, market-validated threats to community and property. That is, the mixture of amplified and muted fears at Suburban appeared to undermine the possibility of student identities and citizen agency consistent with developing—in everyday practice—the republican virtues of moderation, deliberation, and cooperation. Insulated from the experience of living in openly democratic—and therefore inescapably disorderly—communities, students were denied the opportunity to develop conflict management skills and come to see conflicts as abnormal rather than commonplace.[5] In this context, the elite-led violence constitutive of a zero-tolerance culture was seen as being resolute, because their experiences in punishing schools have erased practical knowledge of less violent or less official approaches to managing conflicts.

At Suburban, we observed a community built on an uncritical conformity to a politically right, utopian vision of democracy, where an amplified fear of democratic disorder supported the patronizing of fortress communities of citizens who self-identify through deference to state agency that punishes those whose fears focus on the disorders of an unregulated market. As such, the punishing schools created in this community, like the market-utopian promises made about charter schools, are less innovative, the communities they reproduce are less resilient, and the forms of citizen identity and agency constitutive of these communities provides a political and cultural foundation for a public opinion made more vulnerable to mass-mediated manipulation by public or private leaders seeking to determine our fears.

In a context where only punitive state agency is recognized as an effective and legitimate response to conflict, not only do citizens get deskilled in ways that make democracy less likely, they also become far more vulnerable to divisive, mass-mediated, and elite-insulating images of conflict as frightening and conflict management as about being resolute and unyielding rather than about achieving agreements. Even if we accept the self-perception of suburban residents as victims, a related consequence becomes clear: when the "victim" is so entirely separated from the "offender" that they do not even experience the conflict-made-salient directly, "we leave him outside, angry, maybe humiliated . . . without any contact with the offender. He has no alternative. He will need all the classical stereotypes around 'the criminal' to get a grasp on the whole thing. He has a need for understanding, but is instead a non-person in a Kafka play. Of course, he will go away more frightened than ever, more in need of an explanation of criminals as non-human" (Christie 2003, 62).

The punishing school in our affluent community targeted nonconformity and difference as threats, patronizing those who were comfortable with identities that renounced agency. For these citizens, the embrace of freedom as dependence becomes a precondition for them to be recognized as "the community" whose amplified fears insulated the powerful from critical public scrutiny, patronizing suburbanites in ways that disempower—even imprison—them in fortress communities exiled from the disorderly experiences that constitute modern life, spur innovation, and provide opportunities to learn the skills for democratic citizenship. Thus, privileged student identities are only linked to their limited agency to the extent that these support the punishment of others, imprisoning other students for their nonconformist agency; they exchanged official recognition for their support of punishment in suburbia and in the inner cities, where students (and their parents) cycle between the two poles of malign neglect constitutive of their communities: prisons as pockets of fiscal abundance within an otherwise systematically impoverished public sphere (see Wacquant 2002).

Punishing Urban Fears

In our inner-city school ("Urban High") interpersonal conflicts were seen as serious, potentially explosive evidence of an inner-city culture where violence was a way of life—incomprehensible to white teachers—undermining the possibility of education. At Suburban High, on the other hand, these same types of interpersonal conflicts were accepted as a normal part of adolescent life, as conflicts that posed no threat to patronized Suburban High identities.[6] At Urban High, group conflicts were constructed as gang problems. Most references to conflicts, including interpersonal conflicts, at Urban High contained some fear of gang violence, despite the fact that the school's police officer noted that there was little to no actual gang activity at or near the school. But this empirical reality did not inhibit the construction of the school as an inner-city pocket of chaos filled with uncontrollable kids. At Suburban High, however, interpersonal conflicts were not associated with gang violence or even group conflict. Conflict in the Suburban High community was framed as a form of individual harassment, and in a school culture that did not challenge this abuse, this amplified homophobic and class-based fears to undercut the fears of those targeted for hateful harassment.

Since the pedagogy of a zero-tolerance culture sends the message that diversity causes conflict, conflict management focuses on containing differences as invisible and keeping young citizens insulated from experiencing difference, making them more susceptible to problematic mobilization of frightening images of conflict by the mass media. Unexamined, white, heterosexual normativity patronizes normalized students to disempower them, denying to them direct experience with critical conflicts and, therefore, insulating them from the opportunity to develop the understandings and skills needed to effectively prevent, resolve, or reduce the harms associated with these conflicts. Instead, the weakness of de-skilled students is manifest in identities without effective agency, leaving them subject to more aggressive and less accountable forms of power in their hallways and classrooms.

In both schools the adults recognized that it was the students who had leadership skills who were able to handle conflict well and in ways that strengthened the school and prepared the students to be active and productive participants in (sometimes disorderly) democratic politics. But in neither school did we observe a serious effort to identify and transfer these skills through a cultural recognition that conflict is normal, varied, and an opportunity to lead. Instead of embedding skill development into the daily routines of our schoolchildren, we encourage their cynicism and wrath with flavor-of-the-month public relations activities such as "Peace Week" or peer mediation programs that few at either school were aware of and that did not seek to engage the natural leaders in the student population. In this context, to seek adult intervention is to escalate the conflict: children see that adults favor punishment as the response and, since they experience even more directly than adults do that this approach has failed to prevent conflict, see that upping the ante in this way most likely makes a situation worse. A process that starts with too little adult attention to education and ends with too much adult attention to enforcement at the other end leaves the kids in charge but without the intellectual or relational skills to understand power—a whole series of teaching moments lost by educators, parents, and legislators failing to lead. In this context, conflict and democracy become spectator sports, dramatic commodities for consumption that teach us there is safety in being passive and dependent citizens of a juvenocracy.

Leaders constructing a zero-tolerance culture encourage adults to fear children, citizens to fear informed agency and democratic governance, and middle-class parents to fear power-poor parents in ways that disempower both. In punishing schools, this has paralyzed effective mentoring relationships, encouraged reactive and punitive leadership even in our affluent schools—despite opposition (and resistance) from teachers —and supported a juvenocracy in place of community, thereby producing young leaders without leadership skills. Those in closest proximity to the conflicts, whom research indicates are likely the most ambivalent about strictly punitive approaches to conflict management, are the least empowered to act. Teachers and parents at schools like Suburban High are choking on self-esteem and respect-building programs designed in response to urban school conflicts (Simon 2007) and nationalized by leaders far from both schools who are more interested in building electoral coalitions than in ensuring that we have an education system that will support active democratic forms of citizen agency. Teachers and parents at schools like Urban High are starved by programs that work better in affluent suburbs, where affluence can provide private resources to supplement antitax and antiunion attacks on the public sector that blame teachers for their fear of students, parents for being too busy, and both for squandering public investments being diverted into less innovative, more costly, and poorer performing charter schools.

The key conflicts for Suburban High were internal, and we analyzed these to highlight the ways that even our most affluent suburbs' schools are becoming more like penal institutions. The students, teachers, and parents at Urban High also shared a common discursive construction of the central conflicts and approaches to conflict management constitutive of their school culture, but the consensus at Urban High focused on tracing the roots of their inner-city school conflicts to the neighborhoods in which their students live. While Suburban High students and teachers experience their palatial building as a prison, the students, teachers, and parents of Urban High experience their school as a target for punishment from state and local leaders reprimanding their school for the challenges their students face.[7]

At Suburban High, the construction of citizen identities depended in large part on their relocation away from the inner city, punishing Urban High with white and capital flight. Their suburban identities, on the other hand, reflecting what Mike Davis (1998) called an ecology of fear, also punish Urban High in a second way. The construction of identity and citizen agency at Suburban High depended on the absence of the inner-city racial and lower-class "other," an absence that supported the further punishing of inner-city schools when a powerful electoral coalition made salient fears of this left-behind "other" to divert funding from schools to prisons, corporate welfare, and infrastructure investments to support suburban fortress communities outside the city.

Political Utility

Our leaders are punishing our inner-city schools for the challenges they face, as if their decaying buildings, decades of disinvestment, disappearing residential neighborhoods, and status as power-poor communities stand as evidence of parental neglect and uncontrollable youth. This approach to teaching and learning in the inner city reflects a perspective on limited government that Katznelson (1976, 220) wrote encourages "a politics of dependency," where governance is limited to amplifying largely punitive efforts to "manage the consequences of our inability to solve urban problems."

Rather than strengthening the families and communities in our most victimized neighborhoods, this combination of more aggressive punishment in communities less able to hold powerful state and corporate agents accountable further fragments and disorganizes urban communities (Santos 1982) and constructs local political networks that are gradually made more responsive to a nationalized and expressive politics of crime and punishment than they are to the parents, teachers, or students attending punishing schools. Our leaders are also punishing more affluent schools by responding to their amplified fears in ways that disempower them as individuals and undermine the social foundations for resilient democratic community life, while at the same time patronizing suburban parents to the extent that responding to their mass-mediated fears (of difference) reinforces state agency.

Conservative and frightened law-abiding suburban parents are managed as political inputs with campaign rhetoric that amplifies their fears, condensing a wide range of concerns into a fear of criminalized youth and channeling broad social and economic anxieties into a fear of the poor, the different, and the disorderly (Giroux 2003; Ferguson 2000; Aronson 2000; Bauman 2000; Scheingold 1984; Beckett 1997; Sennett 1970; Melossi 1993). This fear—and the frightened and dependent middle-class taxpayers mobilized by it—then justifies more prison construction (suburban and rural job creation for these same frightened taxpayers) in place of investment in education, deepening educational inequalities between affluent suburban and inner-city school districts. At the same time, this fear constructs the poor, their communities, their schools, their children and their parents' fears as dangerous and irrational, appropriately managed as political outputs, a population targeted for extreme, often expressively punitive, criminal justice policy, but also, increasingly, through welfare-to-work social service providers and the public school system itself (Ferguson 2000).[8]

In terms of the cases examined here, the fears of some parents are amplified and the articulated fears of other parents are ignored on two dimensions. First, within the inner-city school those fears that articulate with a punitive educational environment, reinforcing state agency, are constructed as "reasonable and pragmatic," while other fears become problems for the administration and are consistently framed as "beyond our control," and the parents who insist that these fears be heard are constructed as irrational and unstable, as living evidence that "the apple doesn't fall far from the tree."[9] The second dimension is while the "irrational" fears of inner-city parents are marginalized and their children punished, suburban parents are constructed as the law-abiding community. As such, currently prevailing approaches to limited government are designed to reduce their fears; these approaches, then, are the foundation of a crime-control state governing through fear.

Punishing schools thrive in this zero-tolerance political culture. When average Americans were concerned about job loss and financial insecurity, President George W. Bush was focusing on fear as patronage, punishment, and pedagogy to make permanent a new tax system that taxes earned income from blue-collar paychecks and does not tax unearned income in the investment portfolios of the wealthiest Americans, punishing those who work with their hands and patronizing the fears of elites "antagonistic to the public sphere" (Scapp 2003, 215). He increased funds for drug testing in schools even as drug use continued its decades-long decline and shifted drug treatment programs to a core constituency of the zero-tolerance coalition: faith-based religious groups that stand to benefit most from this "votes for patronage" arrangement.

Krugman (2003) argues that this new regime is frightening because it does not recognize the legitimacy of our political system; rather than improve on what we have accomplished, these leaders have long sought to impoverish in order to dismantle (and privatize) foundational programs average Americans depend on, such as Social Security, unemployment insurance, Medicare, the U.S. Postal Service, welfare (largely accomplished with President Bill Clinton's Welfare-to-Work), and public schools. But impoverishing the public sphere also undermines respect for the rule of law and democratic legitimation (the Patriot Act, Guantanamo Bay, the 2000 presidential election, disinformation campaigns before and after the invasion of Iraq), international institutions *that we built* to project our influence and protect our interests (the United Nations, NATO, the World Bank, and other international regimes including the Kyoto Accords, the land mines treaty, and the International Criminal Court), and principles like the separation of church and state (Krugman 2003, 6–7; Cole and Dempsey 2002; Schlosser 1998). The war on terror hastens and makes more visible this transformation, but analysis reveals the same process in punishing schools as well.

In the war on terror the context of being under attack dramatically changed the dynamics of domestic politics, the direction of funding priorities, and the priority ranking of competing policy objectives. When our leaders determined that we ought to fear weapons of mass destruction, this justified resource allocations, including our willingness to send our young men and women into harm's way:

Terrorism can induce a country to scare itself into a kind of paralysis. . . . How he [President G. W. Bush] got from the first widely supported goal of suppressing terrorism to the second widely opposed goal of removing Saddam from power is at least in part a story of *fear*—fear instilled by awful terrorist deeds but also *fear marketed and amplified by the administration's response to terror*. On its slippery slope, "rogue states" became fixed targets that could be identified, located, and attacked, but targets that were stripped of their internationally recognized sovereign rights, which otherwise should have protected them from attack. . . . [T]he United States prefers states it can locate and vanquish to the terrorists it cannot even find. . . . *Vulnerability trumps culpability.* Except that states like Iraq and North Korea are intrinsically more suited to deterrence and containment than to preventive war, so when the doctrine of preventive war is applied to them, it rapidly melts down into something that looks very much like a special case of deterrence—in Tod Lindberg's bold phrase, preemption as "the violent reestablishment of the terms of deterrence" (Barber 2003, 26 and 106–9; italics added).[10]

This leadership choice to amplify the one fear of terrorism—displacing fears of al Qaeda, economic insecurity, environmental degradation, corporate malfeasance, official misconduct and punishing schools—not only impoverishes public debate, but, to the degree that vulnerability trumps culpability, we are abandoning the rational analysis of the conflicts we face and supporting an anti-intellectual, zero-tolerance culture. At the same time, this is a form of limited government that mutes the fears of many Americans. As Cole and Dempsey (2002), among others, have argued, this choice has concrete material, political, and discursive costs: weakened individual rights against invasion by public or private leaders (arguably encouraging official extralegal actions like those in Guantanamo Bay, extraconstitutional creation of charter schools, and tort reform or other legislative efforts to insulate private leaders from accountability), and the incremental colonization of impoverished educational bureaucracies by a laissez-faire business model that is hostile to both intellectual inquiry and the kind of democratic citizenship that is the foundation of American prosperity.

Our responses to these amplified and muted fears are constructing some communities as "virtuous citizens" and others as "disruptive subjects," namely, distributing citizenship as a form of political patronage to some in ways that disempower them and denying it to others to justify punishing them (Yngvesson 1993). The understanding the political utility of amplifying and muting particular fears illuminates the political-cultural foundation for what has been variously referred to as governing through crime (Simon 1997), our culture of control (Garland 2001), education as enforcement (Saltman and Gabbard 2003), or a zero-tolerance political culture. Following Machiavelli, thinking of fear as a powerful political tool is not entirely new. Hobbes nearly equated sovereignty with both fear and the redistribution of it through state agency. Stuart Hall's critique of policing focuses on identifying the political utility of citizen fear by naming police- and politician-initiated, mass-media-amplified moral panics as a mechanism for public and private leaders to manufacture consent for increasingly punitive approaches to crime, social welfare, and governance. While focusing on fear is not new, the analysis of fear presented here contributes to advancing our understanding of frightening citizens and a pedagogy of violence in public schools today.

NOTES

1. "When there is complete attention there is no fear. But the actual fact of in-attention breeds fear; fear arises when there is avoidance of the fact, a flight; then the very escape itself is fear" (Krishnamurti 1995, 92).

2. From 1977 to 1994, according to the Congressional Budget Office, the after-tax income of the poorest quintile of Americans decreased 16 percent, the middle quintile decreased 1 percent, and the after-tax income of wealthiest 1 percent of Americans increased 72 percent. (For race and wealth data, see Conley 2000.)

3. Simon 1997; Schlosser 1998; Phillips 2002; Krugman 2003. While the argument developed here is related to the argument developed by David Garland in *The Culture of Control* (2001), Garland highlights the neoliberal aspects of right utopianism, and our work emphasizes the neoconservative elements.

4. By identifying this coalition and culture as right-utopian, we make explicit the empirically inaccurate claims commonly offered by zero-tolerance leaders who generally insist on framing political debates as if only a social welfare perspective or social democratic politics can be vulnerable to utopianism. Kevin Phillips (2002, xxi) contrasts right-utopianism with liberal "utopias of social justice, brotherhood, and peace" arguing that "the repetitious abuses by conservatism in the United States in turn involve worship of markets (the utopianism of the Right), elevation of self-interest rather than community, and belief in Darwinian precepts such as survival of the fittest." And as Phillips (2002, xiv) also notes this

right-utopian perspective on limited government is without empirical foundation: history shows that in prosperous, free-market democracies, "government power and preferment have been used by the rich, not shunned."

5. We argue, following Hanson (1985), Boyte (1992), Barber (1984), and others, that moderation, deliberation, and cooperation are among the virtues central to the forms of citizen agency that make democracy both possible and desirable. These are practical and intellectual skills that citizens *learn* in schools, families, churches, and on playgrounds, which is one of the many reasons that strong democracy depends on individuals with rights, empowered and constrained by their embeddedness within resilient, innovative, and progressive communities (Kymlika 1989; Huesmann and Podolski 2003; Mayer and Leone 2004; Stevahn 2004; Graff 1992).

6. For a criminological parallel, see Tonry (1995) on differential sentencing for two forms of the same illegal drug, lenient penalties for the form popular in white suburban areas and much more severe penalties for the form popular in black inner-city areas.

7. There is a great deal of politics behind the rapid growth of charter schools in Ohio, in which the state supreme court ruled four times in the past ten years that the state's school funding formula was unconstitutional. Other political issues include lottery funds supported by voters to support schools routinely redirected by state legislators, electoral fear-mongering about high taxes for schools targeted at proeducation state supreme court justices (rather than complying with state law and fixing the funding formula), near-continuous local property tax levies to fund school operations, and a series of urban renewal projects that decimated the mixed-race and mixed-class neighborhoods surrounding Urban High. These issues are forgotten when city leaders criticize the building as a school without a neighborhood. Keeping these issues in mind, we see public and private leaders unwilling to invest in the institutions constitutive of a democratic public sphere, preferring instead to mobilize a right-utopian free-market discourse (and an electoral constituency whose amplified fears about real job loss and rising economic insecurity can be rhetorically linked to this) to punish our schools and weaken our ability to produce citizen identities with the practical and intellectual skills necessary to address in democratic ways the challenges we face.

8. Katznelson (1976) argues that the shift from machine politics to bureaucratic politics made city governments better at service delivery. Governments became better at delivering the resource side of the patronage exchange of jobs (and other forms of public economic support) for votes (and other forms of political support). But as governments became better able to craft policy and produce the political outputs expected from government institutions, this shift also made them less able to mobilize citizens to ensure that the political inputs on the other side of the exchange of jobs for votes would be forthcoming. This weakened governments. One way to think about the combinations of amplified and muted

fears we analyze here is as efforts to revitalize official capacities to mobilize political support (by amplifying or patronizing the fears of particular communities and muting others) by better managing selected fears—and the associated publics —by mobilizing them as political inputs and managing other fears by punishing them with-zero tolerance policy outputs.

9. See Greenhouse, Yngvesson, and Engel (1994) for a detailed analysis of the ways that our ongoing struggles over law, community, and social change impact identity and agency. They argue that in our efforts to manage conflicts we construct meanings for law and community, common sense, individualism, and what is realistic, including some and excluding others in the process.

10. Barber (2003, 109) continues, noting that the "Bush administration admitted as much: at the beginning of 2003, an unnamed senior administration official acknowledged that in the new preemptive strategy 'there is also a deterrent element for the bad guys.'"

REFERENCES

Aronson, Elliot. 2000. *Nobody Left to Hate: Teaching Compassion after Columbine.* New York: W. H. Freeman.

Barber, Benjamin. 1984. *Strong Democracy: Participatory Politics for a New Age.* Berkeley: University of California Press.

———. 2003. *Fear's Empire: War, Terrorism, and Democracy.* New York: W. W. Norton.

Bauman, Zygmunt. 2000. "Social Issues of Law and Order." *British Journal of Criminology* 40(2): 205–21.

Beckett, Katherine. 1997. *Making Crime Pay: Law and Order in Contemporary American Politics.* New York: W. W. Norton.

Boyte, Harry. 1992. "The Critic Critiqued." In *From the Ground Up: Essays on Grassroots Democracy and Workplace Democracy,* George Bennello, ed. Boston: South End.

Christie, Nils. 2003. "Conflicts as Property." In *A Restorative Justice Reader,* Gerry Johnstone, ed., 57–68. Devon, UK: Willan.

Cole, David, and James Dempsey. 2002. *Terrorism and the Constitution: Sacrificing Civil Liberties in the Name of National Security.* New York: New Press.

Conley, Dalton. 2000. "The Racial Wealth Gap: Origins and Implications for Philanthropy in the African-American Community." *Nonprofit & Voluntary Sector Quarterly* 29(4): 530–40.

Davis, Mike. 1998. *Ecology of Fear: Los Angeles and the Imagination of Disaster.* New York: Vintage.

Douglas, Mary. 1992. *Risk and Blame: Essays in Cultural Theory.* New York: Routledge.

Edelman, Murray. 1977. *Political Language: Words That Succeed and Policies That Fail.* New York: Academic Press.

Ferguson, Anne. 2000. *Bad Boys: Public Schools in the Making of Black Masculinity.* Ann Arbor: University of Michigan Press.

Frank, Thomas. 2004. *What's the Matter with Kansas? (How Conservatives Won the Heart of America).* New York: Metropolitan Books.

Garland, David. 2001. *The Culture of Control.* Oxford: Oxford University Press.

Giroux, Henry A. 2003. *The Abandoned Generation: Democracy beyond the Culture of Fear.* New York: Palgrave Macmillan.

Glassner, Barry. 1999. *The Culture of Fear: Why Americans Are Afraid of the Wrong Things.* New York: Basic Books.

Graff, Gerald. 1992. *Beyond the Culture Wars: How Teaching Conflicts Can Revitalize American Education.* New York: W. W. Norton.

Greenhouse, Carol J., Barbara Yngvesson, and David M. Engel. 1994. *Law and Community in Three American Towns.* Ithaca, NY: Cornell University Press.

Hall, Stuart, Chas Critcher, Tony Jefferson, John Clarke, and Brian Roberts. 1978. *Policing the Crisis: Mugging, the State, and Law and Order.* London: Macmillan.

Hanson, Russell. 1985. *The Democratic Imagination in America.* Princeton: Princeton University Press.

Herbert, R., and P. J. Landrigan. 2000. "Work-Related Death: A Continuing Epidemic." *American Journal of Public Health* 90(4): 541–45.

Huesmann, L. R., and C. L. Podolski. 2003. "Punishment: A Psychological Perspective." In *The Use of Punishment*, Sean McConville, ed., 55–89. Devon, UK: Willan.

Katznelson, Ira. 1976. "The Crisis of the Capitalist City: Urban Politics and Social Control." In *Theoretical Perspectives on Urban Politics*, Willis Hawley and Michael Lipsky, eds., 214–29. Upper Saddle River, NJ: Prentice Hall.

Krishnamurti, J. 1995. *On Fear.* San Francisco: Harper.

Krugman, Paul. 2003. *The Great Unraveling: Losing Our Way in the New Century.* New York: W. W. Norton.

Kymlika, W. 1989. *Liberalism, Community, and Culture.* New York: Oxford University Press.

Lyons, William, and Julie Drew. 2006. *Punishing Schools: Fear and Citizenship in American Public Education.* Ann Arbor: University of Michigan Press.

Machiavelli, Niccolo. 1988. *The Prince.* New York: Cambridge University Press.

Mayer, Matthew, and Peter Leone. 2004. "A Structural Analysis of School Violence and Disruption: Implications for Creating Safer Schools." *Education and Treatment of Children* 22(3): 24–39.

Melossi, Dario. 1993. "Gazette of Morality and Social Whip: Punishment, Hegemony and the Case of the USA." *Social & Legal Studies* 2(2): 259–79.

Morrill, Calvin, Christine Yalda, Madelaine Adelman, Michael Musheno, and

Cindy Bejarano. 2000. "Telling Tales in School: Youth Culture and Conflict Narratives." *Law & Society Review* 34(3): 521–65.

National Coalition for the Homeless and The National Law Center on Homelessness & Poverty. 2006. "A Dream Denied: The Criminalization of Homelessness in U.S. Cities." http://www.nationalhomeless.org/publications/crimreport/index.html.

Phillips, Kevin. 2002. *Wealth and Democracy: A Political History of the American Rich*. New York: Broadway.

Saltman, Kenneth, and David Gabbard. 2003. *Education as Enforcement: The Militarization and Corporatization of Schools*. New York: Routledge.

Santos, Boaventura de Sousa. 1982. "Law and Community: The Changing Nature of State Power in Late Capitalism." In *The Politics of Informal Justice*, Richard Abel, ed., 249–66. New York: Academic.

Scapp, Ron. 2003. "Taking Command: The Pathology of Identity and Agency in a Predatory Culture." In *Education as Enforcement: The Militarization and Corporatization of Schools*, Kenneth Saltman and David Gabbard, eds., 213–22. New York: Routledge Falmer.

Schattschneider, E. E. 1975. *The Semisovereign People: A Realist's View of Democracy in America*. New York: Harcourt Brace.

Scheingold, Stuart A. 1984. *Politics of Law and Order*. New York: Longman.

Schlosser, Eric. 1998. "The Prison-Industrial Complex." *Atlantic Monthly* 282 (December): 51–57.

Sennett, Richard. 1970. *The Uses of Disorder: Personal Identity and City Life*. New York: Knopf.

Simon, Jonathan. 1997. "Governing through Crime." In *The Crime Conundrum: Essays on Criminal Justice*, Lawrence Friedman and George Fisher, eds., 171–89. Boulder, CO: Westview.

———. 2007. *Governing through Crime: How the War on Crime Transformed American Democracy and Created a Culture of Fear*. New York: Oxford University Press.

Stevahn, Laurie. 2004. "Integrating Conflict Resolution Training into the Curriculum." *Theory Into Practice* 43(1): 50–59.

Taylor, Michael. 1982. *Community, Anarchy, and Liberty*. New York: Cambridge University Press.

Tocqueville, Alexis de. 1956. *Democracy in America*. Edited and abridged by Richard Heffner. New York: Mentor Books.

Tonry, Michael. 1995. *Malign Neglect: Race, Crime, and Punishment in America*. New York: Oxford University Press.

Wacquant, Loïc. 2002. "Deadly Symbiosis: Rethinking Race and Imprisonment in Twenty-First Century America." *Boston Review*. http://bostonreview.net/BR27.2/wacquant.html.

Yngvesson, Barbara. 1993. *Virtuous Citizens, Disruptive Subjects: Order and Complaint in a New England Court.* New York: Routledge.

Zimring, Franklin, and Gordon Hawkins. 1997. *Crime Is Not the Problem: Lethal Violence in America.* New York: Oxford University Press.

Part III

A New Reconstruction

[*Chapter 9*]

Smart on Crime

Kamala D. Harris

In this essay, I will discuss the intersection between law enforcement and social justice, and what I think is a truly radical notion—the promise of real public safety in all our communities. To that end, I believe that those individuals in law enforcement must take responsibility for crime prevention and reentry and, as a corollary, that progressive advocates and attorneys must embrace public safety as an essential component of their work for justice.

I grew up in the exciting environment of Berkeley, California, in the 1970s. The push for social justice and civil rights was sweeping the country, and in Berkeley people thought of themselves as part of what was called "The Movement." The energy was everywhere when I was growing up. On the schoolyard, I could hear ten languages spoken on any given morning. In the classroom, between math and reading, we learned about César Chávez, about Medgar Evers and the struggle for voting rights, about the abuse of Chinese immigrants who built the railroads, and about all of the people who were being left out of the American dream, people who deserved to be at the table. Everyone was speaking out loudly, trying to make his or her voice heard and fighting for justice.

Coming from that place and that time, it was a shock to my family and friends that I considered choosing a career as a prosecutor. But it made perfect sense to me. Prosecutors have the power to defend people who are too easily forgotten—people of color, immigrants, seniors, the poor, the disenfranchised, and the victimized. These are the same groups of people and communities that progressives are concerned about in terms of fairness and social justice. These communities are also the most likely to be victimized and suffer from crime. Today, African Americans comprise less than 7 percent of California's population but account for more than

30 percent of its homicide victims. Latinos are 36 percent of California's population, but comprise nearly 46 percent of homicide victims. Up to 60 percent of all homicide victims in California are under the age of thirty.

If progressives truly care about the voiceless and the disenfranchised, they cannot afford not to be present at the table where decisions are made that impact vulnerable communities. Defense attorneys and public defenders cannot afford to linger outside the door, content with their roles, fighting to get the good offer, fighting to say the charges should be dismissed, fighting to say the charges never should have been filed.

Similarly, for law enforcement to fulfill the promise of protecting everyone equally, those in law enforcement have to talk critically about the need for systemic changes and start looking at old problems in new ways. They have to begin by challenging certain deeply held assumptions. For example, as an institution, those in law enforcement sometimes hold faulty assumptions about identifying the victims and perpetrators of crime.

As a prosecutor in Alameda County, I used to specialize in child sexual assault cases, and I saw that the girls who had been victimized later reacted by acting out and becoming very vulnerable, most often to pimps and other sexual predators. A number of my victims ended up on the streets of San Francisco being prostituted. This troubled me, not only because I knew about the experiences that had led them to this point but also because of the way they were categorized: as teenage prostitutes, as perpetrators of crime. I believed that these categories needed to be redefined and these young girls needed to be protected, identifying them not as criminals but as victims of exploitation and molestation.

I worked with others to found the Coalition to End the Exploitation of Kids, and through the coalition's work, now, for the first time, San Francisco has a "safe home" where these sexually exploited youth who otherwise would have been held in juvenile hall can go for shelter and support. Properly understood as victims, these young girls can now receive treatment and social services.

But I had to do more than just change local practices. The problem was institutional and widespread, so the solution also had to be institutional and widespread. In my first year as San Francisco's district attorney, my colleagues and I were able to enact statewide legislation that increased the sentence for sexual predators who in the past would have categorized as johns or pimps. Under this new law, San Francisco is now prosecuting people who molest children in exchange for money as child sexual abusers with an additional penalty.

This is the promise and duty of law enforcement: to exercise its immense power in the service of people who cannot defend themselves. A great example of that at the national level happened with the creation of the Civil Rights Division of the U.S. Justice Department. The Civil Rights Division directed the powers of investigation and prosecution toward the end of enforcing desegregation, voting rights, and other civil rights laws. In a local example of how to direct law enforcement efforts in a creative way, many cities have worked to create community policing programs in which officers walk a beat and work as problem solvers and partners with community residents to implement crime prevention efforts.

Unfortunately, these days, the role of the district attorney as a leader in justice, violence prevention, and the public good has become narrow. Today, the public's expectation of the district attorney is limited mostly to incarcerating people for as long as possible, no matter the crime, no matter how much it costs to incarcerate them, and despite the documented fact that our current prison system rarely prevents offenders from committing new crimes when they come back out. California has the highest recidivism rate in the country. Nearly 70 percent of parolees from California's state prisons re-offend within three years of being released.

That's just not a smart way to approach public safety. To get serious about ending crime and keeping our communities truly safe, prevention as well as punishment must be considered. For many crimes, there needs to be a much smarter way of thinking about the business of law enforcement.

By focusing exclusively on punishment, our criminal justice system actually ignores the fact that the vast majority of crimes, including serious crimes, often do not result in an arrest. In 2002, in California, only *18 percent* of crimes committed resulted in an arrest. If our criminal justice policy dialogue focuses exclusively on punishment, we are devoting all of our resources to the 18 percent of criminals we arrest and 18 percent of crimes committed, missing the other 82 percent.

Crime prevention and crime reduction strategies are the only practical approaches to addressing the vast majority of crime—crimes that never result in an arrest. We need to craft a new plan for preventing and reducing crime, and we need to insist on new measures of success. This plan should include strategies that invest serious resources in preventing crime at the front end.

The power of the prosecutor should be proactively engaged to protect the vulnerable. If a law enforcement system is to meet our rightful expectations, the public should expect prosecutors to think of the impact of their work not only on individual victims and their families but also on the community as a whole. For example, prosecutors need to talk about prosecuting people who are dumping environmental toxins into poor communities that are suffering silently. Prosecutorial power can be used to promote environmental justice in a proactive way that would have a positive impact on the community. Similarly, prosecutors need to focus their attention and resources on white-collar crime, consumer protection, and crimes like predatory lending.

Many creative prosecutors are also thinking about the long-term effects of how they exercise their authority. Prosecutors and others in law enforcement can, for example, look to long-term approaches crafted by experts in the health field. Deborah Prothrow-Stith, an associate dean at Harvard's Department of Health Policy and Management in the Harvard School of Public Health, has done some groundbreaking research that shows violence should be treated as a public health problem and demonstrates how public health models can be applied to reduce violence among youth (see, e.g., Prothrow-Stith 2004; Prothrow-Stith and Spivak 2005).

We can use a public-health model when we talk about crime and treat crime as a health epidemic. As part of that model, we can look at prevention, at early intervention, at engaging in triage, and in focusing on treatment. I suggest that this model argues for us to invest heavily in preventing crime, because treating the symptoms alone is much more expensive, and it never gets to the underlying cause of the problem.

Prosecutors have important roles to play in crime prevention as community leaders and in their daily work. One place to start with crime prevention is with early intervention with children who are known to be at risk of becoming victims or perpetrators of violence. For example, children of incarcerated parents, especially boys, are six times as likely to go to jail themselves if not properly treated. In San Francisco, my colleagues and I are working with the children of violent offenders and surrounding those children with support through my Victim Services Division. We make sure that our advocates are connecting them with therapy and other support services in the hope of preventing the epidemics of violence and drugs from spreading to the next generation.

For effective early intervention, law enforcement and the progressive community need to address the reality of post-traumatic stress disorder that many children experience because of the violence they witness or experience in their homes and communities. There are seven-year-olds who are unable to sleep at night because of the recurring sound of gunfire outside their bedroom window, yet these same children are expected to go to school the next day and learn. To illustrate this point, a recent series in the *San Francisco Chronicle* reprinted letters from children at an elementary school in a violence-plagued neighborhood in San Francisco. The children wrote letters asking for help but didn't know where to send them. One young boy wrote:

> Hello, my name is Robert. I am 9 years old, and I am in 2nd grade at Malcolm X Academy in Bayview Hunter's Point. The bad people are shooting right by our school. And they are shooting right by my house. And shooting people that they don't know and people that's good and poor people, too.

If these children get no treatment, sometimes they will act out and wind up arrested for low-level crimes. Once trapped in the system, they might become hardened criminals. As a society, we have to intervene early with children in these situations to help prevent future violence.

These are examples of why law enforcement and the progressive community need new ways of thinking. As we design new approaches, we should also create standards to measure our success. The measures should include such questions as: Are we preventing crime? Are we stopping crime? Have we correctly identified who the victims are? Have we ensured that victims receive restitution and that restorative justice principles are implemented? Are our families and communities being strengthened? Have we estimated and established the costs of the current approach and could resources be better invested? Do people feel safer? Are we lowering the risk of the environment in which children live? Are former offenders being reintegrated into their society and reconnected with their families? Have we reduced recidivism, especially among juveniles? These are the kinds of questions, again, that we should be asking as we look forward to working on these issues and achieving long-term success.

Creating a new model demands movement from both sides. Just as law enforcement should own responsibility for crime prevention, progressives must understand the importance of public safety. The reality is that the work to create a new model of law enforcement will meet with stiff opposition. People running for public office are always going to be confronted by the question, "Are you soft on crime, or are you tough on crime?" That debate misses the point of what I believe is the more important question, "Are you *smart* on crime?"

To implement a new vision of public protection, we will need strong new coalitions. We need academics and self-identified progressives to partner with people in law enforcement to identify common ground. So we should not throw up our hands; we should roll up our sleeves and engage together as problem solvers. Progressives can work as partners with police, prosecutors, and departments of correction. The progressive community needs to participate not only in ensuring individual due process for individuals who are in the criminal justice system but also in ensuring public safety, which is, after all, very much a civil rights issue for disenfranchised communities.

Challenging our assumptions, trying new ways of thinking and news ways of doing business can be frightening or unappealing, but it is long overdue. Haven't we been mired in old ways long enough? I think the urgency of addressing our public safety needs mandates that we do things differently. I am certain that if we can move beyond rhetoric and outdated assumptions, law enforcement and the progressive community can work together creatively to forge a new path toward smarter policies. That is the path that will lead us to a safer future.

REFERENCES

Prothrow-Stith, Deborah. 2004. "Strengthening the Collaboration between Public Health and Criminal Justice to Prevent Violence." *Journal of Law, Medicine and Ethics* 32 (Spring): 82–88.

Prothrow-Stith, Deborah, and Howard Spivak. 2005. *Sugar and Spice and No Longer Nice: Preventing Violence among Girls*. San Francisco: Jossey Bass.

Chapter 10

Rebelling against the War on Low-Income, of Color, and Immigrant Communities

Gerald P. López

For nearly three decades, I have been among those promoting an idea of progressive law practice that complements, meshes with, and, at its best, serves as one shining example of my rebellious philosophy. The Center for Community Problem Solving at New York University, which I launched in September 2003 and which I direct (see http://www.communityproblemsolving.org), puts into action a brand of effective and accountable problem solving that aims to earn each day and over time the label "rebellious." We at the Center work with many diverse people and institutions addressing a diverse slate of social, economic, and legal challenges. But perhaps no aspect of our work portfolio more vividly demonstrates how my earliest childhood experiences shape our current vision of practice than our Center's campaign to keep people out of the criminal justice system—everyone from youth we hope never get entangled to those with criminal records we hope never again see the inside of a prison or a jail.

Our campaign can be understood as our Center's opposition to and my career-long battle against the modern "war on crime." Through a set of almost unimaginably irrational, mean-spirited, and ultimately dysfunctional policies and practices, this nation's war on crime closely monitors vulgarly "profiled" individuals and groups, hassles them whenever possible, arrests them often without legal justification and for concocted reasons, prosecutes them perhaps as often to immunize front-line law enforcement officials as to enforce any law, sentences them for far too long, and locks them up in often utterly inhumane settings.

For decades now, we have done our best to hide from the price we pay for our policies and practices. We have long avoided spelling out and debating the extraordinary financial costs of long-term institutionalization. And we have long evaded making explicit and preparing for the complex consequences of imprisonment: "If we really believe these men and women were hard going in, what the hell do we think they're going to be like coming out of prisons and jails?" We only rarely prepare inmates, families, and communities—either while people are locked up or when they are released—for the challenges of reentering the "outside world." Then we hold those with criminal records to standards everyone else need not meet (or at least can fail to meet without facing dramatic consequences). The message rings out: "You'd better somehow make it, even without support, because we'll be watching your every move, and if you slip, you're going right back to where we think you belong." Now that's nasty, no matter where you call home.

Familiar Patterns in the War on Crime

As much as I regard myself and our Center as opposed to this war on crime, I feel bewildered and bothered when I hear this war described as new. It's not that I don't grasp the magnitude of the current crisis. It's not that I don't understand what's both intriguing and maddening about ways in which we inflict and acquiesce in this ugliness. What makes me uneasy and dismayed is that this war on crime is not new. At least it's not new if you're talking about places like East Los Angeles. Let's set the record straight: This nation has been waging a war on low-income, of color, and immigrant communities as far back as I can remember and farther back still. Make no mistake about how much what we're seeing now perpetuates and extends policies and practices long part of life in the United States.

When I was a kid growing up in East L.A. in the 1950s and 1960s, we never knew a world in which law enforcement was not in our face. I'm not talking sometimes in our face. I'm talking each and every day. Maybe you have to live in places like East L.A. and Watts and Compton and Pacoima to know just how much—for absolutely no justifiable legal reason —the L.A. Sheriffs, the Los Angeles Police Department, and the California Highway Patrol routinely rousted us, nastily provoked us, and calculatingly aimed in every way imaginable to get us into the criminal justice system. They thought law enforcement meant relentlessly monitoring and

messing with everyone who lived in L.A.'s already economically and culturally marginalized communities. The actions of law enforcement officials—and the policies and practices of which they were a part—affected
every family I knew. And my own family suffered life-long consequences.

I lived in a large household of parents, children, grandparents, cousins,
aunts, and uncles. Most of those who lived with us came up from Mexico.
Over the years, everyone living with us felt the ugly provocation and real
danger of having to deal with L.A.'s law enforcement officers. Not least
among these family members who got ensnared in the criminal justice
system was my brother—ten years older, a parental figure, a heroin addict
by his mid-teens, an angry pachuco. By eighteen he found himself locked
up, beginning a cycle through various penitentiaries, including Folsom,
San Quentin, and Soledad. During his years in these institutions he got
very little help trying to understand why he could barely read and write,
why he was strung out on heroin, or why he could find a trustworthy second home only through gangs on the street and gangs in the joint.

Back home in East L.A., we tried desperately to figure out how to cope.
Baffled by what had happened to my brother, we had no idea how to
think about—and literally no vocabulary for talking about—his dyslexia,
his addiction, and his gang involvement. The little support we did receive
came principally from the tiny cluster of friends and family with whom
we talked about our not-so-secret secret and from the folks we would
meet while my mom and I waited to board the buses that would take us
on those long trips for those short visits authorities permitted us to have
with my brother. Waiting in those somber lines, we would see people from
other parts of L.A.—people from neighborhoods like Compton, Watts,
Chinatown, Pacoima, Gardena, San Pedro, and Wilmington, in which the
war on crime had been long waged, and people for whom these bus rides
meant getting to see their imprisoned fathers, grandfathers, uncles, aunts,
and children. In our often silent and wary ways, we regarded one another
as both strangers and relatives.

What smacked me hard during those early years was the criminal justice system's absolute disregard for what we knew. No one in the system
ever asked either my brother or other people in the joint or my mother
and father or other family members back home what we were facing;
what problems we would frame; what help, if any, we received in addressing our problems; and what we thought of our capacity with and
through others to do anything to change either my brother's situation or
our own. Not one single person ever asked. Even as a wild, sports-crazy,

and not-much-reflective kid, I still said to myself, "How in God's name can they be running a system where the last thing they ever think of do-ing is asking the people most directly affected, 'What do you think and how can we make it better?'" They didn't have to believe we had all the answers. We certainly didn't think we did. But couldn't someone imagine we had something important to share if anyone indeed cared about effec-tively solving a range of problems obviously implicated?

I realize that there were people all over Los Angeles and all across the country who never were consulted about what they knew and what they thought. In the reigning vision of democracy, we govern ourselves through experts who ask questions typically to confirm what they al-ready have decided to do and to hang on to their power. But let's not conflate the reasons many others are not consulted with the reasons no one made inquiries of my brother and my family. When officials didn't ask us folks from East L.A., it was principally because they could not imagine that we had anything worth saying. For generations we had been perceived and described as genetically and culturally inferior. We were dumb and lazy Mexicans, messed-up and needy "wetbacks," cross-and inter-bred mongrels. We could fill certain lower-echelon economic and social roles. But in the stock account that had taken cultural and cognitive hold over the southwestern United States and probably the en-tire United States, we Mexicanos and Chicanos couldn't possibly have within us anything valuable to offer about how best to solve problems or to govern our shared world.

A Rebellious Response

Even at an early age, I knew enough to say, "Hell no!" I tried with all my might to think through why I felt so repulsed by what seemed to be the reigning approach about how to live and work. Why exactly did I find so unacceptably appalling how we seemed principally to shape our demo-cratic institutions and the problem-solving practices at the heart of our everyday routines and our future trajectories? And, at the same time, I tried to piece together my own contrasting "philosophy." Could I develop a way of thinking and acting that could guide me across contexts to tell-ing cultural and cognitive details that could embrace the lessons of expe-rience and the insights of imagination and that could both appreciate and challenge life as we know it in pursuit of a future we might currently be able only to prefigure?

Back then I didn't know how to pull apart the reigning scheme, to identify all the relevant elements, to see how together they could come to feel seamless, natural, and even inescapable. I didn't even know the word "philosophy" in English, in Spanish, or in the street versions of both through which I so often expressed myself. But youthful energy propelled me forward. And, with the help of many people, I learned over time to contrast the reigning approach with my own rebellious vision of how, through our institutions and through our practices, we can and should shape our lives and choose our vocations in ways both personally rewarding and collectively valuable.

In the reigning approach to organizational and human behavior, experts rule. These experts collaborate principally and often exclusively with one another (and with support staff paid to enhance their expertise). In framing problems and choices, identifying and implementing worthy strategies, and deciding how much and whose feedback qualifies as necessary for effective monitoring and evaluation, these experts issue top-down mandates with which subordinates typically comply (through a wide range of intermediaries) in order to be rewarded for doing their job. This approach and those who operate within its sway show too little interest in regularly adapting aims and means to what unfolding events and relationships reveal; too little curiosity about the institutional dynamics through which routines and habits form; too little time discovering how well strategies work for everyone affected by its reign; and too little belief in our individual and collective capacity to shape a future that does not acquiesce in the limits of today's world.

The rebellious vision challenges the reigning approach along virtually every dimension. The rebellious vision depends on networks of coeminent institutions and individuals.[1] These coeminent collaborators routinely engage and learn from one another and all other pragmatic practitioners (bottom-up, top-down, and in every which direction at once). They demonstrate a profound commitment, time and again, to revising provisional goals and methods for achieving them; to searching for how better to realize institutional and individual aspirations; to monitoring and evaluating from diverse perspectives what's working and what's not; and to picturing future possibilities that extend beyond (even as they take cues from) past events and current arrangements.

The great gap between the problem solving championed by the rebellious vision and that nurtured by the reigning approach can be described as revolving around knowledge: Which institutions and which groups of people do we regard as "expert" sources of valuable knowledge? Which institutions and which groups of people do we believe need to be "in the loop" about information? To what degree and to what ends do our institutional and individual practices actively seek out new and evolving information about what we face and what we do? To what degree and to what ends do our practices—institutional and individual—put to use what we learn? Contrasting answers offered by the rebellious vision and the reigning approach can be discerned in the practices of diverse specialists (including the lawyers and others who serve low-income, of color, and immigrant communities).[2] And they can be detected in the workings of democratic politics, market economies, and civil societies, and in the ideologies and routines of those who directly shape and comment on these spheres.

The divergence between problem-solving methods parallels the contrast between the rebellious vision's and the reigning approach's vying ideas of how we should live. Must we accept what we're now living as our only option? Or can we regard what we're now experiencing as endlessly unfinished, not just in its details but also in the very frameworks that seemingly define our choices? Must we settle for wildly less than we dream in building our relationships, our institutional capacity, and our democratic communities? Must we deride our own ideas of a better life with labels like "naïve" and "adolescent"? Once again, contrasting answers offered by the rebellious vision and the reigning approach can be perceived across institutional and personal realms in minute particulars about a life well led and in large statements about our collective mission.

The Center for Community Problem Solving

When I launched the Center for Community Problem Solving in September 2003, my colleagues and I decided that our mission would draw on and reach beyond the work I'd been doing with others throughout my career. The Center would team up with low-income, of color, and immigrant communities to solve current legal, social, economic, health, and political problems and to improve our capacity to solve such problems. Along the way, we would strive toward our dream of an accountable and equitable democracy—one in which equal citizenship is a concrete everyday reality, not just a vague constitutional promise.

To meet these bold aspirations, the Center puts into action our comprehensive and innovative "rebellious vision of problem solving." Through this vision, we meld street savvy, technical sophistication, and collective ingenuity into a compelling practical force. The power of our rebellious vision lies in extraordinary teamwork—teamwork in fact and not in name only. The Center never works alone. We regularly work with problem solvers of all sorts—including residents, merchants, organizers, researchers, funders, service providers, artists, teachers, corporate executives, journalists, public officials, doctors, lawyers, bankers, coaches, religious leaders, and policymakers. Only by routinely partnering with absolutely anyone who might in any imaginable way contribute can we get to where together we hope to go in the future.

Our vision of community problem solving unites certain key fundamentals:

1. We collaborate with those who live and work in low-income, of color, and immigrant communities. We seek out and share knowledge about existing problems, available resources, and useful strategies.
2. Drawing on this knowledge, we connect those who face problems with those in public, private, and civic realms who help address these problems. We build networks of valuable know-how among diverse problem solvers and help shape and meet common goals.
3. Where problems remain unaddressed even after making such connections, we help fill those voids by scavenging around for resources (in New York City, across the United States, across the globe). We leverage what's available with what may never have been tried, taking on apparently insoluble problems through everything from one-time trouble-shooting squads to more permanent, full-fledged partnerships.
4. All the while, we vigilantly monitor how strategies get implemented and candidly evaluate what works and what doesn't. Together with others, we develop and enforce standards by which to measure effectiveness, raising those standards as we increase our collective problem-solving power.
5. By sharing widely and regularly all that can be learned through formal research and informal exchange, the Center aims to improve our problem-solving capacity. We work to convince all involved

(individuals, offices, organizations, institutions, coalitions, and net-works) that we can and must always get better at working together to meeting life's evolving challenges head-on.

For the past three decades, I have insisted that we need sophisticated and manageable methods for assessing both the problems faced by and resources available to low-income, of color, and immigrant communities. The legal and nonlegal offices, organizations, coalitions, and networks that serve these communities must learn—at least if we are to do our job as well as we should—to document and analyze what problems clients face and, simultaneously, what help they together might find to address these problems. Such research is anything but "academic" or "one-shot" or a "luxury." In our view, studies of this sort must become part of "business as usual" and united with street delivery of services.

Gathering, Sorting through, and Sharing Information

Since 1999, in partnership with the Center for Urban Epidemiologic Studies (C.U.E.S.), I have led a multidisciplinary team in conducting the Neighborhood Legal Needs & Resources Project (N.L.N. & R.P.)—a sweeping study in Spanish, Mandarin, Cantonese, and English of prob-lems and resources in Harlem, East Harlem, Chinatown, the Lower East Side, Bushwick, and Bedford-Stuyvesant. Relying principally on a so-phisticated telephone survey of 2,000 residents and intensive in-person interviews of more than 1,000 service providers, we have the following aims:

Phase One—Information Gathering: Collect comprehensive informa-tion about problems residents face, where they go for help, and how they regard the help they get.

Phase Two—Data Analysis: Analyze the rich data residents and service providers have collaborated with us to generate.

Phase Three—Information Sharing: Team up with those who live and work in these neighborhoods and with a wide assortment of others to share, put to use, and mobilize around what we have learned.

Phase Four—Distribution of Tool Kit and Guide: Make available what we learn and how we learned it to those in New York City, across the country, and in international circles interested in studies such as

the N.L.N. & R.P. and its critical role in developing effective problem-solving systems.

In June 2003, we completed our telephone survey of 2,000 residents.
Already we have learned extraordinary amounts from these interviews.
We are now in the midst of running qualitative and quantitative analyses of the data collected through our surveys with residents and service
providers. At the same time, we continue our march to complete the outreach side of phase one, combining intense background research and a
daily slate of outreach interviews to close in on our goals.

Meanwhile, we keep drawing on everyone—from residents to hip-hop
artists to ad executives—about how best to share and organize around
what we have learned. Ultimately, through a variety of formats and languages, we will share the information gathered to inform and galvanize
the many constituencies implicated in the quality of problem solving in
New York City's low-income, of color, and immigrant communities. And
we shall make widely available the N.L.N. & R.P.'s plan and instruments
and further explore its potential for improving everyday and long-term
problem solving.

Our partners at C.U.E.S. are the first to say they could continue
to crunch the data we've gathered for years to come. But already we've
learned a great deal. And what we've learned from the communities that
have so generously shared with us their experiences and knowledge has
begun to shape our work agenda. Below is only a sample of our efforts to
keep people out of the criminal justice system.

Community-Informed and -Evaluated Strategies

The Reentry Project aims to help people with criminal records deal with a
range of problems, to shape reentry policies and practices, and to improve
available services. We develop community education programs, cultivate
consortiums of service providers, and implement empirical studies of
what works and what doesn't in reentry.

The Reentry Orientation Program connects people coming out of prisons and jails with available resources. Our workshops and guides cover
everything from applying for identification and benefits to getting shelter
and food to finding affordable housing to accessing education and jobs to
managing family and childcare issues to meeting health needs.

The Keeping Our Kids Out of the Criminal Justice System Campaign aspires to prevent our young people from getting entangled in the criminal justice system. Teaming up with teachers, families, and everyone willing to pitch in, we help youth make wise choices, reform our educational and juvenile systems, and raise awareness about incarceration and its alternatives.

The Campaign to Hire People with Criminal Records makes the case for why we all benefit from recruiting, hiring, and promoting people with criminal records. Collaborating with everyone from employers to public officials to the general public, we work to increase dramatically our clients' employment opportunities and social mobility.

The Consumer Surveys of Problem-Solving Resources insist that we must have the equivalent of a "Zagat Survey" of resources available to low-income, of color, and immigrant communities. We have developed and will soon implement consumer surveys—beginning with people with criminal records—to allow diverse client populations to share their opinions of those to whom they turn for help.

The Streetwise About Money Campaign helps our client communities manage their money as wisely as possible. We share knowledge and build skills about how to sort through bank accounts, credit cards, payday lending, check-cashing, credit counselors, and pawnshops, principally through financial education drives, workshops, manuals, and reform efforts.

The Fair & Just Workplace Campaign, in coordination with the New York State Attorney General's Office, reaches out to low-wage workers, employers, and the public. Through workshops, written materials, public opinion drives, and lawsuits, we work to enforce minimum wage, overtime, and healthy workplace laws.

The Public Health Project teams up with low-income, of color, and immigrant communities to better understand health problems, access care, and shape both service and research. We conduct community-based participant-informed research, disseminate findings in accessible formats, and design interventions and mobilize communities based on what we learn.

Radical Hope

My mom died January 24, 2004. For about the last ten years of her life, she suffered dementia's awful wounds. At the beginning, she simply couldn't remember some of what she had lived. In some ways, that might have been a blessing. In any event, at roughly the same time my mother began living with this illness, my brother moved back into my mom's small apartment. He had returned, in part, for the same reason he all too frequently came back: He was using and he was in a jam and he was hiding and he knew my mom would put him up. He had returned, in part too, because he realized my mom needed help that only he could provide.

In the first few years, he and I cleaned up his legal messes and got him help in trying, once again, to stay clean. As always, his situation proved precarious. On a daily basis he felt the impulse to hit the streets and hustle—who knows what exactly, but a fix if nothing else. But my brother sensed my mom's precipitous decline. He understood he couldn't both hit the streets as he once had and take care of my mom in a way he felt she deserved. Most often, he stayed home, trying yet again to learn to live in ways always a bit foreign to him.

Dementia ravaged my mom. But now and then, she would suddenly emerge lucid. During those moments, she sometimes would ask me, "How are we going to help your brother find a job so he can live out a good life?" Now you could say she was just being a great mother, a great mother to her sixty-four year old son, who happened to be many things, including a life-long junkie and institutionalized soul. And you'd be right: She was a great mother—in fact, she was the perfect mom for me.

But my mom was passing along a message that anchored and propelled her entire life: Not only should my brother not give up, but also neither should we and neither should anybody else. Rather, in her exceedingly radical and practical way, she was insisting we should all think in very concrete terms: "What's the next step in actually trying to live out what we dream for ourselves, for our families and friends, and for the world we aim to make fundamentally a better place?"

Since my mom's death, my brother has been very sick. At first, he contracted a serious infection from sources unknown, then he endured severe complications from diabetes, then he suddenly began throwing up pints of blood from what turned out to be previously undiagnosed bleeding ulcers. Still, at least when gently coaxed, he'll ask me, "Should I stay in L.A. or should I go back to Arizona?"

When I first heard that question, for a moment I thought, "What does he mean?" Then finally it dawned on me. My brother is following my mom's lead, isn't he? He is proclaiming, "I want to see if maybe I can do something with the rest of my life, maybe work again with the other

Chicanos and Mexicanos taking care of horses in Arizona, certainly not just play out my hand without having again put to use what I know and what I can always learn. I want to put it all on the line, see if I've got what it takes, see how I can live again as a full-grown adult, and see if I can make at least some of what I dream come true."

Is that some crazy utopian claim? I don't think so. In fact, for me it's anything but. The absolutely grounded conviction that my mom lived by all her life and that, at his best, my brother clung to is that we can and must strive for something better, knowing there have been moments of "something better" in the past, and there can be such moments again in the future. And through this hope they both seem to be saying that if we can learn to be any good at working together, we can lengthen these moments. And as we do so, we can change along the way both how we think about our living together and how we think about solving problems together (including though our professional lawyering).

Yes, this rebellious conviction is ambitious. Perhaps it's even against the odds. But how do we know what we can individually and collectively accomplish unless, against the reigning approach to how to live and work, we act as if our dreams can come true? Join my mom and my brother. Join millions of people all across the globe. Reject absolutely the "common sense" and "mature" notion that what we're now living marks the limits of what's possible. Imagine we can, with others, shape our lives, our problem solving, and the futures we dare to dream.

NOTES

1. For illustrations of my own efforts to define and elaborate these contrasting visions, see López 1992 and 2004.

2. For only a tiny sample of the wide range of people—from Nobel-Prize winning polymaths to heralded movement activists to radical social theorists to resilient low-income, of color, and immigrant communities and to others still—whose views variously evoke the contrast between the rebellious and regnant visions on how we both solve problems and govern ourselves—see Anzaldúa 1987; Baker 1973; Bruner 1986; Cruse 1967; Dewey 1929; Simon 1997; Foucault 1961/1988; Gaventa 1980; Geertz 1983; Rorty 1982; Rosaldo 1989; Stiglitz 1994; Unger and West 1998; Abel 1973; Austin 1992; Bell 1976; Bellow 1977; Cornwall and Gaventa 2001; Felstiner et al., 1980–81; Goetz and Gaventa 2001; Helper et al., 2000; Hing 1993; Karst 1983; Kennedy 1976 and 1982; Marshall 2000; Minami 1980; Minsky 1975;

Piomelli 2006; Pitkin 1987; Reagon 1983; Roberts 1999; Su 1998; Tversky 1977; Tversky and Kahneman 1973; Rodrik et al., 2002; Taylor-Thompson 1996; and White 1997.

REFERENCES

Abel, Richard L. 1973. "A Comparative Theory of Dispute Institutions in Society." *Law & Society Rev.* 8: 217–347.

Anzaldúa, Gloria. 1987. *Borderlands/La Frontera: The New Mestiza.* San Francisco: Aunt Lute Books.

Austin, Regina. 1992. "The Black Community, Its Lawbreakers, and a Politics of Identification." *Southern Cal. L. Rev.* 65: 1769–1817.

Baker, Ella. 1973. "Developing Community Leadership." In *Black Women in White America: A Documentary History*, Gerda Lerner, ed., 347–52. New York: Random House.

Bell, Derrick. 1976. "Serving Two Masters." *Yale L. J.* 85: 470–516.

Bellow, Gary. 1977. "Turning Solutions into Problems: The Legal Aid Experience." *NLADA Briefcase* 34: 10625.

Bruner, Jerome. 1986. *Actual Minds, Possible Worlds.* Cambridge, MA: Harvard University Press.

Carlson, Ann. 2001. "Recycling Norms." *Cal. L. Rev.* 89: 123190.

Cornwall, Andrea, and John Gaventa. 2001. "From Users and Choosers to Makers and Shapers: Repositioning Participation in Social Policy." Institute of Development Studies, Working Paper No. 127.

Cruse, Harold. 1967. *The Crisis of the Negro Intellectual.* New York: New York Review Books.

Dewey, John. 1929. *The Quest for Certainty: A Study of the Relation of Knowledge and Action.* New York: Minton Balch.

Felstiner, William L. F. et al. 1980–81. "The Emergence and Transformation of Disputes: Naming, Blaming, Claiming . . ." *Law & Society Rev.* 15: 631–54.

Foucault, Michel. 1961/1988. *Madness & Civilization: A History of Insanity in the Age of Reason.* Richard Howard, trans. New York: Vintage Books.

Gaventa, John. 1980. *Power and Powerlessness: Quiescence and Rebellion in an Appalachian Valley.* Urbana: University of Illinois Press.

Geertz, Clifford. 1983. "Local Knowledge: Fact and Law in Comparative Perspective." In *Local Knowledge: Further Essays in Interpretive Anthropology*, 167–234. New York: Basic Books.

Goetz, Anne Marie, and John Gaventa. 2001. "Bringing Citizen Voice and Client Focus into Service Delivery." Institute of Development Studies, Working Paper No. 138.

Helper, Susan et al. 2000. "Pragmatic Collaborations: Advancing Knowledge While Controlling Opportunism." *Indus. & Corp. Change* 9: 443–87.

Hing, Bill Ong. 1993. "Beyond the Rhetoric of Assimilation and Cultural Pluralism: Addressing the Tension of Separatism and Conflict in an Immigration-Driven Multiracial Society." *Cal. L. Rev.* 81: 863–925.

Karst, Kenneth L. 1983. "Why Equality Matters." *Ga. L. Rev.* 17: 245–89.

Kennedy, Duncan. 1976. "Form and Substance in Private Law Adjudication." *Harv. L. Rev.* 89: 1685–1778.

———. 1982. "Notes of an Oppositionist in Academic Politics." Unpublished manuscript on file with New York University Law Review.

López, Gerald P. 1992. *Rebellious Lawyering—One Chicano's Vision of Progressive Law Practice*. Boulder, CO: Westview.

———. 2004. "Shaping Community Problem Solving around Community Knowledge." *N.Y.U. L. Rev.* 79: 59–114.

Marshall, Shauna. 2000. "Mission Impossible? Ethical Community Lawyering." *Clin. L. Rev.* 7: 147–225.

Minami, Dale. 1980. "Asian Law Caucus, Experiment in an Alternative." Unpublished manuscript on file with New York University Law Review.

Minsky, Marvin. 1975. "A Framework for Representing Knowledge." In *The Psychology of Computer Vision*, Patrick Henry Winston, ed., 211–77. http://web.media.mit.edu/~minsky/papers/Frames/frames.html.

Piomelli, Ascanio. 2006. "The Democratic Roots of Collaborative Lawyering." *Clinical L. Rev.* 12: 541–614.

Pitkin, Hanna Fenichel. 1987. "The Idea of a Constitution." *J. Legal Educ.* 37: 166–69.

Reagon, Bernice Johnson. 1983. "Coalition Politics: Turning the Century." In *Home Girls: A Black Feminist Anthology*, Barbara Smith, ed., 343–56. New Brunswick, NJ: Rutgers University Press.

Roberts, Dorothy. 1999. "Poverty, Race, and New Directions in Child Welfare Policy." *Wash. U.J. L. & Policy* 1: 63–76.

Rodrik, Dani et al. 2002. "Institutions Rule: The Primacy of Institutions over Geography and Integration in Economic Development." Unpublished manuscript. http://ksghome.harvard.edu/~.drodrik.academic.ksg/institutionsrule,%205.0.pdf.

Rorty, Richard. 1982. "Pragmatism, Relativism and Irrationalism." In *Consequences of Pragmatism: Essays, 1972–1980*, 160–75. Minneapolis: University of Minnesota Press.

Rosaldo, Renato. 1989. *Culture and Truth: The Remaking of Social Analysis*. Boston: Beacon.

Simon, Herbert. 1997. *Administrative Behavior*, 4th ed. New York: Free Press.

Stiglitz, Joseph E. 1994. *Whiter Socialism?* Cambridge, MA: MIT Press.

Su, Julie. 1998. "Making the Invisible Visible—The Garment Industry's Dirty Laundry." *J. Gender, Race, & Justice* 1: 405–17.

Taylor-Thompson, Kim. 1996. "Individual Actor v. Institutional Player: Alternating Visions of the Public Defender." *Geo. L.J.* 84: 2419–71.

Tversky, Amos. 1977. "Features of Similarity." *Psychol. Rev.* 84: 327–52.

Tversky, Amos, and Daniel Kahneman. 1973. "Availability: A Heuristic for Judging Frequency and Probability." *Cognitive Psychol.* 5: 207–32.

Unger, Roberto Mangabeira, and Cornel West. 1998. *The Future of American Progressivism: An Initiative for Political and Economic Reform.* Boston: Beacon.

White, Lucie E. 1997. "'Democracy' in Development Practice: Essays on a Fugitive Theme." *Tenn. L. Rev.* 64: 1073–98.

Chapter 11

Of Taints and Time

The Racial Origins and Effects of Florida's Felony Disenfranchisement Law

Jessie Allen

Foreword

Since this chapter was written, the Florida government has significantly limited, though not eliminated, its policy of permanent disenfranchisement. In April 2007, the state rules that govern the restoration of voting rights after felony convictions were amended. Those rules now allow some people disenfranchised after criminal convictions to regain their voting rights on completion of their sentences through a nondiscretionary process. This is at least a partial victory for democracy. Moreover, reform in Florida comes in the context of a more general national trend toward liberalizing voting rights for people with criminal convictions. The wider turn toward reenfranchisement is one of a few hopeful developments that may justify calling this volume After *the War on Crime.*

Particularly given the focus of this chapter, it seems important to note that the recent cutback on felony disenfranchisement in Florida, as elsewhere, has not come through the courts. Indeed, courts—federal and state —have rejected one challenge after another to the validity of felony-voting bans, including the equal protection claim discussed here. Instead, state executive and legislative officials have taken action to repeal or shrink obstacles to political participation by people with criminal convictions. Some of these reforms have been quite sweeping. In 2005, the governor of Iowa issued an executive order automatically restoring the voting rights of all people with felony convictions on completion of sentence (Sentencing

Project 2007). In contrast, the Florida reform is decidedly partial, but, because it is Florida, it will affect many more people.

At this point, it is unclear how many of the nearly one-million Floridians *who have fully completed their sentences* but are still barred from voting will qualify for reenfranchisement under the new rules.[1] A long list of serious crimes and designations like "Violent Career Criminal" and "Prison Releasee Reoffender" are disqualifying (Florida 2007, Rule 9). The requirement of paying all ordered victim restitution (Florida 2007, Rule 9) will be impossible for some people who simply cannot come up with the cash. The state originally estimated that some 80 percent of people currently being released from prison and supervision would be eligible based on the crimes for which they were convicted.[2] But at a recent presentation to civil rights advocates, the director of the Florida Department of Corrections suggested that as many as 40 percent of that group ultimately would be disqualified by the need to pay restitution and other requirements (Ispahani and Lewis 2007), reducing the proportion to something under 50 percent of those currently coming off of supervision. So, the best estimates now suggest that even with the rule change, more than half of those disenfranchised will stay permanently locked out of Florida's polling booths.

Advocates of reenfranchisement have expressed a range of responses to the news from Florida. While it has been called "an important step towards resolving [Florida's] democratic crisis" (Wood 2007), it has also been suggested that although "the proposed rules do represent some incremental progress, they still fall far short of a truly fair and effective plan to restore the right to vote" (Ispahani 2007). It really is a glass half-empty, glass half-full kind of issue. Between April and June 2007, some 15,500 people have had their voting rights restored. On the half-full side, that's more people than Florida reenfranchised in the entire year before the rule change. On the (more than) half-empty side, it is "still a drop in the bucket when you look at the entire population of [nearly a million] former offenders whose civil rights have not been restored" (Farrington 2007, quoting Muslima Lewis of the Florida ACLU).

Finally, I note that the new policy in Florida is not avowedly addressed to the racial origins or effects of the voting ban that are the main subject of this chapter. Florida's new governor, Charlie Crist, explains the rule change as part of a state policy "to encourage and contribute to the rehabilitation of felons and to assist them in the assumption of the responsibilities of citizenship" (Schlakman 2007). There is no suggestion that the rule changes will do anything to remedy the racially disparate effects of the state's disenfranchisement policy. (Indeed, they may exacerbate them. The restitution requirement, for instance, will fall hardest on those with fewer economic resources, disproportionately African Americans.) There was also no overt acknowledgment of the ugly racial origins of felony disenfranchisement in Florida. At least one state political operative, however, managed to imply that the policy change addressed that history, without actually mentioning it. "Governor Crist recognizes the need to govern in a tradition of Abraham Lincoln," said Jim Greer, chairman of the Republican Party of Florida. "He recognizes that government has a responsibility to do the right thing for its citizens" (Farrington 2007).

In Florida, once someone is convicted of a crime, he or she is indefinitely barred from voting. Even after serving time, even after years of law-abiding life in the community, most people's only hope of regaining the right to vote is through a complicated, rarely successful, clemency process.[3] This permanent disenfranchisement harks back to civil death, outlawry, and the ancient concept of "attaint"[4] associated with felony convictions. The voting ban has caused much collateral damage in the African-American communities targeted by the "war on crime." Some 18 percent of Florida's black voting-age population was shut out of the polls in November 2004.[5] One in four black men in Florida cannot vote (Sentencing Project 2007).

The loss of voting rights is not part of the sentence. With no definite term and no grounds for appeal, this is a kind of permanent political exile—the democratic equivalent of excommunication forbidden without a criminal trial by the U.S. Constitution's prohibition on bills of attainder (Article 1, Sec. 9, cl. 3 and Sec. 10, cl.1). Under the state's clemency rules, applications may be denied for any reason or no reason. Like kings of old, the governor of Florida, and other members of the clemency board, demand that applicants travel to the state capital to make a personal appearance in a public hearing to express contrition for their past crimes and beg for reinstatement in the body politic. Such favors are rarely granted. As they say in Florida, "clemency is an act of grace." Like "attainted" persons, Florida's disenfranchised citizens are powerless to change their status.

For black Floridians, the taint of felony disenfranchisement recalls the stigma of inferiority historically associated with the denial of voting rights on account of race (Austin 2004, 177). And it turns out that criminal disenfranchisement in Florida is tinged by the historic taint of race in another way as well. A recent federal lawsuit charged that the state's blanket felony disenfranchisement policy was originally adopted after the Civil War as part of a scheme to keep newly freed African Americans from gaining political power (*Johnson v. Bush* 2005).[6] So, the law that makes criminal conviction in Florida an indelible stain of civic inferiority is itself tainted with an illicit past. The state has treated this second kind of taint quite differently, however, than the permanent mark its law makes on some of its citizens. To be sure, the state defendants contended that the law had no racist origins. But they made a second argument, as well, that was ultimately accepted by the court and that raises hard questions about the history of race in this country and who does and should bear the blemish of the way race and race discrimination have helped to shape both our criminal justice and electoral systems.

The state maintained, and the federal court ultimately agreed, that even if the felony disenfranchisement provision was originally designed and enacted in 1868 to strip blacks of voting rights, it is today a legitimate, nondiscriminatory policy because in the intervening years it was amended and reenacted. The framers of the revised modern provision never confronted or disavowed the law's racist origins or put on the record any legitimate policy reasons for reenacting a law with such skewed racial effects. Nevertheless, the court upheld Florida's claim that after the reenactment there is nothing illicit about the provision's continued racial effects—even if they continue to fulfill the law's original racist purpose.

So here is the contradiction: With permanent disenfranchisement, Florida taints its citizens convicted of intentionally bad acts with a stigma whose symbolic and practical effects won't wash out with time, benevolent intentions, or a lifetime of good works. Yet the state fought—and won—a legal challenge to its voting ban with an argument that the law's own malicious intent should not forever stigmatize it.[7] According to the law's enforcers and all but two of the federal judges who eventually heard the argument, the law's silent reenactment "eliminated any taint from the allegedly discriminatory 1868 provision" (405 F.3d 1214, 1224)—even though its racially disproportionate effects still carry out its original racist design. Apparently there are taints and there are taints.

The Disenfranchisement Provision's Discriminatory Origin

Florida's earliest constitution, ratified in 1838, limited suffrage to "free white male[s]," over the age of twenty-one (Art. VI, Sec. 1) and authorized the general assembly to exclude from voting "all persons convicted of bribery, perjury or other infamous crime" (Art. VI, Sec. 4). After the Civil War, Florida faced the need to write a new constitution that would at least nominally enfranchise blacks in order to be allowed back into the Union. It was this 1868 constitution that made criminal disenfranchisement self-executing and widened it to include the expandable category of anyone convicted of any felony. There are no smoking guns in the 1868 constitutional records.[8] But a well-recognized historian of Florida during Reconstruction, Jerrell Shofner, the plaintiffs' expert witness in the recent constitutional challenge to Florida's voting ban, found that "[f]elony disenfranchisement was a way of reducing the effect of the despised black suffrage that Conservatives knew they had no alternative but to accept" (Shofner 2001, 17).[9]

Shofner documented strong circumstantial evidence that the felony disenfranchisement provision was put into the state's 1868 constitution for the purpose of keeping blacks from voting.[10] During Florida's 1868 constitutional convention, two rival political factions battled for control (Shofner 2001, 9–18). The Radical Republicans wanted to enfranchise all black men, and their proposed version of the constitution contained no felony disenfranchisement clause at all (Shofner 2001, 14). The moderate Republicans were working with ex-Confederate Democrats and were willing to sell out black suffrage in order to retain the support of their Democratic allies. The moderate Constitution that ultimately prevailed contained the predecessor of Florida's current felony disenfranchisement law.[11] According to Shofner, it was designed to work with a racially targeted criminal justice system that aimed at disproportionately convicting African Americans (Shofner 2001, 2–3). Along with other suffrage provisions designed to dilute the black vote, felony disenfranchisement could help prevent Florida's newly freed slaves from gaining political power (Shofner 2001, 2–3). Thus the constitution would, in the words of one "moderate" leader— keep Florida from becoming "niggerized" (*Johnson v. Bush* 2002b, 1296).

A hundred years later, as part of a wholesale revision of the Florida Constitution, the felony disenfranchisement provision was amended and reenacted substantively intact. The only surviving record of discussions of the felony disenfranchisement provisions are the minutes of a three-hour subcommittee meeting. Those minutes offer no explanation for felony disenfranchisement policy by the constitutional drafters recommending its adoption. A more limited felony disenfranchisement policy was offered by others and voted down. There is no record of the reasons for reenacting the blanket, permanent ban, and no suggestion of any legitimate, non-discriminatory reasons for continuing a practice that at the time of its re-enactment continued to have a racially discriminatory impact.[12]

Discrimination in Florida's Criminal Justice System

The felony disenfranchisement law that was reenacted in 1968 had a discriminatory effect in part due to continuing discrimination in the state's criminal justice system, for example, the exclusion of blacks from criminal juries. Like the voting ban, racial discrimination in the criminal justice system had its roots in Reconstruction. Directly following emancipation in Florida, the criminal justice system was used as a tool for the continued subjugation of newly freed slaves. Florida enacted the Black Codes and criminalized taking vegetables from fields. In 1868, African Americans were 48 percent of Florida's population, but by 1877 they made up at least 82 percent of the prison population.

The state sanctioned discrimination in the criminal justice system well into the twentieth century. Some members of the plaintiff class that challenged Florida's felony disenfranchisement law were convicted in the 1960s and 1970s when blacks were still systematically excluded from juries (see, e.g., *Porter v. Sinclair* 1967; *State v. Silva* 1972). More recently, a commission formed by the Florida State Supreme Court found that blacks were still excluded from meaningful participation within the criminal justice system as judges, lawyers, prosecutors, and law enforcement officers (Florida Supreme Court Racial and Ethnic Bias Study Commission 1991). The commission concluded that institutional racial bias persists in other ways as well. For instance, the differential treatment of African American and Hispanic youth in the juvenile justice system "results, at least in part, from racial and ethnic bias on the part of enough individual police officers, HRS workers, prosecutors, and judges to make the system operate as if it intended to discriminate against non-whites. It results as well from bias in institutional policies, structures, and practices" (Florida Supreme Court Racial and Ethnic Bias Study Commission 1991, 59–60).

Discretionary charging and sentencing practices in today's criminal justice system also work to disadvantage African Americans. In particular, prosecutors in Florida allow defendants in certain circumstances to plead guilty to a felony offence with the disposition of "adjudication withheld," which resolves a felony conviction without a criminal record (Fla.

Stat. § 948.01(2)). Whites are more likely than blacks to receive this lenient disposition. A study by the *Miami Herald* of nearly 800,000 felony cases revealed that whites were 47 percent more likely to have adjudication withheld (Grotto 2004, A23). Significantly, adjudication withheld also prevents a loss of voting rights.

Equal Protection Doctrine: The Centrality of Bad Intent

In life, people's old, hidden intentions generally count for very little. But if you litigate equal protection claims you become obsessed with this kind of thing. In equal protection, it is the thought that counts. In the 1970s, the U.S. Supreme Court made a series of decisions narrowing the basis on which individuals could challenge government action as racially discriminatory. Beginning with the now canonical ruling in *Washington v. Davis* (1976), the Court held that in order to prove a state law violates the federal constitutional guarantee of equal protection, plaintiffs must show not only that the law tends to harm people of one race, but also that the harm results from a deliberate, subjective intent to discriminate on the basis of race. As the Court later explained, "official action will not be held unconstitutional solely because it results in a racially disproportionate impact. Disproportionate impact is not irrelevant, but it is not the sole touchstone of an invidious racial discrimination. Proof of racially discriminatory intent or purpose is required to show a violation of the Equal Protection Clause" (*Village of Arlington Heights v. Metro. Housing Devel. Corp.* 1977, 264–65). Thus bad motives became the *sine qua non* of a viable claim to equal protection.

The doctrinal requirement of subjective bad intent has been attacked from many different perspectives. Critics have pointed out the relative unimportance of subjective intentions to individuals who suffer harm, the impossibility of assigning a single subjective intention to a legislature composed of many different participants with many different political objectives, the great difficulty of obtaining convincing proof of an intangible mental state, and the corrosive social effects of ferreting out individual racism. As the principal legislative report accompanying passage of the Voting Rights Act put it, the intent requirement in constitutional cases saddles voting discrimination plaintiffs with an "inordinately difficult" proof burden and is "unnecessarily divisive because it involves charges of racism on the part of individual officials or entire communities," and "asks the wrong question" (U.S. Senate 1982, 36).[13]

Be that as it may, this core aspect of constitutional doctrine is now carved in stone.[14] So to prove that disenfranchising one in four black men was a violation of equal protection, the *Johnson* plaintiffs had to prove that the racial results of Florida's felony disenfranchisement law stem from a deliberate racist purpose.

At this point, you might think that time would be a crucial issue. After all, Florida's felony disenfranchisement provision was over 130 years old when the suit against it was filed. But it turns out the effect of time on the validity of originally discriminatory laws had already been decided by the Supreme Court and in the context of a criminal disenfranchisement law at that. In *Hunter v. Underwood*, through an opinion by Justice Rehnquist, the Supreme Court held that even though an intentionally discriminatory enactment took place over seventy years ago, the state remained liable for its ongoing discriminatory consequences (*Hunter v. Underwood* 1985, 233). The Court presumed the Alabama criminal disenfranchisement law challenged in *Hunter* was currently being administered by state officials in good faith, without racial animus. Nevertheless, as the Eleventh Circuit explained in the opinion the Supreme Court affirmed, "Neither their impartiality nor the passage of time . . . can render immune a purposefully discriminatory scheme whose invidious effects still reverberate today" (*Hunter v. Underwood* 1984, 621).

If time doesn't immunize a policy originally designed to discriminate, what later acts or circumstances might? Can subsequent events ever intervene to cut off liability for the continuing racial impact of a discriminatory legislative decision long ago?

Liability for Policies "Traceable" to Unconstitutional Segregation

You might think the answer is simply "no." (Or maybe, "hell, no.") Once a government has acted intentionally to disadvantage some of its citizens by passing a policy aimed at harming those people, the state should remain liable for the continuing ill effects of that original discriminatory decision. A change of heart shouldn't matter so long as the harm continues. This is, in fact, the standard of liability set by the Supreme Court in evaluating whether states have sufficiently dismantled the segregated school systems resulting from the "separate but equal" laws and practices outlawed in the 1950s by *Brown v. Board of Education* (1955).

After segregation was ruled unconstitutional, the Court held that state governments had an affirmative duty to do away with their segregated school systems. That didn't just mean repealing the laws mandating racial separation. The Court held that "a State does not discharge its constitutional obligations until it eradicates policies and practices *traceable* to its prior *de jure* system that continue to foster segregation" (emphasis added; *United States v. Fordice* 1992, 728). Under this standard, if current, facially race-neutral policies have "perpetuated" racial segregation, those policies must also be reformed (*United States v. Fordice* 1992, 729).

For example, a case in the 1990s challenged admission standards to Mississippi's public universities (among other policies) as perpetuating unconstitutional segregated education. Under the state's challenged admissions scheme, 72 percent of Mississippi's white high school seniors were eligible for top universities, compared with only 30 percent of African American seniors. Looking at the history of those standards, the Supreme Court first noted that in the 1960s, requisite test scores had been set deliberately to exclude African American applicants.[15] The Court then went on to describe the current admissions standards as having tinkered with the original formula but not abandoned it. The lower courts had blessed the current standards, characterizing them as "derived from policies enacted in the 1970s to redress the problem of student unpreparedness" (*United States v. Fordice* 1992, 734, citing *Ayers v. Allain* 1990b, 679, and *Ayers v. Allain* 1987, 1531). But the Supreme Court disagreed: "Obviously, this midpassage justification for perpetuating a policy enacted originally to discriminate against black students does not make the present admissions standards any less constitutionally suspect" (*United States v. Fordice* 1992, 734). The Court observed that the challenged admissions standards were "not only traceable to the *de jure* system and were originally for discriminatory purpose, but they also have present discriminatory effects" (*United States v. Fordice* 1992, 734). That placed a burden on the state, said the Court, either to reshape its admissions policy to do away with its discriminatory results or to prove that the current policy "is not susceptible to elimination without eroding sound educational policy" (*United States v. Fordice* 1992, 738–39).

In other words, confronting school segregation more than thirty years after *Brown*, the Court placed the burden of history on the state. Justifying subsequent reforms with nonracial educational goals was insufficient to legitimate the new policies if they perpetuated the segregated system. If a new, facially neutral policy was traceable to an old, racially tainted one, the state is still liable for its racial effects. Under *Fordice*, the only way for a state to defend such a policy is to prove that it cannot be eliminated without undermining sound educational policy. Even proof of pure contemporary motives won't protect state policies that are "traceable" to the old unconstitutional system and that perpetuate its discriminatory effects.

The Eleventh Circuit's Rejection of the Equal Protection Challenge to Florida's Voting Ban

Unsurprisingly, when the *Johnson* plaintiffs challenged Florida's disenfranchisement law, the state contended that the law's reenactment had negated any previous discriminatory intent. The district judge agreed. Explaining that "a new provision may supercede the previous provision and remove the discriminatory taint associated with the original version," he held that the 1968 reenactment "cleansed Florida's felon disenfranchisement scheme of any invidious discriminatory purpose that may have prompted its inception" (*Johnson v. Bush* 2002a, 1339). With no mention of *Fordice*, the district judge relied primarily on a decision from the Fifth Circuit Court of Appeals dismissing an equal protection challenge to another criminal disenfranchisement law. There was no question that the voting ban challenged in that case originated with a discriminatory purpose. It was adopted in 1890, when, as the Mississippi defendants admitted, "southern states discriminated against blacks by disenfranchising convicts for crimes that, it was thought, were committed primarily by blacks" (*Cotton v. Fordice* 1998, 391). The Fifth Circuit absolved the state of liability for any ongoing discriminatory effects, however, because the law had twice been amended and reenacted. The court acknowledged that under *Hunter* the old law was unconstitutional. The provision had been amended, however, in 1950 to remove burglary from the list of disenfranchising crimes and again in 1968, when murder and rape had been added to the list. The court pointed out that the second amendment added "crimes historically excluded from the list because they were not considered 'black' crimes," and stressed that the amendments took place through "a deliberative process" that included approval by two-thirds of the members of both houses of the state legislature and ratification in a popular election (*Cotton v. Fordice* 1998, 391). According to the Fifth Circuit, because the amendment process resulted in reenactment of the criminal disenfranchisement provision, "each amendment superseded the previous provision and removed the discriminatory taint associated with the original version" (*Cotton v. Fordice* 1998, 391).

Recall that in *Fordice*, the Supreme Court held that Mississippi was still responsible for the discriminatory effects of its college admissions standards, *even though the standards had been changed* and somewhat ameliorated since their original discriminatory adoption. But the Fifth Circuit held in *Cotton* that the state was *not* responsible for the continuing discriminatory effects of its criminal disenfranchisement policy because the policy had been amended and reenacted. The Fifth Circuit explained that the revised criminal disenfranchisement policy was "unconstitutional only if the amendments were adopted out of a desire to discriminate against blacks" (*Cotton v. Fordice* 1998, 392). The Florida district judge adjudicating the challenge to Florida's long-standing felony disenfranchisement provision found that analysis "persuasive" (*Johnson v. Bush* 2002a, 1339). Following the Fifth Circuit's lead, he held that Florida's originally discriminatory felony disenfranchisement law had been cleansed by the "deliberative process" of its reenactment (*Johnson v. Bush* 2002a, 1339, citing *Cotton v. Fordice* 1998, 391).

But the Eleventh Circuit panel that heard the appeal from the district court's dismissal was not prepared to follow the *Cotton* approach. Instead, the question the *Johnson* panel asked was whether Florida had "disavow[ed] any connection to the law's original discriminatory purpose by showing that it was later reenacted for independent, nondiscriminatory reasons" (*Johnson v. Bush* 2002b, 1299). Where the Fifth Circuit focused on the formal amendment process through which the Mississippi disenfranchisement provision had been altered and reenacted, the *Johnson* panel focused on the substantive reasons for the continued existence of permanent felony disenfranchisement in Florida.

The *Johnson* panel explained that "[r]etaining an originally discriminatory provision in order to preserve continuity, or out of deference to tradition, or simply due to inertia does not amount to an independent purpose sufficient to break the chain of causation between the original racial animus and the provision's continuing force as law" (*Johnson v. Bush* 2002b, 1302). The panel asked whether Florida's criminal disenfranchisement policy today, with its racially disproportionate impact, still owed its existence to the racist scheme devised during Reconstruction to keep blacks from voting. If the reenactment had an "independent" legitimate purpose, then the likelihood is that Florida would have adopted felony disenfranchisement then, even without the discriminatory policy already on the books. But if there was no such purpose, the old discriminatory decision is still "a substantial or motivating factor" (*Hunter v. Underwood* 1985, 225) for the law's presence and effect today.

The Eleventh Circuit as a whole, however, was not inclined to accept the *Johnson* panel's analysis. The court vacated the panel decision and reheard the case *en banc*, after which it dismissed the equal protection challenge to Florida's voting ban in an opinion that again echoed *Cotton*. The *en banc* court observed that, like the Mississippi law upheld in *Cotton*, "Florida's disenfranchisement provision was amended through a deliberative process" (*Johnson v. Bush* 2005, 1224). The court emphasized that the 1968 constitutional revision did away with another provision that disenfranchised people convicted of some misdemeanors and that the reenacted felony disenfranchisement provision was considered by a subcommittee, the entire Constitutional Revision Commission, and the state legislature, before being ratified by voters (*Johnson v. Bush* 2005, 1224). In other words, like the district judge and the Fifth Circuit in *Cotton*, the *en banc* court focused on the legitimacy of the reenactment's "deliberative process" without making any *Fordice*-like inquiry into the traceability of the reenacted voting ban and its ongoing discriminatory effects, to the original discriminatory provision.

The *en banc* court stated flatly that the challenge to Florida's law and *Fordice* were "not analogous" (*Johnson v. Bush* 2005, 1225). But the distinctions the court drew were unsatisfying. First, the court explained that while Mississippi had no sound justification for the education policy challenged in *Fordice*, "Florida has a valid public policy reason for disenfranchising felons" (*Johnson v. Bush* 2005, 1225). But, as the dissent pointed out, that assertion "begs the very question of the motivation behind the 1968 reenactment" (J. Barkett dissenting, *Johnson v. Bush* 2005, 1245), on which the record is silent. The *en banc* court also pointed to the fact that in *Fordice*, relatively little time had elapsed since the challenged policy's discriminatory origin (*Johnson v. Bush* 2005, 1225–26). But *Hunter* clearly holds that the passage of time does not erase a law's discriminatory purpose. Under *Hunter*, the day before its reenactment, Florida's felony disenfranchisement law was as invalid as the day it was originally enacted. According to the *en banc* court, at the time of the reenactment, the challenged law's discriminatory effects were "minor" (*Johnson v. Bush* 2005, 1226). In one sense the court was correct. In 1968, before the "war on crime," many fewer people overall were effected by felony disenfranchise-ment. The state penitentiaries held a much smaller portion of the popula-tion and many fewer "ex-felons" lived in Florida neighborhoods. But then, as now, the prisons disproportionately housed black men and African American communities lost more than double the proportion of non-African American voters disenfranchised by the felony voting ban—3.13 percent as opposed to 1.24 percent of the voting-age population (*Johnson v. Bush* 2005, 1226, n. 23). The *en banc* majority also expressed reluctance to extend *Fordice*'s reasoning outside the education context, but offered no principled justification for this limit. It is hard to see one. Certainly political participation is at least as important an individual right and state interest as education.

Ultimately, the *en banc* court seemed impatient with the very notion that a law's discriminatory origins could color the validity of its present effects. But of course that was the basic holding of *Hunter*. So the court looked to the reenactment, finding that it negated the law's discriminatory motive "particularly in light of the passage of time" and the fact that "at the time of the 1968 enactment no one had ever alleged that the 1968 pro-vision was motivated by racial animus" (*Johnson v. Bush* 2005, 1224). The idea that the challenged policy was in some way presumptively legitimized if not actually validated by the passage of time and the ignorance of its re-enactors seems particularly short sighted, given the context here. After all, this is a constitution we are talking about, not a temporary plan. Surely if they had been asked, the framers of Florida's Reconstruction constitution would have said they hoped to affect the entire course of the state's future political development. Moreover, as Eric Schnapper has pointed out, the ultimate success of intentionally discriminatory state policies depends on setting up institutional structures that will burden the target group with-out requiring repeated deliberate discriminatory decisions by countless other individual state actors going forward: "Only if one racist decision can affect large numbers of victims over an extended period of time is discrimination administratively feasible" (Schnapper 1983, 834–35).

The "Taint" of Race and the "Chain" of Causation

Both the Eleventh Circuit *en banc* opinion in *Johnson* and the Fifth Cir-cuit in *Fordice* talked in terms of "cleansing the racial taint" of the old discriminatory motive. Neither analysis is true to the metaphor it invokes.

The *Oxford English Dictionary* defines the verb "taint" as "to affect with or as if with a disease" and "to affect with decay or putrefaction; spoil" before it gets to "to corrupt morally." The first noun definition is "a moral defect considered as a stain or spot," and the entry also points to an obsolete usage of "to color or dye." A taint is not something that just disappears because you readjust the thing that caused it in the first place. It is not easily reversible, like switching a light on and off. Think of dye seeping into fabric or of a toxic spill. The pollution that happens in a few hours may take years to clean up.

The "taint" usage comes up a lot in discrimination cases. Particularly with regard to race, the image reflects the understanding that discrimination is the sort of problem that gets into things and changes them in ways that are not easy to reverse. But the Eleventh Circuit held that Florida's stigma of intentional race discrimination can be effectively cancelled by procedural legitimacy. As in *Cotton*, reenactment "removed the discriminatory taint associated with the original version" simply by following the correct formal procedures to revise the law.

The metaphor of a "taint" was also used by Justice Thomas in his *Fordice* concurrence to very different effect. Thomas explains that "given an initially tainted policy, it is eminently reasonable to make the State bear the risk of nonpersuasion with respect to intent at some future time, both because the State has created the dispute through its own prior unlawful conduct, and because discriminatory intent does tend to persist through time" (*United States v. Fordice* 1992, 746–47). Reflecting the dictionary definition and the state's approach to the taint of criminal disenfranchisement, Thomas's concurrence suggests that the taint of discriminatory legislative motives creates a moral and political stain that won't wash out over time or accidentally; it has to be deliberately undone.

Notice that the notion of a discriminatory taint seems to have been transposed here from a way of thinking about race itself—akin to the old "one-drop" rule in which race—specifically being black—is conceived as a kind of taint in the blood that gets in and cannot work its way out, despite the passage of generations—just like, in fact, the transgenerational corruption of the blood legally and symbolically visited on people and their descendants through the old writs of attainder. The image of a law tainted by racism oddly mirrors the idea of a person or a society tainted by race, more specifically, by blackness—it turns the viscerally aversive aspect of racism in on itself. Race prejudice and its effects are a kind of infection of the civic body, a corruption of the societal lifeblood.

It is interesting that the *Johnson* panel analysis, now vacated, moved away from the taint metaphor to hold the state responsible for its racial history and to envision a way for the state ultimately to move beyond that history. The panel majority used some "taint" language but relied more on a common metaphor from tort law, asking whether the 1968 reenactment had "an independent purpose sufficient to break the chain of causation between the original racial animus and the provision's continuing force as law" (*Johnson v. Bush* 2002b, 1302). It is as though the substitution of the bland "chain of causation" imagery moves the issue out of the singularity of race in America and into routine tort causation questions. And the image of a chain is so much cleaner, so much more manageable, after all, than the idea of a taint.

Or is it? Besides the unfortunate association of chains with slavery, the problem to consider here is that the causal chain may run both ways —or maybe in this case the chain makes a circle, the last loop interlocking the first. Because it might be that part of the reason criminal justice remains so relentlessly race-disparate is that the whole network of police and prosecutorial practices was built up from a time when one specific goal of criminal "justice" was to stop blacks from voting by convicting them of disenfranchising crimes. In other words, the adoption of criminal disenfranchisement laws to evade the Reconstruction Acts and the Fifteenth Amendment may actually have contributed in some way to the shaping of a criminal justice system that today falls more heavily on African Americans.

There is no doubt that there were plenty of other incentives to deform criminal justice to convict more blacks. General stereotypes of black inferiority and moral depravity certainly contributed to the criminalization of African Americans. And no doubt there were economic incentives for convicting blacks of crimes that made them available for the convict-leasing programs that to some extent replaced slave labor. But it may not be insignificant to the shaping of law enforcement and criminal justice practices that designating a black man as "infamous" or a "felon" incapacitated him in the voting booth. Remember that in the South, blacks were present in numbers that in a truly representative democracy could have determined the region's political future. In Reconstruction Florida, blacks were 48 percent of the population and a majority in some counties. The history of the successful violent suppression of African Americans' voting in the South is well documented. But links between the more recently uncovered use of criminal disenfranchisement and the racially disparate structure of the criminal justice system have not really been explored. How did the old racially motivated policies of disenfranchising people convicted of crimes, like those detailed in *Cotton* and *Johnson,* contribute to the structures of the criminal justice systems in Mississippi and Florida?

I am speculating here. But it certainly seems worthy of consideration and investigation to try to understand what role criminal disenfranchisement policies have played, if any, in the expansion of states' list of felonies. One way to disenfranchise more people was to make less serious crimes triggers for disenfranchisement directly, even though they were still conceived as fairly petty offenses. Florida criminalized theft of agricultural products and made even such petty larcenies triggers for permanent loss of voting rights (Shofner 2001). Taking home a potato from the field you had planted, for instance, was now grounds for life-long disenfranchisement. Another strategy would be to expand felonies. Rather than making petty misdemeanors disenfranchisement triggers, states could reconceive those offenses as "infamous" crimes or felonies that would trigger disenfranchisement.[16]

For that matter it is worth considering whether criminal disenfranchisement's role in that initial expansion helped to carve a path for the later expansion of drug felonies in the more recent "war on crime." Yoking disenfranchisement to felony conviction created a very concrete reason to shape law enforcement and criminal justice practices and policies in ways that would convict blacks. Along with general racial prejudice and stereotypes of black criminality, the desire to keep black men out of the polls and its expression through criminal disenfranchisement laws may well have contributed to law enforcement and criminal justice practices that would over-convict blacks. In other words, laws such as Florida's felony voting ban that were written into state constitutions on purpose to disproportionately disenfranchise blacks can only effectuate that purpose if proportionately more blacks than whites are convicted of disenfranchising crimes. After the Civil War and the Fifteenth Amendment, American law enforcement/criminal justice systems were expected, and no doubt built, in part, to disenfranchise black men. Today, the dilution of black communities' voting power is deemed a "collateral consequence," a side effect, of criminal justice policies that disproportionately convict African Americans for what we presume are other reasons—legitimate or not. But once, this tail wagged the dog.

I am not saying the old scheme to disenfranchise is responsible for everything that has happened since. And as a matter of equal protection doctrine, I would agree that here the connections between bad intent and bad effects may be too attenuated to support state liability for a constitutional violation. Certainly no such causal contention was advanced by the plaintiffs in *Johnson v. Bush.* Still, staring at Florida's felony disenfranchisement law makes one wonder to what extent the disenfranchising side effect of today's war on crime was once a design goal of criminal justice and to what extent the practices developed in the service of that goal might have shaped, in turn, the practices that today continue to produce that ostensibly unlooked-for racial result.

It is like stumbling on the remains of some old fort, turned up in a contemporary construction project and tracing the way the modern city plan seems to follow the ancient walls in some places. Maybe the original buildings shaped the land itself in ways that made it easier for future development to track their original lines. The discovery doesn't change all the more salient reasons the city developed in its current shape—the industrial revolution, the invention of automobiles—but it adds something to our understanding of our world. If someone asked *why* the city was built as it was—a question that itself is almost unintelligible, of course—the answer would be different after the traces of the old walls had been found and one noticed how closely they aligned with the current city plan.

NOTES

1. According to the Sentencing Project (2007), "Florida had an estimated 960,000 ex-felons who were unable to vote in the 2004 presidential election."

2. There is also some doubt whether the eligibility estimate based on the people who committed felonies last year will hold for those who were previously disenfranchised. Part of the growth in felony convictions and felony disenfranchisement comes from a pattern of designating less serious crimes as felonies. A greater percentage of felony convictions from the past may thus involve serious disqualifying crimes (Bialik 2007).

3. Under the Florida Rules of Executive Clemency some minority of people convicted of crimes are eligible for a process of voting restoration that does not include a full clemency hearing but still takes place at the discretion of the members of the Clemency Board.

4. "Taint, *n.* A stain, a blemish; a sullying spot; a touch, trace, shade, tinge, or tincture of some bad or undesirable quality; a touch of discredit, dishonour, or disgrace; a slur" (*Oxford English Dictionary* 1989).

5. Forty-eight states bar prisoners from voting, and many also ban voting on parole and probation, but Florida is one of only three that permanently disenfranchise everyone convicted of a felony unless they receive clemency. The others are Kentucky and Virginia. The two states that allow voting in prison are Maine and Vermont, and Puerto Rico does as well (Sentencing Project 2007). One of the Florida law's starkest consequences is its disproportionate disenfranchisement of African Americans.

6. Full disclosure: I was one of the attorneys representing the plaintiffs and argued the case before the Eleventh Circuit panel and *en banc* courts.

7. Put this way, this really looks like a no-brainer—at least to those who already view permanent felony disenfranchisement as undemocratic and wrong-headed even without any racist origins or effects. (According to a recent poll by social scientists, this includes a large majority of Americans—80 percent favor re-enfranchising those who have completed serving their sentence (Manza, Brooks, and Uggen 2004, 281)). But there are ways to make the problem of the law's intent morally complex—and to show that the problem reaches far beyond voting rights. Some time ago, Eugene Volokh suggested a harder case. On a voting rights list serve, he contended that some legislative protections of organized labor—such as they are—were created to shut out nonunion African Americans and are still viewed today as creating economic barriers for blacks (Volokh n.d.). Should these laws, like facially neutral voting bans enacted with racist legislative intent, also be overturned? I am no labor historian and cannot speak to the history of the laws Volokh invoked. But the underlying point is a good one. Imagine that there are laws out there that we regard as doing some well-recognized social good. Then imagine that we discover that these laws began at least in part as an attempt to do something racist and that despite their positive effects—say, raising many workers' salaries—they arguably still have harmful effects on proportionately more African Americans. Given the prevalence of out-and-out racial prejudice through most of this country's history and the tendency of legislators to use whatever leverage they can find to advance political agendas, isn't it likely that very many of our laws were passed, at least in part, to promote racist goals? Do we really want to invalidate all such laws? What, if anything, should rehabilitate the constitutionality of laws with this kind of proven racist history?

8. In this respect, Florida's criminal disenfranchisement law differs from those of other Southern states where there is an extensive record of post-Reconstruction use of criminal disenfranchisement to deplete black political power. Alabama's criminal disenfranchisement provision "was motivated by a desire to discriminate against blacks on account of race and the section continues to this day to have that effect" (*Hunter v. Underwood* 1985, 233). Indeed, the Fifth Circuit has acknowledged that criminal disenfranchisement was used to obstruct black suffrage in the South in general: "[S]tate defendants do not dispute that

[the challenged disenfranchisement statute] was enacted in an era when southern states discriminated against blacks by disenfranchising convicts for crimes that, it was thought, were committed primarily by blacks" (*Cotton v. Fordice* 1998, 390; see also *Baker v. Pataki* 1996, 938, *en banc*, Feinberg, J., concurring; *Ratliff v. Beale* 1896, 868: tracing devices, including criminal disenfranchisement, added to the 1890 Mississippi Constitution to "obstruct the exercise of the franchise by the negro race").

9. Expert Report of Jerrell H. Shofner, page 17, October 24, 2001, filed in document 121 of the appellate appendix to *Johnson v. Bush*, 405 F.3d 1214 (11th Cir. 2005).

10. The district judge who dismissed the plaintiffs' claims acknowledged this evidence: "Plaintiffs have presented to this Court an abundance of expert testimony about the historical background of Florida's felon disenfranchisement scheme as historical evidence that the policy was enacted originally in 1868 with the particular discriminatory purpose of keeping blacks from voting" (*Johnson v. Bush* 2002a, 1338–39).

11. Compare Radical Const. art. VI, § 3, reprinted in H.R. Misc., with 1868 Const. art. XIV, § 2.

12. "In 1968, . . . the percentage of Florida's African American voting age population disenfranchised on account of a prior felony conviction [for which they had completed serving their sentences] (1.97 percent) was more than double the rate for non-African Americans (0.9 percent)" (Brief of Plaintiffs-Appellants of *Johnson v. Bush* 2002).

13. Plaintiffs in *Johnson v. Bush* also challenged Florida's felony disenfranchisement law as a violation of Section 2 of the Voting Rights Act. The Eleventh Circuit rejected this claim at the same time that it dismissed the equal protection challenge (*Johnson v. Bush* 2005, 1227–44).

14. Though of course the stream of future events will one day have the effect water has on more natural rock formations.

15. In the 1960s, Mississippi's historically white universities required all entrants to score fifteen or higher on the standard ACT test. The trial judge described the "racial taint" of that policy. As the Supreme Court later explained, he was referring to the fact that "at the time, the average ACT score for white students was [eighteen] and the average score for blacks was [seven]" (*United States v. Fordice* 1992, 734, citing *Ayers v. Allain* 1987, 1557, and *Ayers v. Allain* 1990a, 735).

16. Doubtless, this is why the 1867 Reconstruction Act, which established conditions on which the former Confederate States would be readmitted to representation in Congress limited criminal disenfranchisement to felonies at common law. That restriction, however, was never enforced. (C. 153, 145 Stat. 428 Section 5; see *Richardson v. Ramirez* 1974, 48).

CASES CITED

Ayers v. Allain, 674 F.Supp. 1523 (N.D. Miss. 1987)
Ayers v. Allain, 893 F.2d 732 (CA6 1990a) (panel decision)
Ayers v. Allain, 914 F.2d 676 (CA5 1990b)
Baker v. Pataki, 85 F.3d 919 (2nd Cir. 1996)
Brown v. Board, 349 U.S. 294 (1955)
Cotton v. Fordice, 157 F.3d 388 (5th Cir. 1998)
Hunter v. Underwood, 730 F.2d 614 (1984)
Hunter v. Underwood, 471 U.S. 222 (1985)
Johnson v. Bush, 214 F. Supp. 2d 1333 (S.D. Florida 2002a)
Johnson v. Bush, 353 F.3d 1287 (2002b)
Johnson v. Bush, 405 F.3d 1214 (11th Cir. 2005)
Porter v. Sinclair, 389 F.2d 277, 279 (5th Cir. 1967)
Ratliff v. Beale, 20 So. 865, 868 (Miss. 1896)
Richardson v. Ramirez, 418 U.S. 24 (1974)
State v. Silva, 259 So. 2d 153 (Fla. 1972)
United States v. Fordice, 505 U.S. 717 (1992)
Village of Arlington Heights v. Metro. Housing Devel. Corp., 429 U.S. 252 (1977)
Washington v. Davis, 426 U.S. 229 (1976)

REFERENCES

Austin, Regina. 2004. "The Shame of It All." *Col. Human Rts. L. Rev* 36: 173–92.
Bialik, Carl. 2007. "Figuring the Impact of Allowing Felons in Florida to Vote." *Wall Street Journal Online.* http://online.wsj.com/article/SB117823054330591406.html?mod=politics_primary_hs.
Brief of Plaintiffs-Appellants of *Johnson v. Bush*. 2002. October 8. http://brennan center.org/dynamic/subpages/johnson_plt_app_brief.pdf.
Farrington, Brendan. 2007. "State Trying to Speed Along Ex-Felon Voting Rights Restoration," *Florida Times Union* (June 13).
Florida Supreme Court Racial and Ethnic Bias Study Commission. 1991. "Where the Injured Fly for Justice." Reforming Practices which Impede the Dispensation of Justice to Minorities in Florida, Report and Recommendations of the Florida Supreme Court Racial and Ethnic Bias Study Commission.
Florida. 2007. Rules of Executive Clemency. https://fpc.state.fl.us/Policies/Exec Clemency/ROEC04052007.pdf.
Grotto, Jason. 2004. "Herald Analyzed Millions of Prison, Probation Records." *Miami Herald* (Jan. 25), A23.
Ispahani, Laleh. 2007. "Background Memorandum." American Civil Liberties Union

(April 6). http://electionlawblog.org/archives/ACLU%20Florida%20Clemency%20Memo%204-6-07.pdf.

Ispahani, Laleh, and Muslima Lewis. 2007. Personal communication.

Manza, Jeff, Clem Brooks, and Christopher Uggen. 2004. "Public Attitudes toward Felon Disenfranchisement in the United States." *Public Opinion Quarterly* 68: 275–86.

Oxford English Dictionary. 2nd edition. 1989.

Schlakman, Mark. 2007. "Speed Up Process for State's Ex-Felons to Regain Their Rights." *Palm Beach Post* (June 29).

Schnapper, Eric. 1983. "Perpetuation of Past Discrimination." *Harv. L. Rev.* 96(4): 828–54.

Sentencing Project. 2007. "Felony Disenfranchisement Laws in the United States." http://www.sentencingproject.org/Admin/Documents/publications/fd_bs_fdlawsinus.pdf.

Shofner, Jerrell H. 2001. Expert Report (October 24). Filed in Document 121 of the appellate appendix to *Johnson v. Bush*, 405 F.3d 1214 (11th Cir. 2005).

U.S. Senate. 1982. Senate Report accompanying the Voting Rights Act of 1982. S. Rep. No. 417, 97th Congress, 2nd Session 3, reprinted in 1982 *U.S. Code and Ad. News* 177.

Wood, Erika. 2007. "Restoring the Right to Vote Gains Momentum." *Huffington Post* (April 9).

Volokh, Eugene. n.d. "The Volokh Conspiracy." http://volokh.com.

Chapter 12

The Politics of the War against the Young

Barry Krisberg

The Game

Without question, our young people have paid a heavy price in the so-called war against crime. The most vulnerable political targets of the demagogues on crime policy were adolescents (Krisberg 2005). The next most vulnerable political targets were women who were incarcerated in unprecedented numbers due to mandatory drug laws. The young children of these incarcerated mothers were the civilian collateral damage of the war on drugs, receiving less than benign attention by state criminal justice and welfare officials (Krisberg and Temin 2000). To the extent that obscene levels of spending on the war on crime have led to reduced funding for education, health care, after-school programs, and job training, low-income youngsters have paid an indirect and egregious tax to finance the attack on them by cynical politicians.

The war against the young has taken many forms. The most significant assaults on children in California were new legislative and voter initiatives (e.g., Proposition 21) that were designed to try children as young as fourteen years old in criminal courts. Other states created even lower age limits for youths to be tried as adults. For example, Michigan prosecuted children who were as young as nine years old. Related to this trend of "cracking down" on juvenile crime, many localities adopted aggressive antigang campaigns, including automated police intelligence files that contained the names of tens of thousands of adolescents who were merely suspected of having some gang affiliation. Not even minimal standards of "probable cause" were required to place names in these files, and there were no clear methods through which a young person could remove his or her name from the gang intelligence systems. These law enforcement files were not covered by the usual confidentiality protections that normally apply to juvenile court proceedings. Further, vague evidence that a young person was "gang affiliated" could be used in criminal sentencing to greatly enhance penalties. A recently released documentary titled *JUVIES* presents the tragic story of twelve young people aged fourteen to sixteen who were all sentenced to very long prison terms. In several of the cases, the impact of gang enhancements produced enormous increases in the sentences. For example, the film profiles a sixteen-year-old Vietnamese boy with no prior arrests who is now serving a prison term of thirty-five years to life. He was driving a car when one of the passengers fired a gun. No one was hit by the bullet, and there were no injuries. Still, the young driver was convicted of attempted murder with gang enhancements that will keep him in prison for many decades. There was very little hard evidence that the young man was involved with any gangs.

The hysteria over juvenile gangs, partially fueled by the media, led to a virtual cottage industry of "gang experts" who allegedly could decipher graffiti for gang messages. With little objective evidence, some members the law enforcement community created fantastic mythologies about how Los Angeles street gangs were spreading their ominous colors of red and blue across the county and even around the world. Long before the September 11 bombings of the World Trade Center and the Pentagon, the Patriot Act, and the Department of Homeland Security, the United States was gearing up for a life-or-death struggle against juvenile gangs. Ironically, juvenile crime was dropping during most of this period, and the violent presence of youth gangs was more prevalent on television or the cinema screen than in urban neighborhoods.

During this period, police agencies launched high-profile "made-for-television" crackdowns on gangs. The Los Angeles Police Department organized massive weekend offensives (known as "Operation Hammer") in South Central Los Angeles that resulted in thousands of arrests. So many young people were taken into custody that the L.A.P.D. set up a temporary booking operation at the University of Southern California football stadium. These mass arrests were usually for minor crimes; the arrests resulted in few convictions and virtually no referrals to the California Youth Authority (Krisberg 2005).

Fear of violent juvenile gang members persuaded California juvenile justice officials to send many more youths convicted of crimes to its juvenile prison system without even the pretense of considering alternatives to incarceration. In 1997, that system was almost at 200 percent of its housing capacity. It was at this time that the Youth Authority's traditional emphasis on treatment and education was eroded, with increased use of custodial staff who dressed and comported themselves more like prison guards than counselors. Youth Authority employees were being organized by the California Correctional Peace Officers Association (C.C.P.O.A.), which also represents the prison guards. This movement away from the rehabilitative model was illustrated by the practice of having some Youth Authority residents receive their educational programs in cages. These were steel mesh devices that were the size of a telephone booth. The teacher would pass the student his or her textbooks or lessons through a small slot in the cage. The Youth Authority also instituted the use of attack dogs in some of its facilities to prevent escapes and quell riots. Juvenile correctional facilities continued to utilize the attack dogs long after the Department of Corrections decided to abandon this practice. Funding for rehabilitation, mental health, and medical care in state juvenile facilities was severely cut back. In the mid-1990s, the director of the Youth Authority adopted the rhetoric of the prison guards union and claimed that his facilities were among the "toughest beats in the state."

At the local level, correctional boot camps and the ideology of "tough love" dominated community conversations about youth crime. Schools jumped into the war against the young by creating mandatory suspension and expulsion policies such as "zero-tolerance" programs that claimed to be making schools safer. Many urban schools required that youth pass through metal detectors to enter school buildings. Some public school districts debated requiring students to wear uniforms to classes so as to discourage "gang clothing." Students were pressured to submit to mandatory drug testing if they wished to participate in extracurricular programs and sports teams. More police than ever before were assigned to work on high school and junior high school campuses; other school districts hired their own private security officers. Unannounced searches of student desks and lockers became much more common. Students who were allegedly wearing gang colors were summarily kicked out of school.

There are only partial data on how many young people fell victim to pernicious zero-tolerance policies. The California Department of Education website reported that there were almost 25,000 students recommended for expulsion in fiscal year 2002 to 2003. Of those students, approximately 83 percent were actually expelled (California Department of

Education 2004). In recent years, the numbers of California pupils expelled from school has increased steadily. While there were some limited legal challenges to these new rules, the general picture was of informal and arbitrary enforcement practices that were not guided by due process or equal protection of the law. By all accounts, students of color were the most likely targets of these zero-tolerance policies. Data from the Oakland Unified School District for 2003 to 2004 showed that white students accounted for just 6 percent of the 4,297 students who were suspended that year. African American students made up 71 percent of those suspended. The very limited data on the reasons for school suspensions and expulsions suggest that most of these severe actions were not taken against students who brought weapons to school or engaged in violence. For example, in the Berkeley Unified School District the overwhelming majority of suspensions and expulsions were for "defying authority," i.e., talking back or arguing with teachers and other school staff (Berkeley Unified School District 2002).

Another crucial aspect of the war against the young was the movement to recriminalize juvenile status offenses. These are offenses such as truancy, curfew violations, running away, and "incorrigibility" that are only violations of the law if committed by minors. In the 1970s, there was a national reform movement to divert these youths from secure detention centers, keep them out of the formal juvenile court system, and expand the use of community-based organizations to deal with these family issues. California enacted legislation in 1978 (A.B. 3121) to remove status offenders from locked facilities and the formal justice system. Young women historically had been the primary targets of the status offense laws. Whereas young men were about as likely as girls to be arrested for juvenile status offenses, it was young women who were incarcerated for these behaviors. The perverse and prejudicial logic behind these policies was that girls needed to be protected from themselves, especially their nascent sexuality. The new law limiting the application of juvenile status offense laws significantly reduced the number of girls in state and county juvenile correctional institutions.

There was a rediscovery of the alleged value of strict enforcement of laws against truancy and the need to reestablish curfews for juveniles and increased incarceration for runaways. Many communities passed new local ordinances to restrict the behavior of young people. Courts and probation agencies used the pretext of violations of probation or violations of court orders to charge youth with offenses that could result in their incarceration. Thus, youths who were brought to court were ordered to attend school regularly, to be home before a specific time, or to cooperate with their guardians. Young people who allegedly failed to meet these rules could be sentenced for more serious charges. In a practice known as "boot strapping," youth who got into aggressive arguments with their parents or guardians could be charged with domestic violence. Children who were placed in foster care or group homes could be labeled as delinquents if they left these placements without official permission. Law enforcement and school officials asserted that threatening young people and their parents with criminal prosecutions would reduce truancy rates. All of these severe restrictions on young people were loudly justified as measures required for increased child protection.

The campaign to arrest and incarcerate young people for status offenses was sold to the public based on heightened fears about child abductions and sexual exploitation of young children. In California and across the nation, there were well-financed media campaigns focusing on missing and exploited children. The federal government pumped millions of dollars into publicity about missing children through the National Center on Missing and Exploited Children. Despite these millions of taxpayer funds, there is no documented case in which the center actually found a missing child.

Parents were frightened to death about the potential kidnapping of their children by strangers. Faces of children showed up on milk cartons. Other commercial enterprises sold identification and fingerprinting equipment to petrified parents. Schools and nonprofit groups started training programs to teach young children to avoid abduction. Despite these scare campaigns, the evidence grew that most of the missing and exploited children had either been taken by their noncustodial parents, usually in the context of bitter divorce proceedings, or they were teenagers that had run away from home. Some research suggested that many of these runaways were actually escaping from abusive living situations. The Federal Bureau of Investigation estimated that there were fewer than 200 abductions by strangers a year in the entire nation. Of course there were a very small number of child kidnappings and murders such as the Adam Walsh and Polly Klaas tragedies that galvanized worldwide media attention and further fueled the hysteria about missing children. Motorists were often greeted with highway signs and broadcast "Amber Alerts" telling us about the latest missing child. Many of these alerts proved inaccurate and created false impressions about the frequency of child abductions.

Young people are virtual sitting ducks for politicians and other public officials who want to push "get tough" crime policies. The immediate costs to cynical elected officials of fighting the war against the young appear to be minimal. Adolescents cannot or do not vote. Young people do not sit on the boards of director of corporations, foundations, universities, religious organizations, or large nonprofit organizations. Few unions regard young people as their constituents; rather, adolescents are often viewed as economic threats to older unionized workers. Youths were not invited to be active participants in the political discussions and decision-making forums that led to the war against the young. In the mainstream political process, youth are often used as "window dressing" and as a means to create campaign photo opportunities.

A school-based curriculum on civic engagement of the young is sorely lacking. Education in the politics of social justice is almost nonexistent in most public educational settings. Young people do not belong to well-heeled political lobby groups such as the American Association of Retired People, the National Rifle Association, or the Chamber of Commerce. The conventional media rarely seeks out a youth perspective on critical public policy questions. The viewpoints of adolescents are generally not measured by influential public polling organizations. The organizations that seek to be advocates for young people are chronically underfunded, understaffed, and largely ignored by the political establishment.

Adolescents in this society are a lucrative market for a broad range of commodities including tobacco, alcoholic beverages, fast food and snacks, trendy clothing, grooming aids, expensive electronic toys, music, and movies, to name a few products. Genuine aspects of youth culture are often co-opted by the media, which sells these images to young and old alike. For instance, the mass media embraced a powerful portrayal of violent, sexually promiscuous, drugged, urban, minority youths that is retailed to suburban and rural youngsters so that they can spend their disposable income to cultivate the "Gangsta" look at the carefully protected and sanitized suburban shopping malls. These harsh racist stereotypes promoted by the media are, in turn, used by adults to justify the need to increase social controls on the young.

The great American criminologist Marvin Wolfgang observed that fear of the young by adults is as old as human history. He wrote about a Sumerian tablet that revealed deep-seated fear that young people were the "barbarians at the gates" that would bring down the social order. Whether it was the sexually explicit young people of the 1920s Jazz Age, the rock and roll rebels of the 1950s, the culturally subversive hippies of the 1960s, or the hip-hop generation of the 1990s, adolescents have almost always signaled that the social norms could be changed, sometimes in ways frightening for adults. These concerns may be on the rise as the baby-boom generation is aging and facing retirement and senior citizens become the largest voting block in the nation. These fears intensify as young people of diverse racial and ethnic backgrounds make legitimate claims to be seen and heard. The perception that the young are wildly out of control and need tighter regulation is a longstanding and powerful cultural theme easily exploited by politicians, some religious leaders, and the media.

The Players

While we can comprehend "The Game" in sociological terms and focus on the structural forces that led to bad social policies for the young, it is equally important to expose the perfidy of those power-hungry politicians, government bureaucrats, and academic mountebanks that have fueled the war against the young. I would like to present a brief review of three dramatic California instances in which powerful and influential adults betrayed our young people. Besides talking about the main villains in the piece, I will discuss the smaller roles that others played in these examples of bad public policy.

A.B. 136 and the Rise and Fall of Chuck Quackenbush

For more than a half century, California law mandated that persons under the age of sixteen were to be tried in juvenile courts regardless of the gravity of their crimes. While there were very limited examples of persons between the ages of sixteen and eighteen being tried as adults, the vast majority of minors were handled in the juvenile justice system and served their sentences in the California Youth Authority, the mission of which was to pursue the goals of treatment and rehabilitation, not punishment. Before 1994, the maximum sentence that could be given to a youthful murderer under the age of sixteen was to be confined in the Youth Authority until age twenty-five. Other states began amending their laws to permit serious juvenile offenders to be tried as adults and placed in prisons. For example, New York State revised its sentencing laws in 1978 to allow young offenders above the age of fourteen to be handled in the adult criminal justice system. Throughout the country in the 1980s, states debated and passed new laws that sent more youths to the adult system. California was virtually alone among the large urbanized states to resist this urge to stiffen penalties for very young juvenile murderers.

All this changed as a politically ambitious Republican Legislator Chuck Quackenbush launched a media-focused set of hearings to support his bill, A.B. 136. The proposed legislation dropped the age at which children could be tried for murder in criminal courts and could face a potential prison sentence of life without the possibility of parole. Quackenbush used a time-tested method to push his agenda: he organized events at which the surviving relatives of murder victims talked about the tragic loss of their family members and publicly shared their unremitting sorrow.

The media, especially the local television evening news, has come to adore these stories. Cynical news directors often say, "if it bleeds it leads," and the focus on the suffering of ordinary citizens is compelling television. Not only is the viewer drawn to the drama of the tragic testimony, but there is also an emotional "rush" to viewers as they realize that the story is about someone else and not them. This is not unlike the emotional charge that is offered by horror movies or suspenseful television dramas: we get a chance to vicariously experience the pain or fear of others without paying the price. Some years ago, Danish sociologist Svend Ranulf (1938) pointed out that this sort of very emotional news coverage is often used by totalitarian regimes to build support for repressive government actions. Most important, this sort of journalism generally does not address questions about why these terrible events occur or what the citizenry might do to make their families safer. Violence is portrayed as the random and irrational acts of strangers, despite the fact that most violence occurs among people who are well acquainted with each other.

Quackenbush used A.B. 136 to strengthen his image as a crime-fighting conservative. He broadened his political rhetoric about A.B. 136 to encompass other conservative social concerns such as the alleged decline in personal responsibility and the claimed corrosive nature of the welfare system. As he noted, "Once you bring government into the family, you really are zapping the energy of society. People think, 'Why should I bust my tail to raise a family? Government will take care of all of that for us'" (Hubner and Wolfson 1996, 259). Quackenbush's argument for A.B. 136 also suggested, without providing any evidence, that the juvenile justice system was incapable of handling the "new breed" of young murderers.

Pushing all the fear buttons, Quackenbush warned that "The Little Monsters we have today who murder in cold blood are very dangerous individuals. They have to be punished and walled off from society for a very long period of time, if not forever" (Hubner and Wolfson 1996, 260). He asked if voters were willing to bet their lives or those of their family members on the ability to rehabilitate young killers. He went on to explain, "The way you turn things around is to make crime hurt. If you hurt a person in this society, then society has to hurt you back. It's very primitive, but people understand it" (Hubner and Wolfson 1996, 261).

These arguments certainly resonated with a strain of American social values that suggest that "an eye for an eye" or social revenge is an appropriate and effective response to crime. Further, there were several academic "players" such as James Q. Wilson, Charles Murray, and John DiIulio who were providing seemingly valid intellectual cover for these political arguments. These professor-crime warriors told us that America was about to be overrun by a generation of "super-predators" who were psychologically damaged and possessed lower-than-average intelligence and would only respond to blunt social reactions to their criminal behavior (Wilson and Hernnstein 1985; Murray and Cox 1979; DiIulio 1995). Employing language designed to scare white, middle-class voters, John DiIulio wrote about a coming "Crime Bomb" carried by the new generation of "fatherless, Godless, and jobless" juvenile super-predators who would be flooding America's streets (DiIulio 1995).

The highly questionable science produced by these conservative academics was trumpeted by right-wing think tanks and given enormous coverage in the press. They were invited to present their flawed research to legislators, to the U.S. Congress, and to other gatherings of elected officials.

More moderate members of the California legislature could not resist the pressures from the fear-mongering right wing, the strong, publicity-savvy victims' advocacy groups, and the hysterical media. A.B. 136 was quickly passed and signed into law in 1994. This was the same year that Californians were discussing the "Three Strikes and You're Out" ballot proposition for habitual and violent adult offenders. Trepidation about violent crime was on the political and media front burners, with the rhetoric flame turned up high.

A.B. 136 affected a relatively small number of young defendants, but the break with past juvenile justice traditions emphasizing the possibility of rehabilitation for very young criminals signaled the start of a stampede among elected officials to demonstrate who could be tougher on juvenile criminals. A few years later, this trend resulted in another politically motivated campaign to pass Proposition 21, which amended juvenile law to move the state's juvenile sentencing system toward becoming the harshest in the nation.

And what of the payoffs for the major player behind A.B. 136, Chuck Quackenbush? The formerly obscure Santa Clara County lawmaker used the publicity gained via his support of A.B. 136 to spearhead a statewide campaign to become elected as California's insurance commissioner. Virtually all of Quackenbush's well-funded television advertisements centered on his role to toughen laws against juvenile criminals. This might be an appropriate electoral theme if one was running for governor or attorney general, but crime control was not part of the job description of the insurance commissioner. Despite this logical disconnect, Quackenbush became California's elected insurance commissioner. Politic pundits declared that the former Notre Dame University graduate was a rising political star who might be destined for higher statewide or even national elective office.

Then something happened to derail the Quackenbush political bandwagon. A very high-profile series in the *Los Angeles Times* written by top investigative journalist Virginia Ellis (2000) presented an alarming set of facts. It turned out that Commissioner Quackenbush had made several secret deals with major insurance companies that allowed them to escape fines for mishandling up to thousands of claims resulting from the terrible Northridge earthquake. Quackenbush ignored the advice of his own legal staff that might have produced hundreds of millions in fines for the offending insurance companies. Further, the investigation revealed that Quackenbush and his aides had "strong-armed" some of these same corporations to donate more than $12 million to nonprofit foundations he created. Ellis uncovered confidential documents showing that Quackenbush used his powers as insurance commissioner to create a "political slush fund directed by highly paid consultants, to further his quest for higher public office." Pressures to have Quackenbush resign his office grew rapidly, but even in his last days in office the erstwhile crime fighter approved contracts that obliged taxpayers to pay more than $1 million for his legal fees and those of his top staff for the investigations of wrongdoing.

Commissioner Quackenbush received no jail time for these alleged felonies. He resigned his office and was able to move to Hawaii to avoid further legal entanglements. It does not appear that he was made to "hurt" for the damage he inflicted while in public office. Tragically, while

Quackenbush is now a long-forgotten subject of trivia questions in California politics, the harm to young people created by A.B. 136 continues.

Many liberal legislators argued that the passage of A.B. 136 would calm the panic over juvenile violence and would really only harm a very small number of youths. In 1994, 234 young people between the ages of fourteen and sixteen were arrested for homicide in the state of California (California Department of Justice, Criminal Justice Statistics Center, 1994). Opponents countered that A.B. 136 would just whet the appetite of ambitious politicians for more "raw meat" juvenile justice law reform. Unfortunately, Californians did not have to wait very long to see who was correct about these future predictions. After the enactment of A.B. 136, virtually every legislative session contained additional bills that made it easier to try juveniles as adults by expanding the list of crimes that could result in adult prosecution. Other bills moved the burden of proof from prosecutors to defendants to show that young people should *not* be transferred to criminal courts. Yet even these further "crackdown" measures did not satisfy the players.

The Fight over the Alameda "Super Jail" for Youth

Expanding local capacity to incarcerate more young people was another aspect of the California war against the young. Beginning in the late 1990s, the state legislature voted to reallocate federal funding that was meant to support the construction of new prisons to renovate and expand local juvenile correctional facilities. Legislative staffers thought that this move would force the Department of Corrections to give greater consideration to alternatives to prison for adults. Further, there was a general consensus that local juvenile detention facilities were in a state of disrepair; many of the buildings were over fifty years old and were plainly inadequate for their current mission. The Chief Probation Officers Association had tried to get a bond measure before the voters to help remedy these conditions. However, California voters had consistently rejected bonds for the improving or expanding juvenile correctional facilities or even for building new adult jails and state prisons. To meet the financial needs to expand the adult incarceration capacity, state and local officials did an end-run around the voters, relying instead on private financing to support prison and jail expansion. This method of public financing entailed higher interest rates to be paid to private investors, adding as much as an additional one-third to costs of prison and jail construction. Under President Bill Clinton, the federal government began making grants to the states to partially defray the costs of building new lockups. The California share of these funds exceeded $275 million per year. In the early years of this federal program, almost all of the grants went to adult facilities. Although most of the monies could be used for renovations and improvements, the federal program mandated that there be some, if only token, expansion in the number of custody beds.

The legislature assigned to the Board of Corrections (B.O.C.) the job of working with counties that wished to improve existing juvenile facilities or to build new ones. The B.O.C. created a protocol for counties to submit plans for improving and expanding their juvenile detention facilities. Counties received small planning grants and could apply to the B.O.C. for a share of the federal monies. This led to a virtual boom in detention bed construction across the state. Grants were given to forty of the fifty-eight counties, and, collectively, these projects expanded the detention bed capacity by 3,150 new beds, or a 50 percent expansion in juvenile beds. Besides the expanded capacity, the B.O.C. grants partially paid for replacing another 1,300 detention beds. This all happened during the late 1990s while juvenile arrests continued to decline. Moreover, California had traditionally possessed one of the very highest rates of juvenile detention in the nation. Thus, the Golden State, which used secure juvenile lockups more than any other large state, was creating the ability to greatly increase its power to incarcerate more young people.

The case of Alameda County and its proposed expansion of detention provides a fascinating case study of how an irrational public policy can be promoted. The county operated an aging 299-bed detention center that was located in the northern part of Alameda County, close to the neighborhoods in which most detained youths lived. The facility was in urgent need of repair and probably replacement. There were few youth-advocacy groups in the community that opposed spending funds to improve the conditions of confinement in the old juvenile hall. The county hired a Georgia-based planning firm that specialized in helping build new adult prisons to conduct a study of the needed renovations. Amazingly, the Georgia group proposed that the county build a new 540-bed juvenile hall to be located near the existing jail in the city of Dublin, far from the neighborhoods in which most detained youths lived. There were few accessible methods of public transportation that would permit the families of these incarcerated young people to visit their children. It was asserted that the existing detention center could not be retrofitted, because it sat on top of a major earthquake fault line.

The data provided to support the vast expansion of the juvenile hall were suspect, at best. The Georgia-based planners apparently misinterpreted Alameda County juvenile justice data, showing supposed increases in juvenile arrests and detention bookings, even though the Probation Department's own statistics showed a significant decline in these juvenile crime trends. The plan justifying more detention beds assumed a 50 percent growth in the county's youth population. However, these data relied on projections of population growth in the suburban and rural parts of the county. In fact, the growing numbers of new county residents who were moving into high-priced gated residential communities were unlikely to be candidates for the new expanded juvenile detention center. Rising real estate values were leading to more "gentrification" of traditional urban communities, driving the poorest families to seek housing in other Bay Area counties. The plan also used data on the highest-recorded monthly detention hall populations, exaggerating the real level of crowding. Finally, the Georgia group assumed that the Alameda juvenile justice system was functioning in an optimal manner, making maximum use of alternatives to secure confinement. None of these assumptions were true, but these premises allowed the plan to conclude that Alameda County must increase its detention bed capacity by 81 percent.

The county assembled a facility-planning group and applied to the B.O.C. for funding. They secured grants of almost $30 million to pay for needed renovations and approximately another $3 million to subsidize bed expansion. It should be noted that these B.O.C. funds would cover only a small proportion of the costs of the new 540-bed juvenile hall. Further, it was unclear how the financially strapped county would find the funding to add all of the additional staffing that would be required to operate the new facility.

At this point, the players who were mostly county bureaucrats and some elected officials were operating with little public scrutiny of their ambitious game plan. Enter a small band of dedicated youth organizers calling itself Books Not Bars (B.N.B.). This group questioned the need for the expanded detention capacity that would result in many more young people, especially minority youths, being locked up. In addition, B.N.B. questioned the perverse investments in more juvenile jail beds just as local budgets for youth programs, public school funding, welfare supports, and health care were being slashed. The proposed Dublin detention complex became known as "the super jail for kids." B.N.B. held a number of public forums and rallies that raised serious questions about the value of the county's plans. Theses idealistic and politically involved young people worked closely with a number of local and nationally respected juvenile justice research and policy groups such as the Center for Juvenile and Criminal Justice, the Commonweal Institute, the Youth Law Center, the National Juvenile Law Center, the Justice Policy Institute, and the National Council on Crime and Delinquency to support the case that the super jail was ill conceived and that more alternatives to detention should be created.

The mobilizing efforts of B.N.B. received intense media attention as the B.N.B. pled its case before the county board of supervisors. The group traveled to a statewide meeting of the B.O.C. to protest the grants to Alameda County. The B.O.C. decided to avoid the adverse publicity and voted to ask the county to revise and resubmit its application for funding. This was the first time the B.O.C. actually turned down, if only temporarily, a local proposal to build more detention beds.

Next, the game turned ugly as the supporters of the super jail felt the need to discredit all those who questioned their plans. In a whispering campaign, B.N.B. was labeled as a subversive organization with ties to radical political entities. More establishment adult critics of the plan were accused of withholding their views from county planners, even though the actual planning process involved only the input of the Georgia firm and local officials. Juvenile justice officials announced to the media that the existing building was unsafe and prone to severe earthquake damage. How could the local officials disregard the potential harm to the incarcerated children? When confronted with the question of why the juvenile court and the probation department leaders were willing to wait several years for the building of a new facility to "save these endangered children," and why there were no emergency steps to move the children to safer housing, these inquiries were met with silence.

Referencing Proposition 21, the backers of the super jail told the community that this new law required the building of a much larger detention capacity. Yet only about 12 percent or about 40 of the detained youth were there pending trial as adults. It was claimed that the detained population contained a high percentage of very violent youths, however, at least 25 percent of the juvenile hall residents were being held while awaiting placement in community group homes. Another group of young inmates was locked up for violating court orders or the rules of probation, not for new crimes. When pressed to bring in national experts to look at the existing youth in confinement and propose viable alternative programs, county officials decided to defer this analysis to a more global and more costly study of the entire juvenile justice system. This study was scheduled to be completed after the ground was broken for the expanded juvenile hall. The request for proposals for this study explicitly instructed the bidders not to focus on criticisms of the juvenile court or to revisit the need for a new and expanded juvenile hall.

The proponents of the super jail were eventually undone because residents of the Dublin community opposed the situating of the super jail in "their backyard." These suburban activists joined in common cause with B.N.B. to raise many additional questions about the need for such a large facility and the logic of placing it many miles from where the detained youth and their families resided. The Dublin activists found that county officials claimed to have performed a thorough analysis of alternative locations for the super jail, but no such study could be located. The super jail planners had to retreat and restart the process. Next, the sheriff proposed that the county take over an abandoned jail located in downtown Oakland that had been closed because the sheriff lacked the funds to operate it. Now the county juvenile justice leaders were fighting among themselves as B.N.B. was steadily but surely converting more members of the community, especially those in faith-based groups, to the view that the super jail was a big mistake. Several of the largest religious congregations in Alameda County went on record as opposing the super jail.

At their best, the Alameda proponents of the super jail could only marshal a three-to-two vote of the board of supervisors to go forward with the Dublin juvenile facility. The two opposition votes came from supervisors Keith Carson and Nate Miley, who represented the predominantly impoverished, minority communities of the county. The strongest support for the super jail came from Supervisor Scott Haggerty in whose district the new detention complex would be built, thereby creating an important revenue source for the local construction businesses. Supervisor Gail Steele also represented many of the more prosperous suburbs. She also was viewed as the champion of the probation officers' union that stood to benefit financially as more officers were hired to run the bigger facility. The last supervisor, Alice Lai-Bitker, represented a predominately white and politically conservative suburban community. She was heavily lobbied by youth advocates to oppose the super jail and actually switched her vote to oppose the project. The politically powerful sheriff announced that he would actively support a challenger to Lai-Bitker in the next election. Supervisor Lai-Bitker reversed herself again and rejoined the backers of the super jail. Despite this announcement, the sheriff still vigorously supported an alternative candidate to Lai-Bitker in the upcoming election.

Although few county employees were willing to be quoted for attribution, it was clear that county administrators were demanding loyalty to their agenda. One top county public health official was told that he would lose his job if he publicly questioned the need for the super jail. He declared that his job with the county did not mean the loss of his right to freely express his views about what was best for the public health of young people.

The opposition from Dublin residents, combined with the continued crusade by B.N.B., caused the players to retreat. With successive votes of the board of supervisors, the size of the facility began to shrink, although no new planning data were presented to justify these alterations. Next, the county planners reconsidered the safety of rebuilding the new facility on the existing site; apparently, the problematic earthquake fault was less serious than it had seemed. In the end, the board of supervisors voted unanimously to rebuild on the existing site and to add the minimum number of beds required to qualify for the federal funds. The super jail was dead and the tens of millions of taxpayer dollars that were invested in the planning and design of the Dublin facility resulted in a compromise that would have been acceptable to the youth advocates at the very beginning of the struggle. There were significant personnel changes in the top leadership of the probation department and the juvenile court, and this meant that some of the most forceful advocates of the super jail were no longer in the game.

The Remix

In the vernacular of contemporary music, a remix is a blending of components to reach a new creative level. One version of the remix involves sampling from classic popular music of the past fifty years that is combined with complex rhythmic additions and the innovative use of the spoken word. This form of the remix seems very applicable to finding the strategies to "beat down" the players and their game on behalf of young people. Expressed in more formal social science jargon, we might think of the remix as a pathway to social reconstruction.

The brief case studies presented in this paper suggest some ways to resist the war against the young. Some of the best of these approaches use very conventional methods of research and the presentation of solid evidence to stand up to the players. Public demonstrations and community mobilization proved to be crucial tools against the players and the game. Many of these direct community action strategies were very successful during the civil rights movement and the mobilization to end the Vietnam War. These successful social justice campaigns taught us the value of forging broad community coalitions that bring diverse groups to the table. These organizing efforts rest on a profound respect for all people, including the need to listen and respond to their immediate concerns.

The remix used litigation strategies, voter mobilization, and publicity to expose injustices and to educate the public. While there was ongoing dialogue with the players ("keep your friends close and your enemies closer"), the progressive groups never lost sight of the lesson that real social change needed to happen at the grassroots level.

The current generation of social reformers consists of a variety of very dedicated youth organizers who are savvy about using the mass media and come armed with research data to back up their arguments. Contemporary advocacy groups exhibit an impressive ability to sustain a diversity of ethnicity, gender, and age in their organizations. I remember that, after an early meeting with representatives of B.N.B., I confided with a colleague about how polite and respectful these young people were with us "old heads" from the 1960s. We were a lot angrier at their age, I concluded. My very wise colleague educated me that "They are just a whole lot smarter than we were in the 1960s," and had gotten everything they needed without resorting to confrontational tactics. The new generation of social justice advocates show a very sophisticated grasp of how to balance confrontation and accommodation. Most important, the new generation of reformers is focused on getting results.

In this remix of old and new, justice reformers can make a real difference in the lives of young people. First and foremost, strategies of social reconstruction demand that the players not be let off the hook. The cynical leaders in the war against the young must be publicly held to account for their actions. Second, we should not assume that most citizens know the abuses being practiced in their name. Helping the media to expose abusive and corrupt government practices is an important part of social reconstruction. Equally important is the ability to put forth real-world examples of what a better social policy should resemble. People must be inspired by positive and practical solutions to seemingly intractable problems. The players want us to believe that "nothing works."

Recently in California, the justice reformers have turned the tables on the players by using the tool of voter initiatives to usher in progressive policies. For too long these ballot measures brought us reactionary social policies such as Three Strikes and Proposition 21. Just a few years ago, advocates of progressive reform of state drug policies successfully passed Proposition 36, which allowed minor drug offenders to be diverted to treatment programs in lieu of jail. This measure was almost universally opposed by criminal justice system officials. Most establishment politicians avoided taking a public position on the measure. The proponents employed sophisticated polling and focus group techniques to craft their message. They learned that most Californians reported that someone in their immediate family was suffering from an addiction problem, and they felt that jailing their family members was an expensive and counterproductive approach. Proposition 36 passed by a wide margin.

Another progressive reform measure, Proposition 66, is designed to amend the pernicious Three Strikes Law and is supported by 65 percent of Californians as measured in a recent public opinion poll. The "Yes on 66" campaign is utilizing similar and sophisticated electoral strategies to those employed for passage of Proposition 36. Progressive reformers have also learned that recruiting financial supporters, especially via the Internet, can enable a serious statewide campaign to build momentum. Another voter initiative, Proposition 63, places a modest tax on millionaires to help fund badly needed programs to prevent and treat mental illness. Neither of these bold reforms could have successfully survived the onslaught of special interests if the game had played out only in the legislature and governor's office.

The remix has rediscovered the enormous power of giving young people back their voice. Jerome Miller, a champion of the old school justice reformers, built public support for closing the terrible youth prisons in Massachusetts in the early 1970s by using this approach. As commissioner of the Department of Youth Services, Miller set up public forums around the Bay State that featured youthful inmates who told their stories of maltreatment to civic and religious groups and the media. Their message was compelling and persuasive. Current reformers are also very attentive to the value of empowering young people. Groups such as The Beat Within work with incarcerated young people, encouraging them to write down their experiences and then communicate these powerful insights to the public. Books Not Bars has organized families of incarcerated young people to share their hopes and dreams that their children's lives can be redeemed. Organizations such as Youth Radio teach disadvantaged youths to use the tools of the electronic media to tell their stories.

The players in the war against the young can be very ruthless and the game can be very "cold," but the remix for social justice is showing us that the rules of the game can be changed and the players can be defeated. We have learned that the cynical exploitation of our frustrations, anxieties, and psychic distance from the young is too harmful to our communities for any of us to sit on the sidelines.

Reprinted from *Continuing the Struggle for Justice: 100 Years of the National Council on Crime and Delinquency*, edited by Barry Krisberg, Susan Marchionna, and Christopher Baird. Thousand Oaks, CA: Sage, 2006.

REFERENCES

Berkeley Unified School District. 2002. "Berkeley Unified School District Suspension Report, Spring 2001–2002." Unpublished raw data.

California Department of Education. 2004. "Expulsion Information for 2002–03." http://data1.cde.ca.gov/dataquest/Expulsion/ExpInfo1.asp?cYear=2002-03&cChoice=ExpInfo1&Pageno=1.

California Department of Justice, Criminal Justice Statistics Center. 1994. "Juvenile arrests reported, age by specific offense." Unpublished raw data.

Ching, Carrie. 2000. "Lock Up: Cracking Down on California's Youth. Why Are Big Corporations Backing the State's Prison-Industrial Proposition?" MetroActive (February 17). http://www.metroactive.com/papers/sonoma/02.17.00/proposition-0007.html.

DiIulio, John. 1995. "Arresting Ideas: Tougher Law Enforcement Is Driving Down Urban Crime." *Policy Review* 72: 12–16.

Edwards, Bob. 2000. *Morning Edition* [Radio broadcast]. National Public Radio, Inc. (September 12).

Ellis, Virginia. 2000. "The Fall of Commissioner Chuck Quackenbush." *Los Angeles Times* (Mar. 26–Nov. 30, series).

Hubner, John, and Jill Wolfson. 1996. *Somebody Else's Children: The Courts, the Kids, and the Struggle to Save America's Troubled Families*. New York: Crown.

Krisberg, Barry. 2005. *Juvenile Justice: Redeeming Our Children*. Thousand Oaks, CA: Sage.

Krisberg, Barry, and Carolyn Temin. 2001. *NCCD Focus: The Plight of Children Whose Parents Are Incarcerated*. Oakland, CA: National Council on Crime and Delinquency.

Murray, Charles A., and Lewis Cox. 1979. *Beyond Probation: Juvenile Corrections and the Chronic Delinquent*. Beverly Hills, CA: Sage.

Ranulf, Svend. 1938. *Moral Indignation and Middle Class Psychology*. Copenhagen: Levin & Munksgaard.

Shrag, Peter. 2000. "Prop. 21 Tale of Wilson, Ghost of Politics Past." *Fresno Bee* (February 2).

Wilson, James Q., and Richard J. Herrnstein. 1985. *Crime and Human Nature*. New York: Simon and Schuster.

[*Chapter 13*]

Transformative Justice and the Dismantling of Slavery's Legacy in Post-Modern America

Mary Louise Frampton

Introduction

Slavery was technically abolished in the United States 150 years ago, but the legacy of that atrocity persists at the beginning of the twenty-first century in a "war on crime" that has resulted in the mass incarceration of young American black men, a phenomenon that has been described as the "new Jim Crow" (Scotti and Kronenberg 2001; Glasser 2006).

In the United States we have only 5 percent of the world's population but 25 percent of the globe's prisoners. Our country incarcerates two million people a year, half of whom are African American. A young white male in this nation has a one-in-fifteen chance of being incarcerated; a Latino, one-in-ten; a black, one-in-three (Oliver 2001; Pattillo, Weiman, and Western 2004, 1–7; Robinson 2004, 2). This apartheid system is the scourge of a society that promises equal opportunity for all.

How did we allow this shameful situation to develop? I suggest that one critical factor in this complex equation is our failure as a country to deal honestly with the crimes of slavery and racial prejudice and our unwillingness as a society to confront these evils directly. Our desire to be shielded from this reality enables us to avoid the painful process of probing deeply into the multiple wounds that slavery and racial inequality have inflicted on us as a people, to cleanse our injuries, to repair the harm we have caused by making reparations, and to allow for true healing for both whites and blacks. Until that transformative type of restorative justice is accomplished, I do not think that we will be equipped to understand fully or reform a criminal justice policy that has the effect of denying a large proportion of black men the freedom they obtained 150 years ago. Unless that recognition and acknowledgment occur, we will continue to allow those who resist true equality for African Americans to exploit the racialized fear of white America and to convince the majority of people that our public safety requires the mass incarceration of black men.

As such, a transformative justice project is unlikely to be embraced by the majority of Americans in the near future. However, we must develop more immediate strategies for changing our criminal justice policies and beginning to dismantle this postmodern Jim Crow taint on our society.

A Century of Apartheid

If after the Civil War the United States had properly reconstructed its white privileged society, if the Freedman's Bureau had done the job for which it was intended, if "40 acres and a mule" had become a reality (Foner 1988, 50, 51, 68–71, 158–64)—in short, if former slaves had been granted economic and social freedom as well as physical freedom—the gaping wound in our history that slavery inflicted might have begun to heal. Instead, we placed a dirty bandage on it and congratulated ourselves for our good deed in emancipating the slaves. The Supreme Court justified this approach by ruling that the Constitution did not protect African Americans from private discrimination (Oshinsky 1997) and gave free rein to states to systematically codify the subordinate position of black people in the United States (Oshinsky 1997, 9). Over the next hundred years, we maintained a caste system known as Jim Crow that allowed that covered wound to fester.

The roots of this apartheid system were deep and varied: "For the planter, emancipation meant the loss of human property and the disruption of his labor supply. For the poor white farmer, it had . . . erased one of the two 'great distinctions' between himself and the Negro. The farmer was white and free; the Negro was black—but also free. How best to preserve the remaining distinction—white supremacy—would become an obsession" (Oshinsky 1997, 9). The enormous hostility against African American men was particularly evident in states in which blacks outnumbered whites and true political and economic freedom for African American men had the potential for dismantling white supremacy (Oshinsky 1997, 9).

In analyzing the new Jim Crow, the darker psychological undergirding of the old Jim Crow is of particular significance. In the minds of many Americans, the segregation of black men was justified by the "national obsession with the violent rape of white women by black men"; indeed, "revolt and rape by dehumanized black hordes was a classic white male nightmare" (Brownmiller 1975, 217). The myth of the "black rapist oversexualized black men and, by equating their sexuality with bestiality, stripped them of humanness" and "justified . . . [their] repression, segregation, and disenfranchisement" (Helg 2000, 588, 594). Such a stereotype was even used "to justify lynching and terrorize African Americans into conformity with Jim Crow and the racial etiquette": indeed, four thousand lynchings of African Americans occurred between 1889 and 1930 (Helg 2000; Davis n.d.).

For those who doubt that this myth is still deeply embedded in the American consciousness today, a review of websites and blogs provides potent evidence of its tenacity (Gaede 2004; Hutchinson 2004).

The War on Crime: Jim Crow's Newest Incarnation

Our Refusal to Acknowledge Legacies of Slavery and Jim Crow Allow Perpetuation of Discrimination in the Criminal Justice System

With the international embarrassment of a racially segregated American military during World War II, the end to legally imposed separation in the public schools in the 1950s, and the civil rights movement of the 1960s and 1970s, it appeared that some measure of real equality for African Americans was finally at hand in the second half of the twentieth century. Because overtly white supremacist views had been rejected by most of American society, many people assumed that we could progress seamlessly toward a more just country without directly confronting the severity of the original wound of slavery or the ensuing infection of apartheid.

A careful review of the attitudes of many white Americans in the 1960s, however, shows a more disquieting view. Even as the legal scaffolding of the old Jim Crow system was being dismantled, the majority of white Americans seemed incapable of acknowledging the effects of that apartheid system. In a 1963 poll, two-thirds of whites said they believed that blacks did not suffer from any discrimination in their communities

(*Newsweek* 1963; The Gallup Organization 1964). In 1969, 42 percent of whites told *Newsweek* that blacks had a better chance at a high-paying job than they themselves had, and 70 percent of whites held the view that blacks could improve conditions in slum housing if they had the desire to do so. Defying logic, this same poll also found that while whites insisted that African Americans were no longer the victims of discrimination, three-fourths of them felt that "the Negro is moving too fast" in his demands for equality (The Gallup Organization 2001; The Gallup Organization 1968).

By the late 1970s and early 1980s, the white attitude that "the Negro is moving too fast" in his quest for true equality achieved even greater traction. Just as Reconstruction efforts to provide some measure of both freedom and equality to former slaves after the Civil War were sabotaged, so too were those same prejudices at work a century later. In present-day America, however, the "new Jim Crow" has been cleverly camouflaged in a discourse about public safety and morality.

Is it merely coincidence that just at that critical point when true equality for blacks was in sight the numbers of incarcerated blacks began to rise? That we inaugurated a war on drugs and began building more prisons just as African Americans were beginning to obtain the rights that had been denied to them for centuries? Is it a mere coincidence that before the civil rights movement the vast majority of those incarcerated were white, while at the turn of this new century, half are black (Oliver 2001)? Why is it that the civil rights movement did not insure a continued progress toward social justice for African Americans?

In my view, a focus on our failure to confront and repair the wounds of slavery's legacy helps answer some of these questions. Having suffered from historical amnesia (or, rather, blind spots) we are bound to repeat the mistakes of the past. A nation that is largely unaware of the role of white privilege in its society is incapable of discerning its effects. Instead, our national cognitive dissonance on racial issues leads us to search for any explanation other than race to explain this mass incarceration of young African American men. One such explanation is that this new Jim Crow is simply the result of politics and capitalism. Certainly that is part of the equation, particularly in states such as California in which a partnership of uncommon bedfellows—the prison building industry, poor cities searching for jobs and a tax base, and the correctional officers' union—have jointly exploited and financed a Victims' Rights Movement for their own financial and political gain (Rosenblatt 1996; Beckett 1997; Parenti 2000; Sandy 2003; Samara n.d.). A second explanation is that the moral core of our nation is threatened by skyrocketing drug use, so we have simply enhanced our punishment for drug crimes in response. There is also some validity to this argument. Beginning with President Richard Nixon's war on drugs, the American drug policy has focused on drug use not as a medical or social problem but as a criminal one. Mandatory minimum sentences, asset forfeiture, and broadly drawn conspiracy laws have all contributed to a burgeoning prison population (Scotti and Kronenberg 2003; Roberts 2004, 1302). A final explanation—one not usually voiced but often harbored—is that African Americans simply commit more crime.

These rationales may seem sufficient to those who suffer from the malady of colorblindness. A closer and fuller examination, however, belies these assertions. The fact is that our prisons are populated primarily by nonviolent drug users. All the academic studies have shown that the drug use of blacks and whites is comparable. African Americans account for only about 14 percent of America's nonviolent drug offenses, yet they constitute 35 percent of the arrests, 55 percent of the convictions, and 75 percent of the prison admissions. Study after study has demonstrated that racial bias taints our entire criminal justice system (Human Rights Watch 2000).

Moreover, the fact is that the public support for a drug and crime policy is based primarily on a misapprehension that criminal activity is blossoming in this country and that only strict and retributive consequences can stem the rising tide of violence. Yet the reality is that crime has been on the decline for decades (Roberts 2004, 1275, n. 16; Justice Policy Institute 2000, 3). We should be asking ourselves why it is that the public has been so easily misled by misinformation.

Our Reluctance to Confront Wounds of Slavery and Jim Crow Also Affects Opportunities and Attitudes of Young African American Men

Our failure to heal the wounds of apartheid has also allowed a culture of crime to develop in poor areas of major metropolitan regions where jobs are virtually nonexistent (Cashin 2004, 237–48). The poverty rate for blacks is much higher than for whites; indeed, the average net worth of the white family is more than seven times that of the average African American family (Conley 2001). This economic caste system—a direct result of our unwillingness to provide (monetary) reparations along with many governmental policies with thinly disguised racial motivation —has resulted in desperately poor inner cities populated largely by people of color. In many such areas, the job of meeting the drug demands of middle- and upper-class white America is the best employment available (Cashin 2004, 245, n. 19).

There is another devastating consequence of our society's failure to repair the wounds of slavery and racial prejudice. Prominent African American scholars have documented a culture of despair among many young African American men that can lead to the "self-hate" about which Randall Robinson writes so eloquently. Recounting an encounter with a young black man, Robinson inquired, "How can somebody just take a gun, put it to someone's head, and pull the trigger without remorse?" The young man replied, "I thought you understood, but you do not understand at all. When you are where I am, it doesn't make any difference which way the gun is pointed. How can I value another life more than I do my own?" (Robinson 2004, 5, n. 2). Robinson attributes much of this despair to a lack of historical connection: "There is no greater crime that you can commit against a people than to strip them of their story of themselves" (Robinson 2004, 6).

Dismantling the New Jim Crow by Changing the Public Discourse on Crime and Race

In my judgment the best mechanism for confronting the legacies of slavery and Jim Crow and for healing the wounds that those practices inflicted is a transformative justice project that includes a significant educational and historical component and a reparations fund. Yet, in this day and age, most white Americans and even some black Americans are reluctant to directly confront issues of race. Until more people are able to recognize and accept white privilege and "unconscious racism" (Lawrence 1987), how do we have a discussion about racial prejudice in our criminal justice policy? How do we begin to change the public discourse so that the majority of people who might reject the concept of the "war on crime" as the new Jim Crow can nevertheless be persuaded to consider alternatives to the mass incarceration of black men? How can we plant the seeds?

Changing Crime Reporting: Converting
Racialized and Simplistic Approaches

At the Thelton E. Henderson Center for Social Justice at Boalt Hall School of Law at the University of California, Berkeley, we are taking some initial steps in that direction. Our work is based on the premise that fear, particularly racialized fear of violence, governs most of our criminal justice policy and that public policy will not change until a vibrant constituency demands change. There are two prerequisites for this change. First, the public must be provided with information that encourages it to view the issue of crime through a less racialized and more accurate lens. Second, people must be informed about the successful alternatives to incarceration and be provided access to the tools necessary to develop such programs in their communities. An obvious place to provide this new lens is the media. For this reason, we have developed a project called "Communities in Justice," in partnership with the U.C. Berkeley School of Journalism and the *Oakland Tribune*, to develop models for changing the way that crime is reported.

The research demonstrates that people's views about crime are profoundly affected by what they read in the newspaper and see on television (Iyengar 1991; Graber 1984; Zillman and Brosues 2000; Sherizen 1978). Those views then result in a criminal justice policy that perpetuates the fears and stereotypes that were developed to justify both the old and new Jim Crow. The studies show that the media can report on crime in a way that will change public perception. First, the empirical research shows that "news organizations report violent crime in a way that scares readers and viewers" (Stevens and Dorfman 2001, 7). Second, this research also demonstrates that "readers and viewers feel helpless about reducing violence in their communities" (Stevens and Dorfman 2001, 7). Hence, the challenge is to report on crime in a more accurate manner that reduces both the fear and the sense of helplessness.

The first problem with current crime reporting involves the cumulative choices of what is included in the news. Four clear patterns have evolved in the research. First, violent crime is emphasized. Second, the more unusual the crime, the greater the chances of its being reported. To be more specific, newspaper and television journalists report a small percentage of individual violent incidents at great length and with great precision. Unfortunately, this approach gives readers and viewers an inaccurate picture of both the crime in their communities and how violence affects them economically and emotionally. If the media were reporting accurately, the public would know, for example, that the number one violent felony arrest in California is domestic violence; indeed, this is one type of violence that is not on the decline (Stevens and Dorfman 2001, 13, 33; Meyers 1997). Third, even when real crime rates are declining, the coverage of crime remains constant or actually increases. Hence, even though crime in fact has decreased since 1993, almost 70 percent of people are sure that it is rising and identify the media's coverage of violent crime as increasing their personal fear of being a victim. Youth fare worse than their elders in news portrayals, so although violent crime by youth in 1998 was at its lowest point in the twenty-five year history of the National Crime Victimization Survey, 62 percent of those polled insisted that juvenile crime was the rise (Stevens and Dorfman 2001, 14, n. 26; Blackwell, Kwoh, and Pastor 2002, 180).

Last, and most disturbing, a disproportionate number of perpetrators on the news are people of color, especially African Americans, people of color are underrepresented as victims, and interracial crime is covered disproportionately (Blackwell, Glover, Kwoh, and Pastor 2002, 13; Dorfman and Schiraldi 2001). All of these factors enhance, rather than dispel, the violent stereotype of the African American man.

Another set of difficulties with the way that crime is reported is that reporters continue to cover crime and violence by talking only to law enforcement and criminal justice officials and experts. Moreover, they report a crime as a single event. Research shows that when crime is reported as a singular discrete event—the way most crime is reported—the reader or viewer will place all the blame on the perpetrator and occasionally on the victim. When the crime is reported in context and in depth, the reader tends to blame environmental factors, other people, and other situations. Readers develop not only a much more sophisticated and nuanced view of crime, but also a sense that there are a myriad of ways to prevent it (McManus and Dorfman 2003; Brooks, Schiraldi, and Ziedenberg 2000; McManus and Dorfman 2000).

Empowering Communities to Prevent Crime with a Public Health Approach

In addition to reducing the public's fear of crime, the media needs to communicate and demonstrate that ordinary citizens can both prevent crime and develop responses to crime that are more successful than incarceration. Most people understand that the criminal justice system is broken; they just believe they lack the expertise or the power to fix the problem. They assume that only courts and law enforcement agencies have the means and knowledge to make changes. Yet the reality is that there are many very successful violence prevention and restorative justice programs throughout the United States that incorporate regular (lay) people. Many in the media tend to ignore the fact that people are developing predictable, effective ways to reduce and prevent crime, and thus fail to provide the information that could make their readers and viewers feel less helpless. By reporting on such programs and telling the success stories, the media can encourage their patrons to try such approaches in their own communities.

For example, the media should report that since the late 1970s a new medical/scientific field has emerged that studies violence as a public health epidemic (Winett 1998). Like doctors who study heart disease or lung cancer, these specialists analyze the interactions among the victim, the agent of injury, and the environment, and then define the risk factors. Epidemiologists have identified the risk factors for violence as the ready availability of firearms and alcohol, racial discrimination, unemployment, violence in the media, lack of education, abuse as a child, witnessing violent acts in the home, isolation of the nuclear family, and belief in male dominance over women and girls. The U.S. Centers for Disease Control and Prevention initiated a program on violence prevention as early as 1983, and, in 1984, the U.S. Surgeon General declared that violence was a public health epidemic. Yet, the media's coverage of violent crime is largely devoid of this information (Stevens and Dorfman 2001, 8, n. 24, and 11–12).

Some comparisons will illustrate the point. Until the 1960s, traffic deaths and injuries were blamed on crazy or careless drivers and the media covered the issue with a focus on those bad actors. Then public health experts and injury control scientists studied the issue scientifically and advocated for changes: collapsible steering columns, seat belts, shoulder harnesses, roll bars, airbags, and safety glass. Engineers focused on ways to build roads that were safer. Legislators passed laws requiring seatbelts and imposed stiffer penalties for drunk drivers. As a result, when the media covers automobile accidents today, they report about use of seatbelts, alcohol use, and environmental conditions. Public attitudes about tobacco use have experienced similar changes. Historically it was the smoker who was blamed for having lung cancer. The stories that identified the connections between smoking and lung or heart disease consistently quoted researchers from the Tobacco Research Institute that refuted such links. Today the news reports that tobacco companies share in the responsibility for the illness and death resulting from smoking by manufacturing, marketing, and selling a product they know to be harmful and addictive (Stevens and Dorfman 2001, 11).

Similarly, if the media reported about environmental and other risk factors when it covered violent crime, the public would develop a more sophisticated view of the issue and could pinpoint the risk factors in their communities that they could work to eliminate.

Pursuing Restorative Justice Alternatives to Incarceration

A third way in which the media could change the public discourse about crime would be to provide information about the successful restorative justice programs and other alternatives to incarceration that enable individuals and communities to actively participate in responding to unlawful behavior and in repairing the harm caused by crime in their neighborhoods. The purpose of restorative justice—an ancient method of resolving disputes that is practiced in indigenous communities and in many countries around the world—is both to encourage accountability by the offender and to heal the wounds to victims, the community, and even the offender resulting from the crime (Van Ness and Strong 2000; Braithwaite 1989; Zehr 1990). Crime itself is viewed not as a transgression against the government or the state but as a violation against people and relationships, a tear in the fabric of our society. Indeed, for most of human history, the response to what are now called "crimes" was restorative justice because people understood that crime results in injuries to victims, neighborhoods, even the offenders themselves. A restorative justice model provides for participation by all the parties affected by the crime in the resolution of the problem and the repair of the damage so that true healing can occur (Van Ness and Strong 2000; Braithwaite 1989; Zehr 1990). In our modern society we have lost sight of the importance of such participation and have allowed ourselves to believe that only the criminal justice system has the expertise to solve these problems.

By focusing on the assumption of responsibilities by the offender, the examination of the needs of both the offender and the victim, and the healing of relationships, restorative justice is subject to objective and substantive evaluation. The success of a restorative justice project is measured not only by procedure, but also, more importantly, by outcome —whether the offender took responsibility, whether the harm has been repaired, whether the community is safer, whether the parties were empowered to be sufficiently constructive to avoid similar problems in the future. Restorative justice practitioners point out that once a crime has occurred, there is both a danger and an opportunity. The danger is that the community, the victim, and the offender will emerge from the criminal justice process further alienated, damaged, and disrespected and feeling both less safe and less cooperative. Too often this is what happens in our current criminal justice system. The opportunity is that injustice is recognized, equity is restored through restitution, and participants feel safer, more respectful, and more empowered (Schwartz, Hennessey, and Levitas 2003). Hundreds of small restorative justice programs throughout the country are providing this opportunity. Unfortunately, most of the public is not aware of these programs and too often their reach and influence are limited. By enhancing the visibility of such successful programs, we can encourage the development of similar restorative justice models that can both reduce the incarceration rates and repair the damage to communities.

Unfortunately, there is a dearth of rigorous research on the effectiveness of restorative justice programs to reduce the disproportionate incarceration of people of color. Hence, the Henderson Center for Social Justice is beginning to work with schools, juvenile justice authorities, and community organizations in Bay Area counties to research and develop restorative justice best practices and to assess their efficacy using both quantitative and qualitative measures. This research dovetails with efforts that counties are required to undertake pursuant to the Juvenile Justice Delinquency Prevention Act to reduce the disproportionate contact of minority juveniles with the juvenile justice system. Because this statute requires recipients of federal aid to determine whether children of color have disproportionate contact with juvenile justice systems, to analyze the reasons for that "DMC" (disproportionate minority contact), and then to develop intervention plans to increase the availability and quality of juvenile diversion and prevention programs, many juvenile justice authorities and educational institutions recognize the importance of working with both academic researchers and community organizations to craft successful approaches.

Coming full circle then, when the media reports crime in a less racialized and more complex manner and also reports about successful violence prevention and restorative justice programs that provide alternatives to incarceration, the public discourse can be profoundly altered. Hence, we are working with editors and reporters at the *Oakland Tribune* to develop interactive web pages that encourage dialogue with the readers. These pages will report crime data that include maps and neighborhoods and will show, for example, how alcohol outlets are risk factors for crime. They will provide information about violence prevention and restorative justice programs in similar communities and will include research on violence epidemiology and price tags for the current levels of crime. Research and case studies of successful restorative justice programs can form the basis of news stories that demonstrate the positive ways the community can become involved in developing both violence prevention programs and successful alternatives to incarceration.

The project is also working with the judges in the local juvenile court to create restorative justice models that will reduce the incarceration of youths of color. By partnering with the local schools to institute restorative justice peer courts that approach issues of crime and violence as opportunities for young offenders to be accountable to their victims, we are hoping to encourage young people to both take responsibility for their actions and receive help for the problems that were the risk factors in their behavior. When young people are given the opportunity not only to repair the harm that they caused but also to identify factors that will reduce the likelihood of future offending, their self-confidence is enhanced. This is a sea change from the current school to juvenile hall pipeline in California that results in high school expulsion rates and juvenile hall referrals for children of color (Insley 2001; Siman 2005; Harvard Civil Rights Project and the Advancement Project 2000).

Conclusion

These are small interdisciplinary beginnings. Yet they have already had effects. The *Oakland Tribune* has already changed the way it reports about crime and its editors are beginning to educate their colleagues in newspapers around the country. Law students and journalism students—the lawyers and journalists of tomorrow—are seeing crime and the criminal justice system with entirely new eyes. The hope is that with our small efforts coupled with the efforts of hundreds of other scholars and activists over the next several years, we can change criminal justice policy, reduce the incarceration rates for people of color, foster healthier communities, and even some day encourage a broader discussion about transformative justice and reparations for the legacy of slavery.

REFERENCES

Beckett, Katherine. 1997. *Making Crime Pay: Law and Order in Contemporary American Politics*. New York: Oxford University Press.

Blackwell, Angela Glover, Stewart Kwoh, and Manuel Pastor. 2002. *Searching for the Uncommon Common Ground: New Dimensions on Race in America*. New York: W. W. Norton.

Braithwaite, John. 1989. *Crime, Shame and Reintegration*. Cambridge, UK: Cambridge University Press.

Brooks, Kim, Vincent Schiraldi, and Jason Ziedenberg. 2000. "School House Hype: Two Years Later." Justice Policy Institute, Washington, DC. http://www.prison policy.org/scans/jpi/shh2.pdf.

Brownmiller, Susan. 1975. *Against Our Will: Men, Women, and Rape*. New York: Simon & Schuster.

Cashin, Sheryll. 2004. "The Failures of Integration: How Class and Race Are Undermining the American Dream." *Public Affairs*: 237–48.

Conley, Dalton. 2001. "The Black-White Wealth Gap." *The Nation* (March 26).

Davis, Ronald L. F. n.d. "Creating Jim Crow: In-Depth Essay." http://www.jimcrow history.org/resources/pdf/creating2.pdf.

Dorfman, Lori, and Vincent Schiraldi. 2001. *Off Balance: Youth, Race, and Crime in the News*. Washington, DC: Youth Law Center.

Foner, Eric. 1988. *Reconstruction: America's Unfinished Revolution, 1863–1877*. New York: HarperCollins.

Gaede, April. 2004. "White Women, Black Men and the Issue of Rape." *National Vanguard*. http://www.nationalvanguard.org./story.

The Gallup Organization. 1964. *Gallup Poll #699*, October.

———. 1968. *Gallup Poll #761*, May.

———. 2001. *Gallup Poll Social Audit. Black-White Relationships in the United States, 2001 Update*, July 10: 7–9.

Glasser, Ira. 2006. "Drug Busts = Jim Crow." *The Nation* (July 10).

Graber, Doris. 1984. *Processing the News: How People Tame the Information Tide*. New York: Longman.

Helg, Aline. 2000. "Black Men, Racial Stereotyping, and Violence in the U.S. South and Cuba at the Turn of the Century." *Society for Comparative Study of Society and History* 42: 576–604.

The Harvard Civil Rights Project and the Advancement Project. 2000. "Opportunities Suspended: The Devastating Consequences of Zero Tolerance and School Discipline Policies."

Human Rights Watch. 2000. "Racially Disproportionate Incarceration of Drug Offenders." In *Punishment and Prejudice: Racial Disparities in the War on Drugs.* http://www.hrw.org/reports/2000/usa/Rcedrg00-04.htm#P284_59547.

Hutchinson, Earl Ofari. 2004. "Race Was Inevitable in Bryant's Case." *Feature Report* (February 2). http://www.thehutchinsonreport.com/020204feature.htm.

Insley, Alicia C. 2001. "Comment: Suspending and Expelling Children from Educational Opportunity: Time to Reevaluate Zero Tolerance Policies." *American University Law Review* 50: 1039–73.

Iyengar, Shanto. 1991. *Is Anyone Responsible? How Television Frames Political Issues.* Chicago: University of Chicago Press.

Justice Policy Institute. 2000. "The Punishing Decade: Prison and Jail Estimates at the Millennium." Washington, DC. http://www.prisonpolicy.org/scans/punishing.pdf.

Kennedy, Joseph. 2003. "Drug Laws in Black and White." *Law and Contemporary Problems* 66: 153.

Lawrence, Charles. 1987. "The Id, the Ego and Equal Protection: Reckoning with Unconscious Racism." *Stanford Law Review* 39 (January): 317–88.

McManus, John, and Lori Dorfman. 2000. "Youth and Violence in California Newspapers." Berkeley Media Studies Group 9.

———. 2003. "Distracted by Drama: How the Press Portrays Intimate Partner Violence." Berkeley Media Studies Group 13.

Meyers, Marian. 1997. *News Coverage of Violence against Women: Engendering Blame.* Thousand Oaks, CA: Sage.

Newsweek. 1963. "How Whites Feel about Negroes: A Painful American Dilemma." October 21: 44–55.

Oliver, Pamela. 2001. "Racial Disparities in Imprisonment: Some Basic Information." *Focus* 21 (Spring): 28–31.

Oshinsky, David M. 1997. *Worse Than Slavery: Parchman Farm and the Ordeal of Jim Crow Justice.* New York: Free Press.

Parenti, Christian. 1999. *Lockdown America: Police and Prisons in the Age of Crisis.* New York: Verso.

Pattillo, Mary, David Weiman, and Bruce Western, eds. 2004. *Imprisoning America: The Social Effects of Mass Incarceration.* New York: Russell Sage Foundation.

Roberts, Dorothy. 2004. "The Social and Moral Costs of Mass Incarceration of African American Communities." *Stanford Law Review* 56 (April): 1271–1307.

Robinson, Randall. 2004. "The Importance of Slavery Reparations: What America

Owes to Blacks and What Blacks Owe to Each Other." *African-American Law and Policy Report* 6: 1–13.

Rosenblatt, Elihu. 1996. *Criminal Injustice: Confronting the Prison Crisis.* Boston: South End Press.

Samara, Tony. n.d. "Prisons, Punishments and Profiteers." Louisville, KY: University of Louisville. http://www.louisville.edu/journal/workplace/issue6/samara.html.

Sandy, Kathleen R. 2003. "The Discrimination Inherent in America's Drug War: Hidden Racism Revealed by Examining the Hysteria over Crack." *Alabama Law Review* 54 (Winter): 665.

Schwartz, Sunny, Michael Hennessey, and Leslie Levitas. 2003. "Restorative Justice and the Transformation of Jails: An Urban Sheriff's Case Study in Reducing Violence." *Police Practice and Research* 4: 399–410.

Scotti, Roseanne, and Steven Kronenberg. 2001. "U.S. Drug Laws: The New Jim Crow?" *Temple Political and Civil Rights Law Review 2000 Symposium* (Spring): 303–10.

Sherizen, Sanford. 1978. "Social Creation of Crime News: All the News Fitted to Print." In *Deviance and Mass Media*, Charles Winick, ed. Beverly Hills, CA: Sage.

Siman, Adira. 2005. "Challenging Zero Tolerance: Federal and State Legal Remedies for Students of Color." *Cornell Journal of Law and Public Policy* 14: 327–64.

Stevens, Jane Ellen, and Lori Dorfman. 2001. *Reporting on Violence; New Ideas for Television, Print and Web.* Berkeley, CA: Berkeley Media Studies Group.

Van Ness, Daniel, and Karen Heetderks Strong. 2000. *Restoring Justice.* Cincinnati: Anderson.

Winett, Liana. 1998. "Constructing Violence as a Public Health Problem." *Public Health Reports* 113: 498–507.

Zehr, Howard. 1990. *Changing Lenses: A New Focus for Criminal Justice.* Scottdale, PA: Herald.

Zillman, Dolf, and Hans-Bernd Brosues. 2000. *Exemplification in Communication: The Influence of Case Reports on the Perception of Issues.* Mahwah, NJ: Lawrence Erlbaum.

Afterword
Strategies of Resistance

Van Jones

In light of the present reality of 2007, we are desperately in need of new rhetorical and political strategies. There's something happening in the country that is a kind of musical chairs of racialized policing and racialized oppression. In the 1990s, this policing and repression was aimed at the black super-predator and gang banger, and also included the transferring of various weapons technology from the Pentagon to the local police. The focus of the police was on black males and the war on drugs. And so, as a black male, I was always terrified and mad at the police and couldn't comprehend why other people didn't understand what I was feeling.

Now this policing and repression has shifted a bit and is now about this different racialized "other." Suddenly, people are giving a little sigh of relief. There is something about this process of the policification of our society that requires that people imagine this is all about some group that's not theirs. People think, "Well, I'm not doing anything wrong, so it's not about me." But there are different rationales to policify the society.

A recent experience of mine illustrates this new reality. The other day I traded on racial privilege in the BART (Bay Area Rapid Transit) station. I saw these BART police, these paramilitary BART cops, who are wearing all black and carrying big rifles—it's like Robocop in the BART. I'm a thirty-six-year-old black guy and so usually, up until very recently, if I saw any kind of cop, I would be going in the other direction. But I was, like, "Hey, wassup?" They were, like, "Hey, wassup?" "Wassup?" And I realized, this must be how white people feel when they see a police officer because these cops aren't after black people, they're the antiterrorist cops.

That's their whole deal. So they're after the Arabs and the Muslims—and not me!

We have a problem about understanding what this racialized policing and racialized oppression is. It is so awful that it is hard to look at. One of the things going on is that there has been a shotgun wedding between the prison-industrial complex and the military-industrial complex. One can see that marriage in my previous example of weapons technology from the Pentagon showing up in the BART system. But it seems sort of normalized because it's not really about me. This war on crime is really a series of wars: the war on drugs, which is really war on black people, and the war on terror, which is a war on immigrants, Arabs, and Muslims; and it's that farfetched.

These two wars are basically the same thing: they are fought against a faceless racialized enemy that's both at home and abroad. An open-ended war gets declared, and there's no particular strategy to resolve it except to policify and take away rights, and there's no endgame. That's the war on drugs. It's the war on terror. And when the outcomes are examined, are we actually safer? Probably not.

So what we face now is the prospect of a seamless web of repression, from west Oakland to Baghdad, with the U.S. government being violent inside the U.S. border, violent at the U.S. border, and violent beyond the U.S. border. We are facing a national surveillance security state.

A national surveillance security state is not the same as the drug war we were fighting in the late 1980s and 1990s. It's qualitatively different. It merges the struggles for immigrant and refugee rights, for peace and freedom, and for racial justice into a new soup out of which could emerge a vibrant new resistance. This soup of struggles might create a situation from which individuals may not be able to find their way or their allies, and they find themselves, given their particular community, struggling alone under worsening conditions and against worsening odds.

So, the challenge is for us to look at our world and these struggles as they are and then begin to imagine what modes of resistance might present themselves so that we can escape the racialized oppression and policing our people face. People must confess that when the bull's eye is not on their forehead, it is easier to look the other way. That is the real danger and seductiveness of what we are dealing with.

There is a strategy to deal with the problems of racialized oppression that I think is important, and that I want to mention, though it's not my own: Prisons are rank expressions of racism and capitalism, reminiscent of slavery as an institution, and they should be abolished. I think that's a fine strategy. That is one option for dealing with our current problems.

I want to suggest some other rhetorical strategies that may seem unorthodox from a good leftie like myself, but that may actually shake up the current thinking on racialized oppression and policing.

Progressives need to own this question of community safety and make it ours. We cannot continue to be pummeled and beaten by profiteering incarcerators and the right-wingers who profess to somehow be the guardians of public safety. I live in a low-income community of color and I refuse to be lectured by some white guy Republican from the suburbs about the need for public safety when he actually has it. The strategy by which he has it isn't more police and more prisons. The safest communities are the communities that have the best jobs, the best education, and the best opportunities for young people. So if we want to have a strategy for community and public safety, let's use a strategy that's working in the suburbs. In my community there needs to be a level of rhetoric that matters in these kind of struggles. We've got to be able to say: "Actually, *we* are the custodians of a real community-safety strategy, and you, sir, are a profiteer. You, Mr. Professional Incarcerator, Mr. Right-Wing Cheerleader for your professional incarcerating friends, are actually complicit in a self-dealing bureaucracy. You want to talk about bloated governmental bureaucracies? Don't talk to me about the welfare system. Talk to me about the prison system. The prison system is a self-dealing, swollen government bureaucracy, with a monopoly on public-safety dollars. And the worse it performs, the more money it gets. The worse it performs, the less safe my community is. That is a self-dealing bureaucracy. That is a monopoly with predictable results."

Why should we not say: "You, with your twenty- to thirty-year unbroken run of massive budget increases, you should now be subject to accountability measures and evaluation." We're going to evaluate teachers and test the students twenty-seven times a year. Can we test the wardens? Can we evaluate the wardens based on how well the people who come through their institutions do? One has to begin to run back against the incarcerators, the rhetoric, and the logic that they use to destroy the things about which we care.

We can say: "You are a monopolist. We want you to have to compete for your public-safety dollars with coaches, with counselors, with art teachers, with ballet instructors, and if, in fact, it turns out that art teachers can do with dimes, can create more community safety, more peaceful communities than you, Mr. Incarcerator, can do with dollars, explain to me why it is you deserve to maintain your monopoly on those funds." This is one rhetorical strategy that may hold some promise.

A second strategy is to say that we can't really resolve this thing inside of the tug-of-war as it is currently presented to us. Bill Clinton got a lot of flak in 1996 for his strategy of triangulation. But, he won! So I'd like to think about what a triangulation strategy would look like for us. From a big-picture point of view, the welfare state is fighting the warfare state. The old-style liberals, the old Democratic Party is fighting desperately somehow to defend the old welfare state, the Great Society, the New Deal, all the achievements of the last century, and they are losing. They are losing out to this right-wing vision of a warfare state that the government shouldn't be in the business of helping people, but it should be in the business of keeping order domestically and globally. This vision of a leaner, meaner, primarily violent (for lack of a better term) state—this is the debate as we find it: The nanny state versus the Robocop state. Who's going to win that?

It's conceivable that we can say that we want a third way out. We don't actually want to defend some of the precious programs of the glorified New Deal and Great Society as they were, and we don't want that sort of warfare state either. There's a vision of the U.S. government, capitalist government, as a potential partner to those of us who are trying to solve problems in our communities rationally, effectively, and efficiently. Why is that important? It's important because there's a crisis of imagination at the progressive end of the ledger, and if we can't imagine a new role for the U.S. government or for government in general, then we're left defending the old role, which has basically been discredited.

The right is proposing a new role—again, what I would call the warfare state. I would say that the problem makers in our community right now have government support. The incarcerators create more problems than they solve because they take damaged people, add damage to them, and send them back in the community and call it justice and term it a public-safety strategy. That's not justice, and it's not a public-safety strategy. You add damage to damage, you get more damage. Hence, the incarcerators actually are the problem makers. The polluters are the problem makers. From my point of view, the warmongers are the problem makers. And they get billions.

The problem solvers get pennies: the teachers, the nurses, the coaches, the counselors, environmentally speaking, the little eco-entrepreneurs that are trying to come up with world-saving technologies that will give us energy without poisoning us. They get pennies. In contrast, the big polluters —oil and gas interests—received $87 billion dollars from the U.S. government last year.

Is there a way for us to not talk about left versus right, nanny state versus Robocop state, but instead about getting the government on the side of the people who are trying to solve the problems, who need a partner to solve those problems well? Is that a rhetorical strategy that can then let us talk to ordinary people about the results that we want (safe, healthy communities) and the strategies to get there (public-private community partnerships) that don't put us on the side of, frankly, fairly discredited ideas of government largesse?

I'd also like to bring up political strategy, and this is a little bit more of a head-scratcher. It's difficult to think politically any more on the left because we are so accustomed to such a crisis response. A lot of our identity politics are important but often add up to less than the sum of our parts. It's sort of like asking which crisis are you going to respond to with the most urgency when every crisis needs urgency. But if you look at what the right wing has been able to accomplish (in the 1980s, Reagan gave the courts to the right wing; in the 1990s, Newt Gingrich gave Congress to the right wing, and then in 2000, Bush gave the executive branch and the Pentagon to the right wing), it has allowed all three branches of government to be dominated by what you could describe as the military-petroleum complex in alliance with the religious right.

There is no ethnic politics that can go up against that. People can't do their black power or women's power thing against that and win. It's all important, but against the military-petroleum-religious right alliance, everything else is going to obviously be inadequate.

What we have to do is hold onto the gains in our racial-justice struggles and our gender-justice struggles and our disability rights struggles and our lesbian-gay-bisexual-transgender rights struggles. But we also have to begin to think politically about how we can build a governing majority again. How can we put together, for the lack of a better term, a New Deal coalition for the new century? What would that look like? Can we give ourselves permission to say that what we have to do to solve the prison crisis, what we have to do to solve the immigration crisis, what we have to do to solve the warmongering that's swept the country, what we have to do to solve any of these problems is that we have to be able to govern. We have to be able to govern in a new way, govern in a new direction, govern on partnership principles, both domestically and abroad, govern with the idea of restorative justice, a healing form of justice and not an add-damage-to-damage justice, govern with a view toward restorative economics as opposed to the suicide economics of massive consumption at 20 percent more than the Earth can regenerate.

Can we give ourselves permission politically to say that we want to govern? This is difficult for the left because it has been a protest bloc for so long. We look at the government as a source of rights and something that can defend rights, while the right wing looks at it as a big piggy bank to reward its various constituencies.

In sum, the present success of the right, the domination of the incarcerators, and punitive logic require of us a new rhetoric. Some of this rhetoric uses the argument of the right against it, but some of it is honest, hopeful, and aspirational. It requires new strategies that are not just responses to crises and identity based but politically based and vision driven.

The success of the right also requires the left to have a different relationship with the U.S. government as a whole. In order to be successful, in order to provide a way out, we have to be able to say that we actually want the U.S. government to lead the world, not in war, not in incarceration, not in pollution, but in human rights, in world-saving, green technologies, in showing a rainbow planet how a rainbow country can pull together and solve tough problems. If we're willing to do that, I think we can conceivably escape this noose and, much more important, bring the genius of America, the best side of America back into the forefront of our national life.

About the Contributors

Jessie Allen is an associate council at the Brennan Center for Justice, New York University School of Law. She also works as a litigator and public educator regarding felony disenfranchisement laws.

Elijah Anderson is William K. Lanman, Jr., Professor of Sociology at Yale University. His books include *Code of the Street* and *A Place in the Corner.*

Katherine Beckett is Associate Professor of Sociology at the University of Washington, Seattle, and author of *The Politics of Injustice: Crime and Punishment in America.*

Todd R. Clear is Distinguished Professor of Criminology at John Jay College of Criminal Justice, City University of New York. His books include *Community Justice* and *What is Community Justice?*

Mary Louise Frampton is the director of the Center for Social Justice at Boalt Hall School of Law, University of California, Berkeley.

Angelina Snodgrass Godoy is an assistant professor of Law, Societies, and Justice at the University of Washington, Seattle, and author of *Popular Injustice.*

Ian Haney López is a professor of Law at Boalt Hall School of Law, University of California, Berkeley. He is the author of *White by Law* (NYU Press) and *Racism on Trial.*

Kamala D. Harris is the District Attorney of San Francisco. She is the first woman and the first African American to hold the position in the state of California.

Steve Herbert is an associate professor of Geography and Law, Societies, and Justice at the University of Washington, Seattle. He is the author of *Citizens, Cops, and Power* and *Policing Space.*

Van Jones is founder and executive director of the Ella Baker Center for Human Rights in Oakland, California.

Barry Krisberg is president of the National Council on Crime and Delinquency and serves as clinical professor of psychiatry at the University of Hawaii. He is the author of *Crime and Privilege* and *Juvenile Justice*.

Gerald P. López is Professor of Law at the New York University School of Law, where he is also director of the Center for Community Problem Solving. He is the author of *Rebellious Lawyering*.

Mona Lynch is Professor of Justice Studies at San Jose University.

William Lyons is an associate professor of Political Science at the University of Akron, Ohio, where he also directs the Center for Conflict Management. He is coauthor of *Punishing Schools*.

Jonathan Simon is Professor of Law at Boalt Hall School of Law, University of California, Berkeley, and author of *Governing through Crime*.

Loïc Wacquant is Distinguished University Professor of Sociology and Anthropology at the New School for Social Research in New York, and a researcher at the Center for European Sociology in Paris. He is the author of *Deadly Symbiosis*.

Index

9/11. *See* September 11, 2001

Abu Ghraib, 101
Academics, 11
Adjudication withheld, 171, 172
Administrative (regulatory) agencies, 53, 59
Adolescence, 193
African Americans, 3, 8, 9, 10, 15, 17, 27, 28, 30, 50, 73, 74, 77, 82, 88, 93, 125, 127, 145, 168, 169, 171, 174, 180, 190, 207, 208, 210, 211, 214
Aid to Families with Dependent Children (AFDC), 24
Alameda County, Calif., 146, 198, 199, 201
Alcoholic, 76
Al Qaeda, 39
"Amber Alerts," 191
American: exceptionalism, 39; punitiveness, 13
American Association of Retired People, 192
Anti-terrorism and Effective Death Penalty Act of 1996, 44, 55
Anti-terrorism police, 223
Apartheid, 211
Apprendi v. New Jersey, 57
Arabs, 224
Asians, 11
Attaint, ancient concept of, 168
Authoritarianism, 39, 40
Automobile accidents, 215
Azpuru, Dinorah, 41

Baby-boom generation, 16, 193
Baghdad, Iraq, 18, 224
Ballot initiatives, 46, 204
Bankruptcy, 59
Barrios, 97
Bay Area Rapid Transit (BART), 223

Bay Area (Northern California), 199
Beckett, Katherine, 26, 45, 64
Berkeley, California, 145
Berkeley Unified School District, 190
Black Codes, 171
Black Panthers, 28
Blacks. *See* African Americans
Black suffrage, 17
Blumstein, Alfred, 61
Boalt Hall Center for Social Justice, 18
Bolivia, 38
Books Not Bars (B.N.B.), 199, 207
"Broken windows policing," 15, 55, 110, 111
Brooklyn, New York, 66
Brown v. Board of Education (1954), 174
Burger Court, 51
Burton, Representative Dan, 39
Bush administration, 56, 139n. 9
Bush, President George H. W., 7
Bush, President George W., 5, 56, 128, 135

California, 31, 146, 187, 193, 198, 204
California Correctional Peace Officers Association (CCPOA), 189
California propositions: Proposition 21, 200; Proposition 36, 204; Proposition 63, 204; Proposition 66, 204
Campaign to Hire People with Criminal Records, 17
Cancer, lung, 216
Capitalism, 23, 27, 30, 32, 224
Capital punishment. *See* Death penalty
Carceral, 3; apparatus, 25; *-assistential continuum,* 29; boom, 23; growth, 32; hypertrophy, 26; institution, 28; system, 2, 32;
Center for Juvenile and Criminal Justice, 200
Center for Community Problem Solving at New York University Law School, 17, 151

Centers for Disease Control and Prevention, 215
Central America, 39, 40, 41, 43
Chain gang, 94
Chamber of Commerce, 192
Charter schools. *See* Schools, charter
Chavez, Cesar, 145
Chessman, Caryl, 91, 101
Chicago, 67
Child protection, 191
Children, 77, 78, 79, 149, 187, 191
Church, 76, 138,
Cincinnati, 112
Citizens, 130, 136, 137, 138n. 5, 169; citizenship, 38, 167
Civility laws, 107, 110, 117
Civil rights, 7, 55, 145; era 9; movement, 7, 14, 34, 203, 209, 210; revolution, 27, 31
Civil Rights Act of 1964, 6
Civil war(s) 41, 169, 170, 181, 208
Class and caste structure, 25, 97, 98
Clemency, 168
Cleveland, Ohio, 66, 67
Climate change, 16
Clinton, President Bill, 28, 128, 198, 226
Code of the streets. *See* Street, "code"
Cohen, Stanley, 106, 108, 118
Cold war, 2; era, 30
Commonweal Institute, 200
Communists, 41
Community, 2, 4, 14, 17, 18, 49, 54, 55, 133, 199; based control, 106; police strategies 15, 117, 147; prosecution, 117; safety, 14; -safety strategy, 18; supervision, 106
Congress, 14, 53, 195
Conservatives, 45, 52
Constitution, the U.S., 51, 52, 168
Constitutional law, 49, 58
Contingent employment, 27
Convict laborers, 31
Convicts. *See* Prisoners
Correctional facilities, 29
Correctional firms, 26
Correctional health care, 33
Correctional industrial complex, 64
Corruption, 40, 41
Cotton v. Fordice (1998), 176
Courts, 215; court oversight, 32
Crack, 76

Crime, 7, 66, 68, 92, 106, 116, 117, 134, 145, 147, 216; control, 2, 6, 9, 13, 32, 51; deal, 13, 50, 54, 56, 59; debate, 4; decline in, 16, 62, 63, 64; fear of, 7, 10, 39, 41, 45; insecurity, 13; policy, 13, 187; prevention 145, 147, 148; problems of, 11, 12, 97; rates, 1, 40, 45, 62; risk, 3, 5; security, 11; serious, 23
Criminal justice, 12, 19, 38, 116, 117, 134, 169, 180, 187; experts 17; law, 111, 116; offender, 92; policy, 134; problems, 12; supervision, 24; system, 8, 10, 18, 25, 30, 32, 50, 67, 106, 153, 171, 181, 216
Criminal record, 4, 159
Criminology, 92
Crips, 100
Crist, Charlie, governor of Florida, 167, 168
Culture: of control, 137; of fear, 7, 16
Cummings, Homer, U.S. Attorney General, 58

Davis, Mike, 133
Darwinian, 137n. 4
Death penalty, 14, 94, 95
Defense attorneys, 146
Defensible space, 49
Democracy, 2, 3, 12, 13, 38, 40, 52, 57, 130, 131, 132, 134, 136, 166; democratization, 44, 45
Democrats, Democratic Party, 6, 7, 52, 226
Deregulated labor, 33
Deregulation, 109
Deskilled labor market, 25
Desocialized wage labor, 31
Desocialized wage work, 25
Detention facilities, 27
Deviance, 15, 106, 123; deviant subjects, 15
Dictatorship, 12, 41
DiIulio, John, 195
Disability rights struggles, 227
Discrimination, 208, 209
Disenfranchisement (social, economic and political) 9. *See also* Felon disenfranchisement
Disorder, 110, 117, 134
Disorganization, 76
District attorney, role of, 147
Divorce, 191
Douglas, Mary 126

Dred Scott decision. 51
Drug(s), 40, 41, 75, 138n. 5; offenses, 25, 103n. 4, 181; testing, 29, 135; trade, 62; use, 9, 135
Dual-service economy, 28
Dublin, California, 198, 201, 202
Due process, 30, 116
Durham, North Carolina, 67

East Los Angeles. *See* Los Angeles, East
Ecology of fear, 133
Economy, 4, 8, 32
Education, 28, 31, 33, 49
Eighth Amendment, proportionality principle of, 51
Eisenhower, President Dwight, 8
Ellis, Virginia 196
El Salvador, 38, 39, 41
Empiricism, 53
Employment, unemployment, 4, 26, 28, 49; unemployment problem, 4
England, 34n. 2
Environmental justice, 16
Equal protection clause, 172, 181
Ethnoracial exclusion, 27
European Union, 26
Evans, Linda, 32
Evers, Medgar, 145
Executive power, 12
Experts, 91, 155

Family(ies), 3, 133, 138n. 5, 198
Family wealth, 126
Federal Bureau of Investigation (F.B.I.), 38, 62, 191
Fear, 135, 137; -based approach to conflict or difference, 16; of crime, 7, 10, 39, 41, 45
Federal courts, 17, 58
Feedback effect, of incarceration, 5
Felon disenfranchisement, 10, 11, 45, 56, 58, 169, 176, 178, 179, 181; in Alabama, 172, 183n. 8; in Florida 17, 166, 168, 169, 170, 172, 177, 181, 182; laws, 3, 17
Felonies, 34
Felony disenfranchisement. *See* Felon disenfranchisement
Ferguson, Anne, 123
Fifteenth Amendment, 6, 181
Florida, 17, 166, 167, 168, 169, 171, 176;

constitution, 170, 178; rules of executive clemency, 182n. 3
Folsom, 153
Food Stamps, 24
Fordist industrial economy, 27
Fordist-Keynesian social compact, 33
Formalism, 55
"Four freedoms" of FDR, 52
Fourteenth Amendment, 6, 51
France, 24, 33, 34n. 2
Frank, Thomas, 124; 139
Freedman's Bureau, 208
Freedom, 13

Gangs, 27, 28, 39, 46, 131, 187, 188; gang banger 223; gang culture, 38, 192; "-mega," 38
Gangsta rap musicians, 28
Garland, David, 19, 90, 94
Gendered division of labor, 29
Gender-justice struggles, 227
Genocide, 40, 41
Gentrification, 199
Ghetto, 9, 13, 25, 27, 28, 33, 51, 97; (hyper), 34n. 4; poor, 73
Gibson, Timothy, 109
Gingrich, Newt, 227
Giuliani, Rudolph, 118n. 1
Glassner, Barry, 125
Global: economy, 13; warming, 1
Globalization, 30
Goldberg, Eve, 32
Goldwater, Barry, 52
Governance, 12, 13, 15
Governing through crime, 44, 51, 57, 137
Government of poverty, 25, 27
Governors, 196
Grace, Nancy, 99
"Great Migration" from southern states, 27
Great penal experiment, the, 14, 61. *See also* Penal
Great Society, 226
Green technologies, 228
Guantamo Bay, Cuba 101, 135
Guards. *See* Prison, guards
Guatemala, 38, 39, 41
Guns, 75

Habeas jurisprudence, 55

Hall, Stuart, 137
Harsh penal measures, 13
Health care, 31, 33, 199
Henderson, Judge Thelton (Calif.), 58, 213
Heroin, 153
Hispanic youth, 171
Hobbes, Thomas, 137
Homeless, 107, 111, 114
Homicide, 146
Homicide rate in Latin America, 39
Honor, 81
Hope, 160
Horton, Willie, 7
Housing, 31
Human rights, 13, 41, 43, 56; abuses, 40, 228
Hunter v. Underwood (1985), 172, 183n. 8
Hyper-imprisonment. See Imprisonment, hyper-

Identity politics, 227
Immigrants, 34n. 6, 97, 224; Asian, 27; European, 25; Mexican; 27
Immigration, 49; illegal, 68
Imprisonment, 4, 14, 25, 27, 31; hyper-, 12
Incarceration, 1, 27, 30, 51, 56, 62, 63, 66, 107, 147, 160, 187, 190, 197, 204, 207, 215, 228; alternatives to, 189, 213, 216, 217; hyper-incarceration, 26, 32; "mass," 3, 31, 55, 56, 58, 107, 208, 212; rate, 61, 66, 67, 94, 106
Individual responsibility, 31
Inequality 65, 109,
Informal economy 25, 26, 109
Inmates. *See* Prisoners
Inmate wages. *See* Prisoners, wages of
Inner-city communities, 8, 44, 73, 75, 78, 84, 87, 125, 127, 129, 133, 212
International criminal court, 135
Iowa, 166
Iraq, invasion of, 135
Italy, 24

Jail, 2, 8, 27, 32, 99, 112, 152, 197
Jim Crow, 9, 13, 51, 207, 208, 209, 210
Johnson, President Lyndon, 6, 52, 55
Johnson v. Bush (2005), 184nn. 9, 13
Johnson v. California, 57
Judges, 10, 31, 171
Judicial system, 15

Juries, 10
Justice Policy Institute, 200
Justice system. *See* Criminal justice, system
Juvenile: arrests, 198; correctional facilities, 197, 198; courts, 193, 218; delinquency (crime), 65, 187, 198; justice, 197, 200, 217; sentencing, 196

Keeping Our Kids Out of the Criminal Justice System Campaign, 17
Kennedy, Bobby, 52
Klass, Polly, 191
Klein, Jennifer, 52, 59n. 1
Koonings, Kees, 41
Kruijt, Dirk, 41
Kyoto Accords, 135

Labor, 26; force, 26; market, 3, 26; supply, 26
Las Vegas, Nevada, 28
Latin America, 39, 40, 41, 44
Latinos, 11, 54, 146, 207
Law and order, 128; "Law and Order" TV show, 103n. 5
Law enforcement, 41, 149, 171, 180, 188, 191, 214, 215
Lawyers, 171
Legal realism, 53, 54
Lesbian-gay-bisexual-transgender rights struggles, 227
Liberal-paternalist state, 29, 31
Liberals, 52
Liberal theory, 43
Liberty, 48, 54
Lifers, 33
Life without Parole (LWOP), 102n. 3, 194
Lincoln, Abraham, 168
Loitering laws, 111
Los Angeles, 38, 154; East, 152, 153
Los Angeles Police Department, 188
Low-income urban populations, 33

M-18 (mega-gang), 38. *See also* Mara Salvatrucha (mega-gang)
Machiavelli, Nicolo, 137
Mafia, 41
Mandatory prison sentences, 211
Manhattan, 112
Manpower Incorporated 24

Mara Salvatrucha (mega-gang), 38, 39
Massachusetts, 204
Mass imprisonment, 4, 8, 13
Mass incarceration. *See* Incarceration, "mass"
Media, 9, 215
Medicare, 135
Metal detectors, 189
Mexico, 153, 154
Michigan, 29
Military-industrial complex, 8, 18, 30, 224
Military policy, 32
Miller, Jerome, 204
Minorities, 8, 10; minority communities, 9, 45, 49
Mississippi, 174, 175, 177, 184n. 15
Molina, General Otto Perez (Guatemala), 41
Monster, 96, 195
Moralism, 55
Mulcahy, Michael, 111
Murder, 194, 195; rate, 14
Murray, Charles, 195
Muslims, 224

Nanny state, 226
National Council on Crime and Delinquency, 200
National defense, 32
National Rifle Association, 192
National surveillance security state, 224
NATO, 135
Neo-liberal, 13, 38, 44, 45
New Deal, 50, 52, 53, 54, 58, 59, 127, 226, 227
New York, N.Y., 17, 67, 118n. 1
Nixon, President Richard, 6, 212
"No Child Left Behind" law, 59
Northridge (Calif.) earthquake, 196

Oakland (Calif.), 201, 213, 224
Oakland Tribune, 218
Offender: accountability, 18; atonement, 18
"Off-limits orders," 107
Oklahoma City bombing, 44
"Operation Hammer," 188
Organized labor, 59

Parks, 111, 115
Parole, 29, 91; officers, 31; supervision, 15
Patriot Act, 135

Patronage, 127
Penal: administration, 32; apparatus, 27, 31; confinement, 26; great penal experiment, 14, 61; growth, 26; knowledge, 38; penal order, 38; penal policy, 14, 64, 99; professionalization of, 32; rationalization of, 32; sanctions, 25; severity, 51; state, 23; subject, 15, 89, 90, 91, 92, 93, 94, 98, 99; system, 30, 109; technology, 38; welfarism, 90
Penology, 90, 91; "new" 98; "old," 90
Pentagon, 30, 227
People of color, 107
Philadelphia (Pa.), 67
Phillips, Kevin, 137n. 4
Plata v. Schwarzenegger, 58
Police, policing, 3, 10, 15, 25, 31, 39, 116, 137, 223, 224, 225; use of deadly force, 14
Policy entrepreneurs, 16
Political subjectivities, 11
Politicians, 16
Politics, 14
Poor, the, 14, 107, 134; blacks, 25
Populist, 58
Portland (Ore.), 67, 112
Post-correctional supervision, 25
Post-Fordist age, 23
Post-industrial populations, 13
Post-Keynesian: age, 23; state, 28, 31
Poverty rate, 211
Powell v. Texas (1968), 110
Pragmatism, 53, 55
Prison, 2, 8, 11, 14, 25, 26, 28, 30, 33, 86, 112, 117, 124, 130, 134, 152, 178, 197, 224, 225; building industry, 8, 210; crime 34n. 3; federal, 33n. 1; growth, 14; guards, 8, 31; industrial complex, 7, 18, 23, 29, 30, 31, 32, 33, 34n. 6, 224; and jail jobs, 26; maximum security, 41; officials, 15; Prison Policy Initiative, 34n. 5; population, 14, 211; sentences, 11; supermax, 103n. 7; as surrogate "ghetto," 28; system, 61, 67
Prisoners, 15, 25, 26, 29, 33, 33n. 1, 34n. 7; wages of, 34n. 7
Prisoners' rights movement, 32, 92
Private prison corporations, 34n. 6
Privatization, 109
Probation, 29, 107, 112
Profit motive, 30, 31

Projects of reassurance, 109
Proportionality principle (Eighth Amendment), 51
Propositions 21, 36, 63, and 66. *See* California propositions
Prosecutorial approach, 32
Prosecutors, 10, 16, 34n. 3, 145, 147, 171
Prostitution, 107, 112
Public defenders, 146
Public health, 16, 49, 148
Public housing, 113
Public safety, 18, 65, 150, 225
Public school children, 16
Public schools. *See* Schools, public
Punishment, 30, 31, 39, 123, 125, 127, 132; sector, 8; privatization of, 26, 31
Punitive: city, 106, 117; policies, 13; state, 89

Quackenbush, Chuck, 194, 195, 196, 197
Quality of life, 15, 44

Race, 2, 3, 6, 8, 9, 12, 14, 37, 54, 97, 168, 180, 224; relations, 3; reconstituting, 9; -making social institutions, 9, 13
Racial: construction, 12; domination, 3, 9, 12; hierarchy, 10; justice, 12, 13; justice movement, 10; meaning, 14; policing, 18; politics, 8, 10; prejudice, 212; subordination, 6, 12, 169, 171
Racialization, 15, 224
Racialized: oppression, 225; political identities, 11
Racism, 10, 23, 30, 88, 224; unconscious, 212
Radical left, 8
Radical Republicans, 170
Ranulf, Sven, 194
Reagan, Ronald, 7, 46, 52
Recidivism, 25, 147, 149
Recidivist violent criminals, 7
Reconstruction: post–civil war, 17, 171, 175, 180, 210; post–war on crime, 90, 203
Red enemy, 30
Re-entry 5, 10, 11, 17, 56, 159
Refugee rights, 224
Rehabilitation, 5, 10, 19, 91, 112, 167, 189, 195
Rehnquist, Chief Justice William, 173
Rehnquist Court, 51
Reparations, 207
Republican Party, 6, 7, 52, 128
Republicans, 225

Restitution, 18, 217
Restorative justice, 18; programs, 18, 217
Revenge, 195
Right(s), 45, 136
Right-utopianism, 137n. 4, 138n. 7
Rio Grande, 45
Ríos Montt, General Efraín, 41
Risk, 13, 53, 54, 97, 98
Robinson, Randall, 212
Robinson v. California (1961), 110
Robinson, William, 46
Robocop, 223; state, 226, 228
Roosevelt, Franklin Delano (FDR) 55, 58
Rural, 192

Safety, 31
San Francisco, Calif., 16, 146, 148
San Quentin, 153
Schnapper, Eric, 178
Schools, 9, 124, 132, 138n. 5, 189, 218; charter, 123, 138n. 7; conflicts, 16; public, 3, 135, 199, 209
Schwarzenegger, Arnold, 5, 58
Seattle, 15, 67, 108, 111, 112, 113, 114, 115, 116, 118n. 2
Seattle Police Department (SPD), 114, 115
Security, 49, 54, 55, 106
Segregation: racial, 49, 106, 174, 209; hyper-, 55
September 11, 2001, 12, 16, 18, 48, 52, 188
Sex offender, 94, 96
Sexuality, 29
Shakur, Afeni, 28
Shakur, Tupac, 28
Shofner, Jerrell, 170
Simon, Jonathan, 96
Slavery, 3, 13, 27, 57, 207, 210
Smuggling, 41
Social: change, 14; conflict 14; control, 4, 15, 46, 106, 107, 108, 111, 117, 118, 192; insurance, 54, 55; justice, 14, 16, 203; movements, 14; norms, 193; prison, 27; welfare, 25, 137; work, 49
Social democratic politics, 137
Social Security, 53, 135
Soledad, 153
"Southern Strategy," 6
Sovereignty, 137
Snow, David, 111
Spacial control, 107

Spain, 24
State: charity, 25; power, 15
Status offense 190
Stevens, Justice John Paul, 57
Street, 75, 77, 78, 82, 83, 85, 88; "code," 15, 74, 79, 80, 83, 87; "culture," 74
Stuntz, William, 57
Sub-poverty jobs, 26
Suburbs, 56, 130, 132, 133, 192, 225
"Super jail" for youth, Alameda County, 197
"Super *Mano Dura*" (antigang initiative), 41
Supreme Court, 57, 108, 110, 172, 173, 174, 208
Surveillance, 30

Taint, 178, 179, 182n. 4
Tallahassee, 66
Taxes, 135
Taxpayers, 134
Taylor, Texas, 114
Teachers, 123, 132, 134
Temporary employment sector, 26
Tennessee, 29
Terrorism, 1, 11, 12, 16, 56, 68, 136
Texas, 29
Thelton E. Henderson Center for Social Justice, 213
"Third Wave" transitions, 39, 45
Thirteenth Amendment, 6, 56
Three-strikes laws, 5, 45, 195, 204
Torture, 102
Tough-on-crime politics, 64, 94
Transnational, 38; crime, 40
Trespass law, 111, 113, 115
Triadic institutional nexus, 30
Truancy rates, 191
Tucker, Karla, 103n. 9
Tupac Shakur. *See* Shakur, Tupac

U.C. Berkeley School of Journalism, 213
Underclass, 125
Unemployment rate, 26
UNICOR (Federal Prison Industries program), 34n. 7
Unions, 13, 59, 192
United States, 12, 15, 23, 24, 25, 26, 30, 31, 32, 33n. 2, 45, 50, 54, 152, 207, 226, 228
United States v. Booker, 57
United States v. Fordice (1992), 179
Universal Declaration of Human Rights, 52

Urban: marginality, 33; planning, 49; policing strategies, 15; public spaces, 15; renewal, 109; revolts, 28; withdrawal, 28
U.S. Postal Service, 135
U.S. Surgeon General, 215
Utopianism, 137n. 4

Vagrancy, 108, 111
Victims, 18, 43, 82, 93, 130, 146, 167, 216, 217; rights movement, 195, 210
Village of Arlington Heights v. Metro Development Corp. (1977), 172
Violence, 43, 79, 80, 82, 86, 123, 131, 147, 148, 197, 211, 213; domestic, 214; state, 45; violent crime, 59n. 3, 213
Volokh, Eugene, 183n. 7
Voting, 145; rights, 145, 166, 168
Voting Rights Act of 1965, 6

Wage labor, 25, 27
Wales, 34
Wal-Mart, 24
Walsh, Adam, 191
War: on Arabs, 18; on crime, 1, 2, 3, 5, 6, 7, 9, 10, 16, 17, 33, 37, 38, 44, 45, 50, 56, 59, 89, 90, 124, 151, 152, 168, 178, 181, 182, 187, 207, 209, 224; on drugs, 16, 18, 38, 109, 124, 210, 211, 223, 224; on Muslims, 18; on terror, 1, 16, 18, 38, 44, 56, 124, 135, 224; on youth, 187, 190, 192, 193, 197
Wardens, 31
Warehousing, 28
Warfare state, 18, 226
Warren Court, 51
Warren, Chief Justice Earl, 51
Washington v. Davis (1976), 172
Welfare, 225; reform, 24, 28; retrenchment, 28; -state approaches to social problems, 226
Western, Bruce, 26, 64
West Oakland, Calif., 18
White fears, 10
White privilege, 210, 212
Whites, 10, 138n. 6, 19, 207, 208, 210
White supremacy, 208, 209
Williams, Stanley "Tookie," 100
Willie Horton. *See* Horton, Willie
Wilson, James Q., 110, 195
Women, 34n. 6
Workers Compensation, 53

Workforce, 30
Working class, 25
World Bank, 135
World War I, 27
World War II, 126, 209

Youth activists, 17
Youth Radio, 205

Zero-tolerance, 16, 124, 125, 127, 128, 131, 135, 136, 189, 190